ESSAYS 2

ESSAYS 2
GARETH WARDELL

GROUSE BEATER

First published in the UK in 2022

Text © Gareth Wardell, 2022
Cover image © Barbara Rae CBE RA RSA RE,
2018, Fortress Castle (mixed media on paper)

All rights reserved. No part of this publication may be reproduced, stored or transmitted in any form or by any means electronic, mechanical or photocopying, recording or otherwise, without the express permission of the publisher

ISBN 9798834924951

Typesetting and ebook production by Laura Kincaid,
Ten Thousand | Editing + Book Design
www.tenthousand.co.uk

Printed by Amazon

Dedicated to Emma and Nora, daughters, intelligent, good natured, humorous, generous, honoured to know, productive in their chosen vocation, each a joy to see and hug, only occasionally annoying.

CONTENTS

Preface   *xv*

1   Grandfather Reilly   1
My Irish grandfather was an exceptional musician, a fiddle player, a founder of orchestras and a pioneer for the musician's union. He made Edinburgh his home, his piano player his wife, and ten children strong enough to survive two wars and transcend poverty.

2   Adrienne Corri   16
A survey to establish which Scottish woman was truly of an independent mind, actress and writer Adrienne Corrie would be among the top ten. The habit is to describe such women as 'ahead of their time'. In Corri's case it was true all her life.

3   The Independent Novelist   28
The late, respected novelist Frederic Lindsay wove love of his culture warts and all into his novels. His writing was outstanding, his standard of his detective fiction way above that of his popular contemporaries. He began writing late in life and yet achieved a tremendous amount in a short time.

4 Civil Disobedience   45

Countries suffering authoritarian governments, or the repression of colonialism, eventually reach breaking point; people mobilise themselves to participate in civil disobedience. The tactic is to concentrate effort on what will alter government policy, not what will defeat the people one is trying to protect.

5 The Infamous Ledger   54

In 2017 I began keeping a diary of every instance 'England' was used to mean the UK or Britain, and insultingly, Scotland. Within a few weeks the list numbered hundreds of examples. Those published in this chapter are a selected few.

6 An Arts Policy for Scotland   64

I jumped at the chance to compose a policy guide for Scotland's undervalued artistic output, but being reduced to a cerebral role in old age has its frustrations. One is not at the forefront of the arts anymore, merely an observer and a recorder. What to write that will inspire?

7 The Road to Crieff   72

On long car journeys drivers are apt to take in the accompanying traffic, stopping at a petrol station, and not notice much else. A journey from Edinburgh to Crieff turned into a visit down the ages to Roman times, and an appreciation of our old market towns.

8 Collaborators   83

After centuries of often brutal British rule, it is incumbent on a new administration of a liberated country to hold key oppressors to account. Scotland a civilised nation, use of the guillotine is not envisaged. A council of reconciliation is a safe mechanism allowing the guilty to explain their actions and atone for their cruelties and betrayals.

9   The Folly of Nuclear War   93
Humankind is intent on annihilating the species. Warnings of Armageddon have been expressed by the great and the good since Robert Oppenheimer uttered the infamous words, "I have become Death, the destroyer of worlds". Wars in the modern world cannot be won.

10 Embarrassment   100
Acute self-awareness affects us all at some time in our life, from poor eating etiquette to sexual matters and can be so intense it immobilises us. When does it begin?

11 New Zealand Cannot Exist   104
Most people will know a few things about New Zealand, its tourism boosted by the Peter Jackson director of the 'Lord of the Rings' movie cycle. We know it suffers from earthquakes, but what is less well known is how it survives so well when English assert Scotland cannot.

12 Melody Man   108
Everybody should get to know one composer in their lifetime, classical, jazz, rock music, it doesn't matter. It's good for the soul, a civilising relationship. I have been lucky. I managed to know four, three of whom I can genuinely call friends.

13 The Irish Experience   117
As I left Davy Byrne's pub in Dublin's Duke Street, in June 2014, a few months from Scotland's referendum on restoring self-governance, I was conscious of Ireland's struggle for the same goal, how the British State made it a matter of life and death.

14 The Man with the Walrus Moustache   128
I arranged a meeting with a man to discuss a stage project. I asked a friend who knew him, that is, a friend who was a

woman, what he was like. With barely disguised distaste she said, "He's an animal". She was right, but I discovered more to him than carnal lust.

15 Nationalism and Nazis 137
We are taught to detest Hitler and Mussolini, but in their earliest incarnation they were admired by British and American leaders. In contemporary times Brits who would have held them in high regard call the SNP fascists. The slur requires a sharp boot up the nether region.

16 The Professor's Perversion 146
He was an elderly respected professor. No one has claimed such men should be well-adjusted, rational adults fit to analyse the mind of others, but this one was a psychiatrist and his own patient wrapped into one.

17 The Outward Urge 157
For over three hundred years, invasion, colonialism, poverty and a few poor harvests have driven millions of Scots to live in far flung corners of the world. The Union has seen no end to Scotland's forced immigration.

18 The Last Man in Europe 163
A gift of a book discovered an unknown side to George Orwell's life. He loved flowers. We make symbolic use of them, from romantic gifts to funerals. Research led me to a letter of Orwell's and his thoughts on an independent Scotland.

19 The Stubbie 173
An article written for a British car magazine while in Los Angeles - a light-hearted survey of a famous municipal installation often an extra in movies - was noticed by a local Fire Station in Marina del Rey and the staff presented with a framed copy.

20 Give the Bear a Hug 177
The Cold War was courageously dismantled by Mikhail Gorbachev, but the West's imperial urges fires up another Ukrainian crisis, followed by censorship, hysteria, a million refugees and Russia depicted again as the Evil Empire. The answer in these events is to turn fire on one's own government and demand peace.

21 The Arctic Fox 183
Dr John Rae was one of Scotland's greatest explorers, a trained doctor and cartographer, famous for discovering the doomed crews of Captain John Franklin's expeditionary ships and the link to the Northwest Passage, denounced by Lady Franklin so that her husband got all the fame.

22 Bigfoot 197
This was a cat of enormous proportions, an independent cat, the cat of cats, an aristocratic beast. He dominated my life until the house we shared got too small to contain us.

23 The Rise of National Parties 201
Against all odds Scotland's premier national party achieved power and made great strides in progressive policies under the leadership of Alex Salmond only for his successor to squander advances in idiotic, half-baked policies and laws.

24 A Cultural Difference 213
What are the roots of cultural difference between Scotland and England? The two Kingdoms have been at war or wary of each other for as long as they existed.

25 High Hemlines 219
Edinburgh's 'climbing' club is a genteel moniker for a pioneering group of women that decided middle-class life needed a bit of pepping up in the form of adventure and danger.

26 **The Declaration of Arbroath** 226
    When a Scottish MP invokes the Declaration of Arbroath or the Claim of Rights in the House of Commons as the means by which Scots can choose their own destiny, the party in power will always answer it with an evasive reply.

27 **Smart Cars and Smart Visionaries** 233
    Recommending the benefits of driving small, compact cars is a disheartening task in an age where car makers tell us bigger is better. The micro Smart Car was mocked on its first appearance; it was the shock of the new.

28 **Smackeroonies** 241
    The hue and cry over what currency Scotland should use is a clever diversion created by our opponents to scare old ladies and the poor into assuming independence means poverty.

29 **The Polish Stonemasons** 248
    A family of brothers, all Polish, built my place of final existence on this earth. No amount of thanks is enough for the work they put into it, and the friendship they offered.

30 **The Bastardisation of the BBC** 256
    The first director general of the BBC, Lord Reith, a Scot on the make, set the template for the BBC's loyalties. "Assuming that the BBC is for the people, and the Government is for the people, it follows that the BBC is for the Government."

31 **The Gospel According to the Albionites** 272
    Written in 2014, this tongue-in-cheek Gospel languished on the Guardian website until discovered by readers and sent whirling around the ether.

32 George Forrest – Plant Hunter 277
Lionised by botanists and scientists, George Forrest was a masterful collector of plants and shrubs. If all you own is a window box likely one of the plants in it was discovered by him.

33 The Twilight of the Imperium 288
The English are enduring a lengthy period of self-harm the only logical result of which will be a country isolated from the world but presumably happy in its xenophobia. England is not the first Imperial nation to implode.

34 Define Women 294
A once wise institution called Stonewall, established to secure equal rights for gay people that achieved great things for them, now churns out claptrap to keep it in existence. It writes laws demanding governments and government agencies comply with its tablets of stone.

35 Death of a Monarchy 299
The British Royal family has a long history of surviving self-made crises. This century sees an end to the reign of Queen Elizabeth II. Does anyone other than her siblings care?

36 Dreams 308
Psychologists tell us our dreams are our subconscious at work, telling us of anxieties we should address or desires we should suppress. But is the analysis related to political dreams?

37 Postcards of Wisdom 315
More miniature fag packet philosophy, easy to pass, one person to another.

38 My Country to Govern 325
There is a school of thought that argues nation states ought to be abolished to make the world a better place. It will make the world a boring place with no guarantee of peace and prosperity. In the meantime, Scotland has every right to nationhood and to its place in the world.

39 The Colonial 329
Colonialism is racism; it regards the colonised as inferior, a subordinate species.

Acknowledgements	331
About the Author	333
Index	335

PREFACE

A collection of essays is eclectic in nature. This second collection *is* mercurial to an extent but in truth the life of my nation permeates each and every one. My philosophy remains the same since I gave thought to Scotland's ills and aspirations, how Scotland could be Elysium North and not a copy of Hades South, an ideal needing only political courage to attain.

I have come to realise a nation's independence is not about being Left or Right or a born again tattie howker. The people will decide the ideology when free to do so. The aim is liberation, *freeing the mind*. Now that I am one of the walking elderly, more accurately the shambling invalided, I feel intellectually freer than at any time in my life. Thus, I am happy to announce I have not reached the predicted apotheosis and become a selfish sod of the British right-wing, a malady the cynical claim overtakes us all in our later years.

As an observer of human behaviour my essays are attempts to understand events and people who affected them and me, critiques of people one liked or avoided, identifying patterns of behaviour, noting hypocrisy, pricking pomposity, heightening the study by miniature portraits in prose. Insight helps. Peel off the layers of an onion and you get to the real onion, went an old saying beloved of amateur psychologists. I learned the layers of an onion *are* the onion. Polemic compartmentalises experiences in much the same way as assessing human history. History can be viewed as one long imperialistic set of conquests.

For me, writing essays is a consolation. They put to good use years of stage play and screenplay research understanding the best and worst of human nature, and specifically aspects of my nation's history such as the Highland Clearances. Scotland's future remains hanging by a tartan thread. So long as we are ruled by London our rights are water through our fingers. The duty, the priority, of a national government facing down a colonial power, is to lead its people to safety, after that it has the luxury of planning for prosperity. Scotland is attacked from all directions, Westminster, England's colonialism, organises funds withdrawn from us by the UK Treasury and powers withdrawn by Whitehall.

We are one of the lucky countries. We have a wonderful abundance of natural resources, a clever and energetic population, and a healthy set of values. We have opportunities and capacities. The level of higher education producing fine graduates is good despite the loss of Scottish staff to colonial incomers. But our wealth is stolen, our children's inheritance, gone in an instant if we cannot exercise self-determination and keep what we earn.

George Orwell thought parts of Scotland "almost an occupied country" well before most Scots recognised the reality. The colonial always argues they govern us because it does us good. Westminster's dictum could so easily be that of hypocritical remorse exemplified in the headmaster's cliché, "This will hurt me more than it hurts you," as he brings his cane whip-hard down on the buttocks of an unfortunate upstart.

On the subject of the human posterior, sitting in an office chair hours on end writing for a living is guaranteed to widen the slimmest of arses. In time, when you stand up the chair is liable to come with you. I have never been a great advocate of jogging let alone running for exercise, certainly not with my legs. Running is for catching a bus, taking shelter from a sudden rain storm, or escaping a maddened elephant. It holds no practical outcome; there is nothing to show for the effort at the end of it, nothing created that benefits another person or you can sell. A slow walk in an interesting location is healthy enough physically and intellectually. I admit the sedentary life of a writer is not a healthy one but when my wife wants me she knows I am at home.

Most trades have associated physical side effects, the decorator with paint permanently under his fingernails, the dancer with calluses on her feet, the blacksmith with rough skin. Those of us that used a pencil or pen in youth have their index finger distorted where they held it between first and second finger for ten or more school years. Writers suffer from carpel tunnel. It sounds like the place where best to fish but it is a pain that afflicts a nerve in your wrist that causes numbness in your hand and fingers. Eyeballs are given a bashing if the scribbling is done late at night. Robert Louis Stevenson managing to write through the dark hours by the light from a jar of fireflies is quite a feat. Tolstoy wrote most of *War and Peace* by candlelight in the depths of winter. I sit in a warm book-lined study, classical music playing quietly in the background. The most exercise lawyer and biographer James Boswell took when scribbling notes for his *Life of Samuel Johnson* was lifting a tankard of ale from a table to his lips, which he did too often. Unlike spending two sweaty hours in a gym each morning, four hours writing a day has something to show for the effort. Princess Diane visited a gymnasium five mornings a week, but died without a grey hair on her body; exertion and pain for what end? Forced to choose a sport I would choose tennis, a lot of running around in a confined area and minutes in between of doing nothing more than staring at your opponent across a net. Or maybe snooker would be better, not that it qualifies as a sport. If I ever took up physical exercise I would take up Yoga. Anything that says lie down on the floor and go to sleep is fine by me.

I try to achieve the greatest possible clarity of expression in my writing, altering and revising, rejecting everything that obscures meaning. Publishing one's thoughts on almost anything is unsafe these days, high risk; the lazy, the untalented and the envious wait around every corner to pounce on a weakness and shake it as a dog would a rabbit by the neck. A morning's dalliance at the portal of a social Internet site discussing ideas is a good way to develop one's intellectual muscles. In face-to-face encounters one is well-prepared with informed answers. Handling inane opinion repeated by an unseen stranger on the Internet, the guy at the other end making each response a duel, can feel like picking my teeth with barbed wire. Facts, truth, understanding are alien to some so-called Christians.

Speaking as a former dominie, I try not to elevate mere opinion over expertise. Most of what I write about is based on direct experience, observation or project research. For now, I offer a word of caution. There are two kinds of teachers. There is the teacher who teaches you to be a confident person, to make your own decisions and live by them. And there is the teacher who teaches you to *need* them all your days. The former is the good teacher. The latter is a bad teacher. Love of power is the chief enemy of the educator as much as the politician. This is why I argue self-determination is not about left or right, or even being environmentally green. It is about freeing minds. I want no dependents. I want a Scotland where citizens need no masters.

Gareth

1
GRANDFATHER REILLY

My grandfather was not a spontaneous man. Not when I knew him. The only occasion I remember him unconstrained was when he was bedridden and asked impatiently for a book to read. He threw it across the bedroom against a wall with an angry shout "I've read that one!" He had a temper did grandfather Pádraig Joseph Reilly, more out of frustration than anger, evident by his physical inability to lead a normal life in old age. When in his twenties he was run over by the wheel of a Hansom cab. The wound returned to blight his life cruelly as internal wounds do when our physical constitution grows weak.

Born in 1876, granddad hailed from County Mayo, a small town on the edge of the Atlantic called Westport, carved into two by the Carrowbeg River, a place of farms and pubs and Georgian antecedents and no crime. His father, my great grandfather, another Patrick Reilly – the Irish believe in holding tight to their cultural nomenclature – and his wife Mary O'Donnell, were from Donegal. Great-grandfather was born in 1831. He and his wife Mary knew starvation and disease of the Great Famine of 1845 to 1852 when the harvests were full and the potatoes blighted, but their English landlords took the wheat and sold it in England for a healthy profit leaving over a million souls to starve to death, and another two million to emigrate.

From a census of 1891, great-grandfather aged sixty was living in Edinburgh registered as a fish hawker. He sold fish from a cart.

Living in Niddry Street, off the Tron, he must have plied his fish down the High Street. He brought his family with him, Bridget (1865), Mary (1867), Margaret (1872), Ann (1875) and my grandfather Patrick (1876) and James (1878). A grandchild John Farrell is registered, but to which son or daughter remains a mystery. Good Catholics everyone, bred almost a child a year, women as baby machines. There are unmarked graves of children and still-born babies in Ireland to remind us of the poverty that condemned so many to an early grave and the living to a life of anonymous poverty.

What material legacy the Reillys left behind in Ireland is unknown. What is clear is the Reilly clan were survivors. By all accounts great-grandfather could play a medley of Gaelic tunes on the fiddle with the facility of a cricket looking for a mate. That presupposes he spoke in his native tongue, Irish Gaelic. His son, Patrick Joseph, the subject of this essay, inherited the same skill and made his way from relative working class poverty to Edinburgh's bourgeoisie as soon as he had legs to carry him and a few pounds in his pocket to pay his way. He joined 4,015,577 others living in Scotland. The Irish were welcomed as were the Polish and Italians. Scotland was a European country. Unlike the English, they did not bring with them wealth made on the backs of slavery.

Irish census records before 1901 are lost or destroyed. No immigration records were kept of people travelling from Ireland to UK. Ireland was then a British territory, a passport unnecessary. Nothing more might have been heard of Patrick Joseph Reilly, but he had a skill, a singular talent. He could play the violin like the Devil himself. The ability had to come from his father, but life and the human genes remind us it is not always guaranteed to happen. I have heard music lovers regret Beethoven had no son to see the world filled with more revolutionary music. The cleverest of human genes has a way of skipping generations. I am told my grandfather stuck a child's violin under my chin when I was five years of age and plucked it from me just as quick. "The boy has no musical ability", he said, "but his creativity will come out some other way." And so it came to pass. I followed granddad into theatre, the one way open to a person keen on the arts, in my case, to write and direct plays, not to play music in the orchestra pit.

I can recognise a composer on hearing three bars of their music or a single chord, even if the piece is new to me – a useless skill – but I cannot play a musical instrument. I tried the fiddle for a year, hating the discipline and the musty smell of old music manuscripts. My nephew Christopher Devine is a concert pianist and composer. C'est la vie. At least, my drama productions employed many a budding composer, Ireland's Enya being one.

Granddad took to classical music, light lively music at first, the emotional and sentimental melodies of La Belle Époque, and the popular kind you would hear played in a French salon composed by Jacques Offenbach or Gabriel Fauré. Later, *his* first son, another Patrick, became leader of the Scottish National Orchestra throughout the Fifties and Sixties. (An Anglophone manager had the prefix *Royal* stuck on the orchestra's title to remind us who owns Scotland.) Granddad's second son, Walter, decided jazz and the clarinet were his music and instrument of choice. Walter was a born raconteur. He had an innate ability to turn the smallest of events into a humorous anecdote. He lost critical career time developing his jazz technique sent to fight in Normandy, returning home to be greeted by a young daughter at the door, "Are you mah ither daddy?"

I have no idea when or how Patrick Joseph made the move to Scotland and Edinburgh. He packed his Stainer fiddle and Tubbs bow in their case, and settled in the village of Corstorphine on the edge of the capital in the days before an expanding city swallowed up its village communities, or cut it in two with a main road used by thousands of vehicles daily.

His pronounced talent got him enough money quickly to purchase a two-bedroom flat on the top of a Victorian tenement, kitchen, living room, and a toilet shared with the neighbour across an open rear veranda where residents hung out washing to dry. Ablutions were taken in a large tin bath in front of the kitchen range used for cooking. A few years he had live in an Edwardian terrace of flats, Drumdryan Street, in Tollcross the centre of Edinburgh, to be close to his places of work, the University, the Kings Theatre and the Empire Palace Theatre, now known as the Festival Theatre. Above the bar in the foyer of the Festival hangs a large tapestry of one of my wife's paintings of Edinburgh. What comes around comes around a second time if you wait long enough.

In Victorian times there was a magnificent, red, green, blue and gold ornate bandstand in the centre of Tollcross where five roads converge. He and fellow musicians played perched there on Sundays to entertain perambulators out for the day's stroll. In my mind's eye I can see him conducting and playing with his bow as they struck up a Strauss march, coins of appreciation thrown into a tub helped pay his mortgage. The bandstand was removed in 1940 for the war effort on the instruction of Winston Churchill, and together with tonnes of beautiful garden railings everywhere ripped out, dumped in a field and never replaced. Melted down, the cast iron was too brittle to build tanks, one of Churchill's wild ideas.

On warm weekends when not entertaining strollers in Tollcross or Princes Street gardens, granddad hired a charabanc to take his large and growing family to the Pentland Hills for a day's picnic at Swanston village with its white walled thatched cottages, the two storey house once the home of Robert Louis Stevenson. He told me 'Pentland' derives from the Brythonic *pen llian* – the top of an enclosure, the language spoken before and during Roman times. He knew some Greek and Latin but admitted he had lost his talent for the Irish Gaelic by the time he hit thirty. Moving from one colonised and brutalised country to another and you adapt to the ways of the ruling class. You don't have a choice, assimilate or perish.

The other side of my grandparents, on the distaff side, were English. I never knew the Wards, but born out of wedlock I was christened Gareth Ward, altering my surname to Wardell when I reached twenty-one in respect of my mother who got into an unfortunate marriage with an old soldier called Tommy Weddell. They had nothing in common until they had children and had less in common after that. Changing my name was a mistake. My father was Don Carlo Bernini, a Sicilian auto engineer and prisoner of war, the only man my mother professed she loved. Then again, it could never be Gareth Bernini, only Gari Bernini makes cultural sense. The Reilly family decided to keep me though I was farmed out to a convent for a year for what purpose I do not know. The nuns taught me to dislike macaroni cheese as a staple diet, a dish as bland and as pasty white as their wimpled faces.

Granddad Reilly sported a luxuriant moustache flicked up at the ends in the fashion of the day, and a thick head of hair so dense he could keep it in a crew cut late into his seventies. For domestic hours, before the days of onesies, jeans and T-shirts, he wore a grey Irish woollen suit, waistcoat adorned with a fob watch. Around his neck he wound a tartan scarf, the stiff collars of the day discarded. In his last years he used a stout walking stick to keep his balance. He did not smoke, but by all accounts, enjoyed a malt whisky. By the time I began to be aware of his looming presence I was eight years old, and he was too old and infirm for sudden adventure trips.

He was productive in what he achieved as a professional musician as he was in spawning a family, a large family as one did in the days when there were no pensions, welfare state, free medicine or insurance. Your family was insurance for your old age. They were expected to rally around and provide financial help and companionship. In fact, Honora, unmarried, one of his most devoted daughters, elected to look after him in his last years. "Don't let the hospital get me", he implored. "Once in, you never walk out again." All but a few memories I have of granddad was when he was bedridden. He was in his mid-seventies.

His children were fine appropriate looking specimens of the Irish–Scottish race, Celts, three sons, and six daughters, and all six daughters managed to find a husband. His sons were first Patrick, named after himself, and second Walter. The third son, John, died at birth. The girls were given customary Edwardian names, blessed with three names each, Winifred, Millicent, and Kathleen, Honora Emmula Louise, and then Bella and Louisa, as Irish as they are coined. My mother was the youngest, Maureen Constance Reilly, born at an age her mother ought not to have another child, in her early fifties, and a father too old to join in the fun and games a child needs. Six daughters must have been a handful. Sharing clothes was taken for granted, the one meeting a boyfriend taking precedence for the best outfit.

My mother was one hellova handful, wayward, as is said of women not prepared to stay under a man's thumb. She was sixteen when I was born, as slim as a ballet dancer, and had tried to become one. One day, complaining of stomach pains, she was taken to the hospital. Granddad and grandma thought she had a cyst. "Don't let them operate, Maureen!" he shouted as she left the house for Chalmers maternity hospital nearby. Winfred, the eldest daughter, and Honora, the one destined to become my guardian, were first at the hospital ward. "We're here to see Maureen Reilly. Was the operation successful?" Winifred asked. "Operation?" said the puzzled nurse. "Miss Reilly has had a beautiful, healthy baby boy!" Winfred was dumbstruck only a moment. "I knew it. I damn well knew it," she said emphatically, looking around for Honora's approbation. But Honora was not in her eye line. She was flat on her back in a dead faint.

The begetting of so many offspring put an end to Isabella, grandma Reilly's career. She had been a sharp piano player in granddad's orchestra and could put her long flexible digits to most genres, from a Scott Joplin ragtime to a Chopin etude. A kindly soul, devotion to her family was not a sacrifice. Her strong hands and arms were needed for other things, to lift heavy cast iron pots onto a hook over the fire, knead dough to make bread, wash laundry, scrub floors, carry shopping, and iron granddad's shirts and separate collars so he was neat and tidy for his concert dates.

Isabella worked from home before working from home became physically possible in the digital age. In what spare time she had in her crowded domestic life, she taught her sons and daughters to read music and play instruments, they were naturals. Only the sons took up musicianship as a way of making a living. Winfred, a school cook, married a shop owner who left her a widow and house. Bella was a bakery shop assistant until she and her husband

Joe Cairns opened their own fruiters shop in Dundee Street. It made enough money for them to buy a bright red Volkswagen Beetle, one of the earliest in Edinburgh. The Reilly clan were looking up. Joe was marked out as the man who looked like the boxer Max Schmeling because of a severely broken nose, the result of riding a delivery bike into the back of a bus. He was a lithographer turned photographer and watercolourist, had three sons and immigrated to Australia on a £15 inducement ticket. Louisa met a Canadian soldier who took her to Nova Scotia before she discovered he liked booze more than life. Millicent married into the Jewish side of the family, the Biermans, Hymie Bierman fresh from a Nazi camp, another escapee from hell. The Biermans made Edinburgh their permanent home, the rest of the Reilly clan by then domiciled in far-flung extreme cold or hot climates, an age-old outward emigration urge. The Biermans spawned an entire dynasty of their own Michael, Esther, Audrey, and brought the Plotkins to the fold with their David, Miriam, Daniel, Lavie, and enlarged on that through my wife's brother with a Beverley, Barry and a Natalie. I seem to have every Jewish relative in names except a Shlomo.

I grew up in a Catholic household amid a Jewish faith. One broke bread and the other the body of Christ. For weeks on end I lived off unleavened bread. My granddad surely never saw a quiet peaceful moment to himself, either at home or among his orchestra. Procreation in a small crowded flat was silent and furtive. Still, large clans must be the integuments that hold families together during bad times and orchestras too.

Aunty Nora, manageress of Rankin's fruiters, met and married Wong Gee Chic, who bought garnish from her on a weekly basis, the first Cantonese to open a Chinese restaurant in Scotland, in Edinburgh's Chamber Street, to be exact, and another in Glasgow, before she discovered he was already married to another woman in Edinburgh. He paid Aunty Nora off with £15 miserable pounds a month alimony. She had two miscarriages leaving fate to anoint me as a surrogate son. As a companion, I must have been some solace for her loneliness and poverty. Whatever I am today, she made me. But that's another story.

I have a wonderful photograph of a handsome granddad taken in Princes Street Gardens about 1910. The Reilly gene ensured dark hair and brown expressive eyes, nose a little on the large side. He is sitting straight-backed in the centre row of his fourteen-strong orchestra, fiddle and bow in his hand. Around him are two other violinists, a viola player, the double bass player standing. In the wind section he has a clarinettist, oboe player and bassoonist, perfect for playing Debussy or Ravel. The brass section boasts a coronet, a trumpet, cor Anglais and tuba. At his feet sitting crossed legged is the timpani player, arm perched nonchalantly over a snare drum, a musician handy with the bass drum, tambourine, maracas, gongs, chimes, celesta, cymbals and … triangle. Except for the last, the instruments chosen are designed to carry sound across large open spaces. Like all the other musicians except for the piano player, Isabella, whom he married, they are dressed in full tailed topcoats, waistcoats, every button buttoned, bow ties of various kinds, and top hats, as proud as a regiment of victorious soldiers. Every one sported moustache and sideburn in the style of the day, again not including Isabella! Granddad has the widest jacket lapels, watered silk, to denote his status.

Behind the orchestra is the garden's octagonal bandstand, and on it an upright piano and music stands. A half-obscured notice board on the side of the bandstand reads, 'Weekly concerts, subscription membership' – income secured in advance of playing.

Granddad was no slouch. He had risen from poor if industrious Irish stock to the Scottish educated professional class. Playing to crowds gathered around Edinburgh's bandstands was never going to be enough for a clever musical entrepreneur. He soon realised the capital's theatres needed their own orchestra. Musicians were in constant demand for various types of theatrical events, operetta, song galas, musicals, magician's acts, pantomimes and plays. His world was an overture before curtain up, narrative music for dramatic scenes, a jaunty piece at the start of Act 2, a rising crescendo for the play's denouement. Finally, a hurried coda, drum crash, and off to the bar next door to slake a thirst.

Until he arrived on the scene, theatre musicians were freelancers, groups and bands in eternal competition. When a theatre manager wanted an orchestra for a production he lined up their chief musicians and asked how much they expected each evening and matinee on Saturday's, for rehearsals and performances. There was no union branch in Scotland, no scale of fees to follow. The representative of a musician's group was expected to say, verbally, what they wanted in fees. It was granddad's son, Walter, who told me how granddad played a trick to get work and beat rivals. Each representative stated their fee amount one at a time, verbally, only when it came to granddad he said "£6" while holding four fingers on his lapel, the thumb hidden behind his lapel. The theatre manager pretended to think on what was said by everyone but chose granddad's orchestra, the least expensive and by reputation the best and most disciplined. Once he had his musician's feet firmly planted in the draughty orchestra pit he negotiated a long term seasonal rate to give the manager comfort he had an orchestra all-the-year-round he could call upon, a retainer paid for the weeks when not called. This allowed his musicians to play at other venues and gigs when not required for theatre work. The manager was able to boast his establishment had its own orchestra and performance players, and indeed credit on play posters, "So and so" operetta with the 'Kings Theatre Orchestra". By repeating the exercise with the Empire Theatre, granddad's ensemble prospered. There was no need for the slogan, 'Keep it live'. All music was live back in the day.

Along the way his days promoting his musicians mounted up to first class advertising skills. He had to be a good promoter. Life was hard, work uncertain for a freelance musician. The Amalgamated Musicians' Union (which merged with the National Orchestral Union of Professional Musicians in 1921 to form the Musicians' Union) dates back to 1879. Granddad would have been aware of its existence in England. When the Musician's Union formed south of the border he set about opening branches in Scotland, organising meetings with colleagues and passing the Gospel word of mouth, asking musicians not to be cowed by employers blackmailing them with the threat, take the low wage or lose the gig.

The First World War and then the Second almost destroyed his work and achievements. He was too old to be conscripted for either carnage, but manage to eke out a living playing with smaller ensembles of fast aging musicians. He understood human aspiration. Watching the many leave for war and the few return, he knew something had to be done. He had a vision. As a morale booster for the citizens of Edinburgh faced with a war that could have been avoided, he chose virtue. He decided an orchestra was needed to play the great classical works for the masses to enjoy. With the music analyst and musicologist Professor Donald Francis Tovey, he co-founded Edinburgh University's Reid Orchestra, not a difficult task when in time of war itinerant musicians are happy to throw in their lot. The orchestra took its name from the Reid Concert Hall, which until then held concerts played by visiting musicians from Europe. Its policy was part-patriotic, part-educational, a given attached to an institution of higher learning.

In the matter of the killing fields of Brigadier General Earl Haig's slaughter of 750,000 British soldiers on the Western front, Patrick Reilly, no admirer of English warmongering, played it perfectly. Scunnered at man's inhumanity to man, he showed his patriotic duty by keeping people alive rather than seeing them dead. As thousands of young Scotsmen kissed goodbye to wife and family, or girlfriend, he saw his proposal come to fruition. The Reid Orchestra was composed of volunteers, concerts charged at a 'modest fee'. The publicity circulated stated: "A local orchestra for the establishment of regular concerts of the best music at popular prices in Edinburgh; for the instruction and development of native talent; and as a means for the practical study of music in the University of Edinburgh." It was signed *D.F.T.* (Donald Francis Tovey, its first conductor), *July 1919*.

"All music-lovers who have studied on the Continent, deplore the absence in this country of good local orchestras, such as exist or existed in all the larger and many of the smaller towns of Central

Europe." It was to repair this deficiency, and at the same time to provide the University with an instrument whereby the study of orchestration could be made a real, living thing that granddad and Tovey, with the aid of the Amalgamated Musicians' Union, formed their orchestra of all-Scottish players. Granddad's orchestra was the basis on which the Reid orchestra was formed, his players augmented the ensemble.

From the 1917–1918 inaugural season of the Reid Orchestra, here is the list of 1st Violins, in alphabetical order: Miss Emily Buchanan (Leader), Miss Esther L. Cruickshank, Miss M. P. Lunn, Miss Muriel Mackie, Miss Magdalene Seton (Mrs Kirk), Mr E Dearnley, Mr W. Barry Furniss, Mr P. R. Meny, Mr Edwin R. Pope, Mr Patrick J. Reilly, Mr J. H. Smith, Mr A. Douglas Willcox, Mr David C. Hutton.

In keeping with granddad's belief in the philosophy of Adam Smith and Karl Marx, the fifty-strong orchestra and deputies did not perform for profit. The Russian revolution, by then in full-spate, had western politicians shaking in their white spats. Following his advice, the Reid's conductor was unpaid – Tovey had a university salary, and the net takings of the concerts were devoted to the extension of the orchestra and the enhancement of the well-being of its members. They held their first concert in the University's magnificent McEwen Hall in 1917, competitor venue to that other wealthy brewer, Usher. Sunday concerts were held in the voluminous Synod Concert Hall on Castle Terrace, later altered into a cinema, a place of cigarette smoke and raincoats where I saw my first nudist film, entering a nervous last among a gaggle of thoroughly self-conscious, testosterone-driven school boys forced to sit in the only free seats available on the front row. For my half-crown, I saw a lot of bare breasted smiling women, waving energetically, laughing, and carrying large fluffy towels with one hand at tummy height, no mean feat when playing tennis with the other hand.

The Reid orchestra survived from 1917 to 1941, disbanded after the death of Donald Tovey and then resurrected for a few months at the end of 1945. The Reid orchestra was the precursor of the Scottish National Orchestra. Granddad was not a conductor by nature or choice. Eschewing fame, he was content as a member of the violin section for as long as he could play well. There was no earthly reason why he could not have been co-conductor, but there was no earthly reason why he should want to be. The orchestra continued until 1988, taken over in its last years by the university and a new conductor, Kenneth Leighton.

By the 1950s, long-playing records brought music to households that could afford a gramophone, and the radio broadcast concerts played by the BBC Light Orchestra. Expensive to run and administrate local orchestras fell out of fashion, theatre managers turned to jack-of-all-trade musicians. Granddad was in his early seventies, retired, and the old wound took it chance to finish his vocation. He spent his days in sardonic witness at the vacillating progress of classical music appreciation, but was pleased to see it open specialist schools for the gifted. He did not believe a cobbler learned much about his trade that was useful from the teachings of a candle maker. While music was for everybody, outstanding talent required concentrated attention in a specialist environment.

My first strong memory of him was on the death of his beloved Isabella. She had worked herself to death, contracting angina for her pains trying to make ends meet over two wars and food rations. It was 1950. I was four years of age. There were murmurings coming from the main room. I opened the door to see granddad seated, handkerchief held tight, his walking stick between his legs. He was weeping. A musician friend stood behind him in tears, a hand on granddad's shoulder, and two daughters, my aunties, all in a row. They were facing one way, toward where grandma lay in her open coffin, their backs to the window. I had stumbled into a wake and the full flood of human despair. "Someone take the boy out," said granddad. A hand reached down to mine from behind, pulled me back and closed the door.

As his ability to control his bodily functions deteriorated, my Aunty Nora's tasks included cleaning him as he lay face down in bed, groaning in humiliation. On good days he would teach me world politics but never religion. He was more interested in themes than specifics. He had lost interest in the Catholic Church, the Christian right, its sexual hypocrisy, ever since he found prayer about as useful as a dead horse was to pull a cart. Devout Catholicism was not going to remove the colostomy bag and tubes from his anatomy. Socialism had a better chance of keeping body and soul together.

For all his atheism he retained a degree of spirituality. Every so often a large herring gull alighted on his bedroom window sill. It tapped its long yellow beak on the glass pain to mark its arrival. In his imagination it was the spirit of his wife Isabella. It made him tearful each time it appeared. I watched it swallow a hen's egg whole, sideways down its gullet, laid on the window sill by Aunty Nora, with a wink in my direction. The bird was a potent symbol of how the tribal instinct lives on in us all.

When Nora propped him up in bed leaning on an ambush of pillows, I used to lie next to him to hear him tell stories, stories of great European nations, of French art and German music, of Russia and its overthrow of aloof aristocratic spongers. He talked a lot of class divisions but not lovingly. He had read Marx, Engel and Antonio Gramsci. He admired the Red Clydeside revolutionary John MacLean, whose ferocious opposition to the First World War got him imprisoned and the loss of his job as a teacher.

Of the great solo musicians, violinists naturally loomed large followed by pianists. "Great concert pianists appear ten a decade, but only one great violinist" he said, a true insight. His hero was Jascha Heifetz, the premier violinist of his era, a player who introduced one bum note deliberately into his recitals to "reassure my audience I am human". He talked of composers of whom Jean Sibelius was his favourite, destined to die one year after granddad. He also loved the music of Johannes Brahms, "Brahms could have been as great as Beethoven if only he had been bolder", he mused with some regret. I never saw him play; he was too ill to tuck a violin under his chin and hold a tune steady. There were evenings he sat up in bed to play a lament on his violin, but I was not allowed to enter his bedroom. It was granddad's private time. I have no idea where the music took him but I could hear the sadness in every shift of the bow. Years later, and to my shame I placed his Tubbs bow across the arms of a chair, and absent-minded sat down, snapping it in two. His violin hung on the wall until it fell apart for want of care.

Most of all I came to him to hear stories of heroes and derring-do, stories with a sly teaching ethic. One he told begins in Siberia, in the depths of a Russian winter.

> *There lived a poor peasant, as poor as most who lived off the land. In need of food, he packed firewood onto his cart, tethered the horse between the shafts, bade farewell to his wife and young son, and set off for the village to sell his goods. The weather was atrocious; snow flew sideways propelled by a biting wind and gathered in the folds of his face, clothes and scarf. He could barely see feet in front of him. On the rutted path to the village a blackbird flew past his head seeking safety from the snowstorm. The bird was so surprised to see another living thing amid the whiteout landscape, it flew straight into a tree trunk and fell, stunned, to the ground.*
>
> *His life lived close to nature; the peasant stopped the horse, got down from the cart and went to the injured bird's aid. It was still breathing. Lifting it up carefully, in his hands, too cold to revive the unfortunate bird, he looked around for ways to start a fire, an impossible task considering the weather. It was then that he noticed his pony had left some mounds of reconstituted hay behind the cart. They were still hot. He moved swiftly to the biggest mound, parted it in the middle and placed the bird in the dung. In minutes, the bird shook its head, stood up, flapped its wings and let out a cascade of calls in happiness at its luck.*
>
> *It was at that every moment that a cat, sheltering from the storm under a hedge at the side of the path, was alerted to the blackbird by its whistling and chattering. In an instant, it shot through the briar, swiped the bird dead with one swing of its paw, and carried it off in its mouth to be eaten at leisure, nature in the raw, tooth and claw.*
>
> *There is a moral to this story, and being a Russian story, there are three morals. The first moral is, if you do not look where you are going you might end up in it. The second is, if you fall foul of fate don't expect*

*strangers to help you. And the last moral is simply; **if you find yourself in it, don't make a song and dance about it!***

The stories were repeated on asking until the pain he endured in his stomach was too much to bear and I was asked to slip off the bed from beside him and come back later. One day, *later* never arrived. He died of bronchial pneumonia six years after his wife, Isabella, in 1956. They are buried side-by-side on Edinburgh's windy Corstorphine Hill cemetery. The bones of my guardian, Nora, and the ashes of my mother, lie beside them.

The word orchestra is from the Greek meaning the place on the ground floor of an amphitheatre where people, a group, stood or sat on the floor. As musical composition progressed and became sophisticated the word was adopted in the 17th century to mean the place below the stage where musicians assemble. For a lot of his time that is where my grandfather sat with his colleagues playing music for the actors, dancers and entertainers on the stage.

As can be seen, I have related a story of character, a subject polemicists shy from touching upon. My grandfather and the clan he birthed were honourable and upright. He kept a happy band of musicians in work for over two decades, a monumental achievement.

I have an enduring image of him in my mind's eye, slurping breakfast, plate on a tray on his bed, spoon to his mouth, *All-Bran* catching in his thick moustache, his reading glasses perched on his nose at a precarious angle.

And I am happy to add this coda, a hospital, the phobia of his life, never got its clutches on grandfather Patrick Reilly. He died at home in his bed. With luck and kind fate, I hope to do the same.

2

ADRIENNE CORRI

Disappointment turned to niggling annoyance some years back when I read a published list of Scottish-born actors working in Hollywood compiled by the Scottish Film Fund, now absorbed part of a profit-led quango Creative Scotland. It was such a poorly researched piece it deserved to be binned. Adrienne Corrie's name was one missing from the list.

Adrienne Corrie died aged 85. She was a fine actress beset by men too misogynistic to use her talents to the full. She was born in Glasgow, Adrienne Riccoboni, with an Italian father, an English mother, raised and educated in Edinburgh in the 1930s. As an independent mind, she was way ahead of her time in an acting profession dominated by competitive men, predatory men, and weak men. Charismatic women could be feisty when they wanted but were expected to knuckle down, sign the contract and play the female love interest without complaining. Female artistes of outstanding ability are less prone to being captives these days, but there are still too few like Corrie.

A fan on a visit looking for Corri's haunts in Edinburgh or Glasgow would be hard-pressed to find her birthplace even if you had noticed her brilliance, or followed her television and film appearances. The civic dignitaries have yet to acknowledge her existence let alone her status. Only male movie stars such as Sean Connery get praise from their home town, welcomed back to be given the Freedom of the City.

Corri was an actor of considerable range and versatility, as well as a quite beautiful woman. She had cheekbones you could perch a chocolate on- okay, she was an Italian Scot, it goes with the genes. As a theatre director, later film, I was keen to meet her, planning a role crafted for her in a detective thriller, but the project evaded the final investment, the excuse to say my hellos lost. I got as far as a lengthy phone conversation promising not to trouble her until the film was rock solid. To be frank, older than me, she'd have eaten me unsalted if I had ventured into her company unprepared. She was an accomplished bullshit detector.

Corri was a feminist before feminism was a career choice. She hated directors who were cloying or patronising. She received fees half that of her male co-stars, had agents clever at writing small print that left her without repeat fees, and who took months to pay her. If stereotypes have any truth to them, Corri's magnificent chestnut hair was a warning to the unwary. She was tempestuous. Plain as the fire in her eyes, she was wholly incompatible as a partner, and so it transpired for her two husbands, the last, actor Daniel Massey, whom she outlived. He probably handled her as the male Black Widow spider handles its far bigger mate, with a gift, a grab, and a dash for safety.

She did not hate men. In the early stage of her career she responded to men with sincere interest, but rarely was the better for it. Had she been still with us, her successful contemporaries would commiserate on the subject of the unreliability of the male species. In a vocation tempered by easy associations and fleeting friendships, directors tend to make swift use of women, and then flick 'em away.

For Corri it was less her love life that caused her anger, far more how she was used in his profession that so got under her skin. In one infamous television debate about women's rights in the media, Corri got thoroughly scunnered with the carefully couched views of her female panellists. She tore off her neck microphone and stomped out the studio in the full view of the cameras. She would have given BBC's anodyne *Question Time* one heck of a run for its money.

Her obvious talent, the passion she brought to a role, a hot-blooded Mediterranean swinging a strong Scottish accent able to out-argue any man, was rarely handled with care by male directors. A disappointing professional life dominated by men, success infrequent, more lows than highs, she never quite reached the power she so clearly possessed.

An adventurous Corri was destined for the stage from an early age. She left home in her teens and performed with travelling theatre groups, learning her craft with each production, and helping to set up and pack the scenery.

"My family were Italian musicians, and I'm Scots-Italian. They somehow got to Edinburgh. I think I'm a throwback. There are actors on the other side of my family too, because my other Italian name is Riccoboni. They were in the Comedia d'ell Arte. I'm definitely a throwback."

By the time Corri – the temptation here is to call her Adrienne but respect for her holds me back – attended classes at London's Royal Academy of Dramatic Arts (RADA) her parents had moved from Edinburgh to run the Crown Hotel in Callandar, Perthshire. She recounts her days there as happy ones. She maintained a remarkably scandal free private life despite being seen with London's low-life gangsters later in her life That, and a volatile temper, got her cast as the seductive women, a straight-jacket of a career.

Her memorable best role came early in her career, as it does with so many young actors. After a walk-on role in *Quo Vadis* (1951), shot in Rome, she was off to India to appear in her very best film, in my opinion, the one with the finest director, Jean Renoir, the son of Pierre-Auguste Renoir the painter. Like all good actors she responded to sensitive direction, but above all, to an excellent script. Actors need to believe in the script as much as we do.

The River (1951) is a poetic evocation of life among British colonials in post-second world war Bengal, a visual *tour de force*. Based on the novel by Rumer Godden, the film eloquently contrasts the growing pains of three young women with the immutability of the Bengal River around which their daily lives unfold. There are no fast cars, no explosions, and no action men. Melodrama is ditched in preference for contemplative inner characterisation.

Corri, her red hair standing out in splendid Technicolor, is the most mature, voluptuous and spoiled of three teenage girls, all suffering adolescent pangs for a young war hero who has joined their entourage. Corri gives a stand-out interpretation of a young woman on the cusp of womanhood. The subtlety and nuance she manages in one so new to acting is captivating. She is never cloying or sentimental. She gives a quiet, dignified interpretation of the uncertainties and confusions of muliebrity. *The River* isn't often on television, but I urge lovers of cinema to watch when it is broadcast.

Sadly for such a bright talent, but par for the course in respect of Hollywood's attitude to female roles confined to the ingénue, hooker, cookie airhead, or bored housewife – Corri is mainly remembered for her participation in the short but notorious gang rape scene from Stanley Kubrick's adaptation of Anthony Burgess's dystopian novel of hoodlum gangs, *A Clockwork Orange* (1971).

In her key scene she is ritualistically raped by a giant plastic penis shaped as a stool seat held aloft by Malcolm McDowall her attacker, while he dances to *Singing In the Rain*. Despite complaining to Kubrick about the multitude of takes, Kubrick asked for more. He was notorious for manipulating his actors until their patience broke. (A few actors walked off the set never to return.) He argued it caused them to shed any easy techniques, quirks, or shallowness. By the end of the forty-eighth take on day five they must have been so knackered all Kubrick got was a sleep walking thespian exuding pain. Corri initially declined the role of Mrs. Alexander because Kubrick was getting applicants to de-bra in his office while he trained a video camera on them. She made it clear that wasn't acceptable. "But Adrienne, suppose we don't like the tits?" Her answer was one word and to the point: "Tough."

"I liked working with Stanley; he's a curious man," she said in an interview about her experience working on the *Clockwork Orange*.

> *"One has to be very tough with Stanley. He appreciated it. I also used to get his name wrong, I called him Sidney. That used to drive him mad. It's very good for directors; keeps them in their place. We*

choreographed it like a dance scene. We really tried to leave it to the audience, and people think they saw a great deal more than they actually did. I thought it was very well done. I think I've just worked with a lot of tough directors, so one learns how to handle them. The thing with tough directors is often their bark is worse than their bite. You just have to measure it. I always think to myself what all actors should think: if I don't like this film, and I don't like this director, I can always leave through the front door. I can go. I always think that, so therefore you don't get into states. It's just another person you're working with, and if you don't like it, you can just say, "I don't like it." But I've never had to do that – no wait, did it once, but that was a different matter. It wasn't a horror film. I walked out of a crappy production through the gates of a castle dressed as Queen Elizabeth. And then I thought "Now what the hell do? I can't go back. It was a very nasty producer, not a director. I had to walk for a mile dressed as Queen Elizabeth down country lanes, to get a taxi to go back to the hotel. (Laughs.) You hold that in mind, that if somebody shouts at you, you say, "Who are you shouting at, you great twerp? What are you going on for?"

Despite Kubrick's sleazy prurience Corri retained a friendship with the director but it was wasted loyalty. He never offered her another role. Just the same, the scene is the one that stays in the imagination for its ferocity and graphic expression. One Christmas later she gave him a pair of bright red socks, a reference to the scene, in which she is left naked but for knee length red woollen socks.

As a single parent in the late Fifties she succumbed to the need to support two children, Patrick and Sarah, the result of a short-lived relationship with the film producer Patrick Filmer-Sankey, an interesting cohabitation – his grandparent was Hugh Grosvenor, the Second Duke of Westminster.

She held her family together by lowering her standards working on third-rate fare for Hammer Horror populist films in a succession of make 'em quick, pile 'em high, sell 'em cheap B-pictures. Her tenure began with *The Tell-Tale Heart* (1960), adapted from Edgar Allan Poe's story of a timid librarian obsessed with Corri, a flower seller who lives across the street from him and who, like many horror-movie heroines, has a tendency to undress by a window without closing the curtains. Small roles followed that kept the wolf from the door and her children fed. *The Viking Queen* (1967) was a silly sword-and-sandal half-baked epic, in which Corri was an anti-Roman pro-druid princess who snaps and snarls. Next was *Journey into Darkness* (1968). The original novella plotted a young American couple moving to New England learning everyone in their new neighbourhood belongs to a cult which has chosen them as sacrifices.

There were two films in which Corri bravely disguised her beauty: she played a disfigured prostitute in *A Study in Terror* (1965), which pitted Sherlock Holmes against Jack the Ripper, and in *Madhouse* (1974), she was bald and wore a mask to hide her face, mutilated in a car accident. There were other low-budget pulp schlock-horror pictures, and while one can claim she made a living, and found work close to home, you can't claim she made a fine reputation. She made the films without complaint, by all accounts, enjoying the experience.

Later she took minor roles in bigger films, three in her friend Otto Preminger's movies, *Bunny Lake Is Missing* (1965), *Rosebud* (1975), *The Human Factor* (1979), and as the mother of Lara (Julie Christie) in David Lean's sweeping *Dr Zhivago* (1965). Among her dozens of television parts were Milady de Winter in the BBC series of *The Three Musketeers* (1954) and various appearances in episodes of ABC's Armchair Theatre (1956–60). None of the roles stretched her ability nor brought her undoubted talents to the populist fore. Nevertheless, Corri did not waste her student days at RADA studying classic and Shakespearean roles. She had gained acclaim on stage within the profession. She was part of the Old Vic Company (1962–63) and appeared on Broadway in Jean Anouilh's *The Rehearsal* (1963). I'll stop here.

In 1959, rebellious to the end, she had a leading role in John Osborne's *The World of Paul Slickey*, a bitter musical satire on the tabloid press, which received the ire of critics and the public alike.

On the first night, Corri gave the booing audience a two-fingered salute and a "Go fuck yourselves!" before storming off the stage.

"I hate to say this, but I hardly ever see the finished product. I'm dreadful at this. This goes for everything, I'm afraid. I don't ever watch myself, or watch a film I've done. It's a job. I do it to the best of my ability, hang up my costume, and go home for the evening."

Her capacity to take risks and damn the consequences, found her mixing with iffy company by the time the 'Swinging Sixties' monopolised the attention of the seamier end of the British press. In the louche atmosphere of night clubs, casinos, high end bars, and an anything goes culture, film celebrities had a habit of rubbing shoulders with criminals. One would find hard to say who was the more excited by the company of the other. Corri became acquainted with some of the darkest figures in London's *demi-monde*, socialising with hard drinking actors and known police bait, including the Kray twins in the cheap tat of their dimly lit, dimly run *El Morocco Club*, a hang-out for rough sex closet gays such as the bowtie Tory politician with the bass baritone voice, Bob Boothby, a smooth operator prepared to be blackmailed by the Krays so long as they supplied him with rent boys. None of this unsavoury dalliance with the dregs of society did Corri's image any good, not boosted her career. It squandered her time. To begin with, Corri had a clever mind. There was more, much more to Adrienne Corri's talent than the boards and boarding house life of a jobbing thespian.

In 1984 she published a unique semi-autobiographical account of serendipity in her long career. *The Search for Gainsborough* begins with her spotting an early portrait of the actor-playwright David Garrick hanging in a dilapidated Birmingham theatre. Convinced it wasn't by an amateur, she set about proving the work was painted by young Thomas Gainsborough himself. Most of the leading art experts sneered at her attribution, but she persisted. Who was she to tell art experts their job, and a woman too?

She followed the trail with forensic skill, got access to Bank of England ledgers, and ultimately discovered the payment made to

Gainsborough for the Garrick portrait. The find led to a second portrait. In time the experts confirmed her intuition and research, two Gainsborough's now reclaimed for posterity.

What makes the book such an absorbing read is the manner written in diary format. We move from Corri's humdrum theatre commitments to bad hotels, to encounters with pompous experts of the art world, and endless efforts to unravel the documentation, in between trying to keep her domestic life intact, and having a social life among the acting fraternity. Her jottings are a gossipy mixture of art and the movie business. This smattering of diary observations from a house party at director John Schlesinger's gives a fair picture of her short-hand notes. There is no slobbering over celebrity. She is their equal.

> "*September 21st: The list included* [writer and playwright] *Harold Pinter, with* [his wife] *Antonia Fraser standing over him like a guardsman – she is beautiful but they make a funny pair. At one point Harold wanted to check a date for something. Antonia promptly supplies it. "She remembers everything. She is my filing cabinet." Albert Finney and Diana Quick;* [a seven year relationship] *he has got very fat, pudgy all round the waist. She is very pretty. Men are lucky, getting fat and plain don't seem to spoil their chances! Francesca Annis is looking ravishing. John needs to raise four million pounds for his next picture. We reckon if we could sell Diana and Francesca to rich Arabs, it would be in the bank. Alec Guinness is there, Charles Gray, and so on. A good cast. The party breaks up late."*

In this next selected chapter she visits a Gainsborough exhibition at the Tate gallery, and afterwards puts thoughts to paper a mixture of her quest and more film people.

> *December 15th. Wretched. Badly chosen and horribly lit; wrongly dated, at least the early ones. Someone seeing him for the first time would think the man subject to brainstorms. Why should he paint like an angel one day and an idiot the next? I must say, when he is bad,*

> he is awful. Saw the exhibition the first time with David Walker who got engaged by the way Gainsborough will put the figure too close to the bottom of the frame, leaving a great gap to be filled with sky and unconvincing trees at the top. The second time I went there I met little Maurice Binder, who does the screen titles for the James Bond films. He was looking bewildered – a very good artist, he could not make out the datings. "Tell me, Adrienne," he said, "why should a man do a sketch for something ten years after he has painted the picture?"

No sooner has she recounted the meeting than it sparks off a memory with the same Maurice Binder of Bond titles fame.

> "I had a funny moment with Maurice a few years ago. I was making a Hammer Horror, Vampire Circus, and he was working on another stage [in the studio] with white Persian cats, doing the titles for Diamonds Are Forever. [SMERSH villains in Bond films are always introduced the same way, face unseen, one hand stroking a white Persian cat sitting on his lap.] I went to see him and found him fed up, dripping with blood where the blasted things had scratched him. The breed is savage. The cats did not like having diamond collars around their necks. Cubby Broccoli had specified that he wanted "diamonds around a white pussy". I met Maurice in the bar later. "How was I to know he meant a cat?" he said, miserably.

Corrie really did an immense amount of research on Gainsborough and his artistic output, a lot of it foot-slogging between institutions to view work and documents and meet experts. Her intent turned into an obsession and that meant physically chasing possible leads like an fine art hunter. She found his bank account records, what paintings he sold, to whom and when, and for how much.

Corri used her celebrity to great advantage organising meetings with people who could help her advance her theory, and getting answers to letters from people who might endorse it. She met less a wall of misogyny from male experts as a gentle indifference at first to her contention the painting in the Garrick Club was a genuine

Gainsborough. In her search for irrefutable evidence she returned to her hometown of Edinburgh.

> "May 18th: Edinburgh, the National Gallery. The gallery is the most select in the world. They may have only one of a certain artist, but it is the best in the world. Rembrandt, Rubens, Vuillard, and on and on. It is more like a private man's taste than a public institution – I do love it. I went also to the Royal Bank of Scotland. Their Libertarian, Christine Robertson, was sweet; a great enthusiast with a real love of history. I think she found the idea of the picture as rather romantic and did all she could to help. Her bet is that I will have more luck at the Drummond Branch in London where the archives are almost intact, and she will give me an introduction to the Archivist there. She says he is very helpful. I got the feeling that the Royal Bank thought its museum rather a waste of time, but that Miss Robertson was hanging on because she believed in it. I found some very early accounts in the attic. Behind some Victorian papers were bundles of notes in practically mint condition, the earliest dating from 1700, some large documents, and what looked like an early charter, seals and all. I staggered out very dirty straight into two of the directors, and before they knew it, had them on hands and knees on the floor looking at all my finds. I stressed the monetary value of the papers as I have learned to do with bankers. Being Scotsmen they may be tempted to sell them! I told them they could be photocopied and bring handsome dividends. The [hand-written] papers included gave insight into who supported which political factions; who was putting money into the '45 Rebellion, and where their allegiances lay. So much, so long neglected. They might have been thrown out if it was not for Christine Robertson."

As you flit between her musings and research on Gainsborough there are intriguing and unguarded reports of actors she works with in her contractual projects. Two pages on Anthony Hopkins confirm my own observations of a tortured talent prone to outbursts of temper and disappearances from stage rehearsals for days leaving a director ashen faced, and fellow actors to get on with rehearsals regardless, until Hopkins' returns and the cast treat his next explosive walk out with an almost blasé attitude.

"If my original search became a kind of 'pilgrim's progress', I am the richer for it. If I can hand on the lessons it taught me, not just in practical terms, I have been given another dimension for my work, and an explanation s to why it because so vital for me, against all odds, to complete it. One thing is certain – once begun it would admit no denial. Are you looking for Thomas Gainsborough, or is he looking for you? I was asked once at the Royal Academy. I could not answer then, and I do not think I shall ever be able to. Art, unlike mundane work, has the chance to live on and grow after the death of the man who conceived it."

Perhaps she realised after forty a women's acting career is artificially limited. After the book was published her appearances grew fewer and fewer. Only a few actresses stay at the top into their sixties and seventies.

Corri was married to the cerebral Etonian actor, the Canadian Daniel Massey, from 1961 until divorced in 1967, her second try at domesticity. The marriage to Massey was tempestuous. Massey described the relationship in the following terms, "We were agonizingly incompatible but we had an extraordinary physical attraction". (*Wikipedia*.) Massey's traditional misogyny of working husband and housebound wife envisaged a domestic life for Corri but was a serious error of judgement. The last role she was suited to accept was full-time hausfrau. Once she had extricated herself from Massey's patriarchal embraces she resumed her career as an actress.

I can't think of another Scottish actress around at the moment with anything like Corri's beauty or searing ardour, her fire, her love of life. Though opportunity is getting better, good roles are still too few, and an exciting woman's best achievements are sure to be ignored. Believe me, the worst thing you can do to a woman is ignore her!

She was never an international star in the full meaning of that term. I think that was because she never took herself too seriously, or tried to massage her public image as stars do looking for a long career, yet her career lasted over fifty years.

Referring to her search for authentication of the Gainsborough portrait, she wrote, "To make an honest mistake is not the end of the world, but to have lost the wish to find the truth, or to deny it because it is not *your* truth, is bigotry." The epigram could apply to lots of things. Corri's work belongs in the pantheon of Scottish heroes.

3

THE INDEPENDENT NOVELIST

Scotland is doing well for authors of good detective fiction. Some of it may be pulp-fiction standard, but there is any number of men and women making a career from crime stories, a few full-time are very successful. The best of them is no longer with us, Frederic Lindsay. Not all his novels are detective thrillers but all represent literature of the highest quality.

Reading his first novel, *Brond*, I marvelled at the veracity of his dialogue. He had a sharp ear for the vernacular. Savouring speeches of his protagonists and the most minor characters, you know that that person would speak those words. No character's dialogue was interchangeable with another. He had a writer's practised ear for common everyday language. When giving lines to his villainous characters, once again he knew how they talk down to people and the aggressive terms they use.

Lindsay was chased, commissioned and published by the biggest and best in the land, Andre Deutsch one of them. His standing allowed him to pick and choose the best of discerning eponymous publishers. At the time of his death, aged 79, back in 2013, Lindsay's novels had just been introduced to an American audience. Fate takes no prisoners.

Lindsay was highly respected by colleagues and publishers alike, but too often ignored by the media. Was it his politics that put off the unionist press, or perhaps his prose leaning to the poetic? There is an ebb and flow to descriptive passages that is immensely pleasing. This, from his novel *A Charm against Drowning*, is a father in a marriage by name only, trying to save the life of his drug-addicted daughter, the only person he cares about:

> At her endurance he directed a chant drawn from the soiled impedimenta of his unsought childhood. Breathless, he made breath: "Yield not to temptation, for yielding is sin. Each victory will help you some other to win."

He wrote about hard working poor folks living on the edge; he gave their existence veracity. There was nothing stereotypical. At the other end of the social scale he could make the most obnoxious bully of a businessman three-dimensional. You could swear his scoundrels were based on people you had met or known.

One quality had him stand out from lesser novelists. All his adult life, Lindsay was a fervent supporter of Scotland's independence. He was open about it. He did his research and came to the only conclusion one can, the Union is an economic, political and cultural disaster for Scotland. It licences the UK Treasury to steal Scotland's wealth. In this, Lindsay confronted the human capacity for self-delusion. People hold tight to beliefs. Redemption or peace of mind is hard-won if at all by his characters. A recurring motif in his writing is the sense of futility that he saw pervading Scottish society, where one's elected representatives are outnumbered by opponents in Westminster no matter how our MPs vote in Westminster or in Scottish elections. Irrespective of how strenuously or how well one protests or argues about inequality, the other side always wins. It throws loaded dice.

To that end, he was quick to write a sharp letter to a newspaper editor correcting the lies and waffle of its anti-Scots columnists. He took on heavy-weight politicians when it mattered. This letter challenging Gordon Brown was published on the 18th of March, 2010:

> "A friend and I were discussing the role self-delusion plays in human affairs, and he cited an example I had missed. Apparently a few days

ago Gordon Brown expressed hope he might be re-elected to complete the job he had begun. Which job would that be? The assault on the pension funds? The rail link across London? Looking after the interests of the City? Or defending the Union by raising Scottish emigration to 100 per cent?"

Lindsay was a dab hand at knocking spots off BBC's white heather outpost in Glasgow. He railed at the way BBC was irrelevant to Scotland's culture, but disliked more BBC London's ability to make England's agenda the most important of all the UK nations. That meant sparring with Scottish journalists aware of Scotland's democratic deficits, such as Alison Rowat of the *Herald* newspaper. This is from 2nd of October 2003:

> "What a muddle Alison Rowat gets herself into over the tagging on of a Scottish segment to Newsnight (September 26). She tells us it was a sop to prevent the offering of a real Scottish news programme. She draws the contrast between the Scottish segment, starved of funds and forced to deal only with the strictly local, and Newsnight, able to look at American and European affairs from an English perspective. Then, rather than drawing the obvious conclusion that what is needed is a properly funded Scottish programme, with a stroke of logic worthy of Dolly the sheep, she decides we should all be herded back for a full measure of the boring Paxman. Less Rowat, it seems, than Roslin."

Rebuffing newspaper propaganda was a problem when the person writing it happened to be a fellow author, in particular one who liked Lindsay's novels. "I hate doing this and alienating a friendly reviewer!" he told me, mulling over whether or not to he should answer an attack on Scotland's sovereignty.

This happened in the case of Allan Massie, born in Singapore, his father a rubber planter, who became a critic of Scots fiction after an education of memorising the names of the Monarchy and their relationship one with another, and cold showers at Glenalmond College. Massie, not to be confused with another unionist lickspittle,

Alex Massie, spent a respectable quarter of a century writing for the *Scotsman* in the days when Scottish nationalists were considered a small, eccentric clique and actually sounded like they were.

Allan Massie retired to Selkirk in the Scottish Borders where unionists love to congregate for the autumn of their days, a safe haven, gentle hills and no craggy rock faces, relatively free of squabbles over Scotland's lack of equality, a place from where to sneer over a good malt. He must have choked seeing the derelict rail line from Edinburgh, closed by Westminster's employee Dr Richard Beeching, the line reinstated by the leader of the nationalist party, Alex Salmond and not with any help from the British government.

In an acerbic riposte to one of Massie's many anti-independence diatribes, espoused in a pamphlet, Lindsay demolished Massie's weirdly counter-factual dislike of Scotland's natural urges. "Arguing the case for Scotland to remain part of the UK, the Union, is for me, a matter of self-confidence," wrote Massie. "If you feel the lack of that, you will vote for independence." Lindsay responded saying it was *precisely* a renewed confidence in Scots that they had the ability to run their own affairs again that motivated voting for independence. To his credit, Massie did not retaliate. He continued to review Lindsay's novels in a reasonably impartial manner, as reasonable as a man could who was reading the work of a better writer, and who thought Scotland was North England's playground.

"Lindsay's detective novels are unusual in that they gain depth and credibility as the series progresses." The depth of Lindsay's concern with character, Massie went on to opine, "Bears comparison with that found in Simenon, and I can't offer praise higher than that". Their author was, Massie added "at once one of the most interesting and under-rated of contemporary Scottish novelists". *Interesting* and *under-rated* are 'at once' mixed praise. I doubt a reader could name a book written by Massie without checking Google. He wrote thirty, of which twenty are novels.

In his novels, Lindsay dwells on class divisions that exist in Scotland, a corrosive legacy from years labouring under a repulsive

English class system. There are entitled landowners, smug Tory politicians, arrogant bullying businessmen, the bourgeoisie – the educated professional class, all stifling radical progress. Finally, there is the working class, the manipulated, pullulating horde that is *real* political power forever waiting for a leader to tell them how to use it. He is never condemnatory of the poor. They are depicted as victims, the put-upon, dregs at the bottom of the pint who will be with us forever, according to the wealthy.

In all my years of knowing Lindsay I never knew him to make a misogynist remark. It might be because he, like me, had daughters. They teach you respect for the female breed. To suit the dark aspects of his novels, his women tend to be distressed housewives, elderly mother, sex workers, or strident, feisty career women, which does not leave much space for the scientist, artist, sports woman, or business boss. Nevertheless, his women are real flesh and blood, people with feelings, some smarter than the men who prey upon them. You won't find them in tabloid newspapers.

Lindsay was not one for grabbing easy celebrity. He refused to make his private life the core of newspaper interviews. "People who write fiction centring on their own life make for boring novels" he told me. Living in Scotland he understood promotion of good work has few outlets, few ways the outstanding will be brought to public notice, an interview on a BBC Scotland radio show for five minutes by a pseudo arts interviewer more show business personality than erudite inquisitor. That and a couple of brief newspapers reviews are about as much as any writer can expect.

And referring to *Idle Hands* one of the Detective Inspector Meldrum series, Massie wrote, "The ability to create believable heroes out of policemen is rare, and Lindsay's DI Jim Meldrum is both credible and endearing. *Idle Hands* is a complex and satisfying crime novel. Lindsay is a profoundly serious writer using the conventions of the mystery novel to approach 'the dangerous edge of things'." Massie was not exaggerating. Author and book critic Fintan O'Toole in the *Irish Times* thought it, "A most satisfying and chilling read."

Massie noted in Lindsay's detective oeuvre each novel gained in depth and credibility as the series progressed, as would a talented aspiring painter or composer with each succeeding painting or composition, only Massie thought this unusual. In most cases, Massie claimed, the opposite is the case and the quirks the author has given his central character "become, in successive books, merely tics". Massie thought Meldrum's drinking habits, his late nights and marriage problems, cliché – misleadingly he called it "drawn from central casting" – the good detective whose personal life is a mess. "He has become more interesting because he has become more convincingly troubled, more uncertain of himself, worried, low-spirited, finding it difficult to express the sympathy and affection he feels".

The diminutive journalist Alan Taylor, founder of the *Scottish Review of Books*, attending Lindsay's funeral, joked, "I loved his detective stories but worried Meldrum would survive his cases, so affected mentally and physically was he by the gruelling chase and outcome". It was a fair scrutiny without acknowledging Lindsay's Meldrum was the reader with a conscience and scruples, not a television automaton handling a case a week.

Frederic Lindsay, known to friends and family as Eric, was born in Glasgow in 1933, the son of a plumber father and teacher mother. On leaving North Kelvinside Secondary School, he worked as a library assistant in the Mitchell Library, before studying at Glasgow University, where he got a first in English. Life as a teacher was marked out before him. He taught at Annan Academy and lectured at Hamilton College of Education, his wife, Shirley, on her way to becoming a respected head of a primary school. They met at his local library where he worked as an assistant. Their marriage endured their lifetime, Shirley succumbing to cancer only a few years after his death.

His attachment to Scotland's democratic ills began at an early age. I have a true story the measure of the man. Alec Douglas-Home was due to give a talk on a better deal for Scotland – devolution. He promised greater political powers could be handed to Scotland, originally a Labour party policy abandoned when Ireland took its independence. It was the eve of a general election, ultimately won by the Conservative party. On learning Douglas-Home was canvassing in his district, the young Lindsay did an audacious thing. He decided to test Douglas-Home's commitment face-to-face. The Scottish public generally believed Douglas-Home's concern for Scotland's prosperity was genuine; an answer to the poor economic return Scotland receives for handing its wealth into a UK pot, wealth often squandered on wars and English vanity projects.

The last to be a card-carrying member of the Tory party, Lindsay resorted to subterfuge. To gain access to the meeting at which Alec Douglas-Home (pronounced Douglas-*Hume*) was the main speaker, Lindsay dressed up as a typical Scottish land-owner in tweed shooting jacket, a pair of cavalry twills, brogue shoes, waistcoat, the *de rigueur* blue tie, and finished the image with a stout walking stick. (He would need a Barber jacket and green wellies today!) Lindsay got his moment during the question and answer session. He asked Alec Douglas-Home how he intended to keep his promise to give Scotland more political powers. Lindsay prefaced his question with calculated flattery, he was a believer in the work-hard-to-prosper ethic of the Tory party, but he also thought "local decision making a good thing". In an effort to deflect the question and save the future prime minister embarrassment, his election manager began answering for him. Lindsay slapped him down requesting firmly his "constituent MP answer", adding, "I have travelled miles to hear him!" Unsurprisingly, Douglas-Home spluttered and waffled making obvious his promise was *personal* not Tory Party policy at all. Predictably, quietly, once elected, the Tories dropped mention of autonomy for Scotland.

I met Eric, as family and friends called him, when he was a lecturer at Hamilton College of Education, a red brick building where they taught teachers to teach. As a married man, I was given free lodgings there as a hall supervisor in the female section, a job that was part therapist for angst ridden students, and part policeman keeping testosterone driven male students out of female dormitories, a thankless task. It was the time I learned a woman's sex drive could be as strong and all-consuming as any man.

Lindsay lived with his wife in one of the lecturer's houses. Hamilton College had a drama department, a progressive idea at the time. I was having trouble understanding the content of lecture papers on drama theory written by the head of the College's drama department, a bearded Englishman who had adopted all the mannerism of an absent-minded professor but not the intellect. This was an early lesson in Scottish drama techniques as taught badly by an economic migrant. Holding passages in the thesis circled in red, and a puzzled scowl on my face, I asked Lindsay what I was missing. "He can't write for toffee," he said straight out, without a trace of the malicious. I liked him immediately.

He enjoyed a clever joke but could deliver a clunky one. A bad joke could easily appear in his novels if the speaker was not careful. One I remember him telling me and then reading in *Brond* his first novel. It concerned an Irish fishing boat. When Lindsay told the joke he always enjoyed the telling of it, his cachinnation funnier than the joke.

> *A trawler man falls overboard in a storm and the skipper of the trawler shouts to the mate to throw him a buoy. The mate picks up the cabin boy and throws him towards the waving trawler man in the sea.* "Not a real boy!" *shouts the skipper,* "A cork buoy!" *The mate answers back,* "And how the hell am I to know which county he comes from?"

Lindsay did not dominate conversations. He was a listener. I think it was he who taught me that social skill by imitation. Listening to people without losing concentration takes a lot of practice, especially if they are boring or self-interested which the same as boring. As a lecturer in English, myself in drama, I never considered that one day we would work together on his first book as a £2.5 million film, he as script writer, my role as initiator, script editor, finance finder and producer. At that time he'd written and published only poetry and some educational papers, and I had never made a drama film in my life.

His first book was *Brond*, a powerful political indictment of English colonialism, published in 1983 by MacDonald in Edinburgh. It was immediately hailed by critics as "a Glaswegian *Day of the Jackal*". One reviewer likened it to "a political thriller written by Kafka". Justifiably, the novel is still high in the list of the 'The 100 Best Scottish Novels'.

Brond contains all the hallmarks of his later work: an original storyline morally-driven. It contains sophisticated parallel plot lines, an innocent as central character, and a clever villain representing and protected by the power elite, in this case England, the *Brond* of the title. He chose '*Brond*' to keep it close to James Bond, the popular British spy of the time.

The dark novel is a superb study of how and why power does *not* lie in Scotland, how we are manipulated by an aggressive, domineering, colonial neighbour. I had not encountered a Scottish writer who could write with such a powerful political subtext and insight, and moreover, authentic dialogue. There was metaphor and symbolism everywhere, characters drenched in frailty and ambition. Here was a writer who understood human psychology. And best of all, he knew how the British State works to keep its territories in line. Lindsay was 46 years old when he wrote *Brond*, a late starter by any yardstick.

The plot of the novel is essentially how the British State manipulates Scotland in ways unseen by the general public. Brond is an agent of the state, MI6, searching for an IRA bomber. We never get to know his full name. The central character is Robert the narrator, a student attending Glasgow University, who witnesses Brond kill a young boy in cold blood, the son of an IRA man on the run, the boy murdered to flush out the father. The scene is a clear demonstration of the brutality of the British State. You know no one will be punished for the killing. Robert, partly unwell, becomes confused and is soon seduced into Brond's world, a witness to the state's crime. Brond asks Robert to collect a parcel from a 'friend', actually a local gunrunner.

Brond got up out of a deep armchair. He was wearing slippers and had the air of a man at home. There was a decanter on the little table beside the chair and he had a glass in his hand. He held out the other in what

I thought was greeting me until he tugged at the parcel under my arm.

"You've brought my little surprise at last."

I felt astonishing relief at parting with it.

"You're welcome," I said. "I'm glad to be shot of it."

I assumed the demeanour of someone ready to leave, but he offered me a drink in a tone that didn't allow for refusal.

I sat in the chair facing his. My feet gave me messages about the depth of the carpet. There was a power hi-fi system flanked by records. He seemed to be a man fond of music.

"Whisky?" he asked again patiently.

"Please."

"You don't have a preference?"

I didn't understand.

"A favourite blend or a malt perhaps?"

"A malt," I said.

He smiled

I twisted in my chair to watch him.

"Water, soda…?"

"Water," I said.

Usually when I drank whisky I filled up with lemonade – a very sound lemonade. Just recently I had discovered tonic water and liked better than anything the odd sharpness it added.

"Ideally," Brond said, "the water should be from the burn that feeds the distillery. I had business once with the managing director of – one of the malt whiskies, and he took a flask out of his safe in his office. It was water from the well in Ross-shire they used in reducing the malt for maturing." As he spoke he poured a little water from a tall beaker into each glass. "Is that admirable or fanaticism? Either way we can only manage water from the tap here. Fortunately, it is the softest city water in the world."

He held up his glass and smiled at me through its amber light.

"Here we are," he said, "in this warm room with a glass of Laphroaig. What have we done to deserve it?"

Everything under my eye was clear and sharp edged so that I knew about the grain of the table as well as the light changing in the glass *and each of Brond's words separately like objects we could weigh in your hand. He sat opposite me. The table stood at the height of my knees as I lay back in the deep chair. The parcel lay on the table beside us.*

"*Slainte!*" *he said, grinning as if a private joke.*
The whisky plucked at my temples.
"*So what's inside?*"

In one page, Lindsay gives us all the hallmarks of his later work. Ever the moralist, he shows us the banality of evil. First of all, the dialogue rings true. The student narrator's observations are those we might make caught in a similar situation, what he sees in the room, what he makes of the objects, his inability to assess Brond accurately.

On the surface normality and domesticity would be humdrum but here nothing is what it seems. The atmosphere is tense, the undertones sinister. It begins with a mystery – what is in the parcel? We soon discover it is a gun used in an assassination. Delivering it, seeing it, the student becomes complicit in the British operative's plans. Brond is an agent of the British State, one given the right to kill with impunity. The student is drinking a toast with an approved government hit man. There is greater meaning in the domestic situation than first meets the eye. There is political intrigue. The character of Brond represents colonial power. He treats the indigenous student as a friend, almost as a compatriot, puts him at rest by complimenting his country's most famous export, whisky. The MI6 agent is manipulating the indigenous student, wants him to think he, Brond, the colonial agent, is comfortable assimilating another nation's traditions, respectful even, when it is the reverse that is happening. He knows water from a burn better than tap water. He is familiar with the efficacy of good 'soft' Scottish tap water in whisky as a substitute for the real thing. Brond knows the correct Gaelic toast and can pronounce it, Slainte!" He doesn't say "Cheers!" Brond is in charge. Brond is the power.

Lindsay had harboured an ambition to write at least one novel before his time was up. On hearing Hamilton College was about to close, putting him out of work, he realised that, "Unless I got down to writing something substantial, the assumption that I would one day write a novel could be curtailed by a bout of senility."

He wrote three more novels, published between 1984 and 1992; *A Charm against Drowning, After the Stranger Came,* and *My Life as a Woman,* his first novel to hit American bookshops. Each differs markedly in tone and subject matter. When he got the itch for another novel he was drawn to the true story of Detective Lieutenant John Trench of the Glasgow Police, who, in attempting to prove that there had been a miscarriage of justice in the Oscar Slater case, faced dismissal from the force and persecution by his ex-colleagues.

> *"Interested in the fate of the whistle-blower and the political background to the story, I moved the events to Edinburgh and to the present and turned it into the novel* Kissing Judas. *The central character was a police detective called Jim Meldrum only because that's what the story required. As far as I was concerned it was a one-off book, a study in integrity and what it cost.*
>
> *Then I had a call from my agent to say that Hodder & Stoughton wanted to publish, and were offering a contract for another two books about this detective Jim Meldrum. Almost by accident, I had the opportunity to do a series of crime novels featuring the same character. Four years later, I've had four Meldrum books published, and finished a fifth."*

"A study of integrity and what it cost" was my comment to Lindsay. In all his books I found only one novel rushed to a deadline in the series. I risked my safety saying it to him, but he smiled and told me I was correct. "I had only six weeks to complete it."

Lindsay's detective novels stand out not for their handling of police procedural detail, the stuff of the conventional thriller, but for their understanding of human nature. That includes a view of women as play things by powerful and deceitful men, often depicted in sordid scenes that grab the macho by the scrotum. As far as pointing out deplorable instances of misogyny, Lindsay was well ahead of the times.

It is not a surprise to learn BBC Scotland ignored him. No matter what book or adaptation was offered, all were declined – his work was infused with life under 'benign' colonial rule. He wasn't perturbed. "BBC Scotland is an irrelevancy" he said.

Aside from approaches to BBC, his detective novels were not filmed for television. They merit a two-part series each defying conflation into an hour's crime solved episode, and anyhow, BBC Scotland has never had a decent drama budget.

With his politics known there was no way BBC Scotland would touch his work. Indeed, it was Channel Four that funded his political thriller *Brond* through my film company, all of it shot in Glasgow. *Brond* was transmitted in the USA. I saw it as a national corrective to *Scotch on the Rocks*, the cheap thriller co-written by Tory MP Douglas Hurd, produced by BBC Scotland, broadcast just before the 1979 referendum on devolution.

In Hurd's novel, hard-line nationalists are depicted as deluded fools or west coast thugs. Lindsay had no truck with crude caricature. His novels depicted the relationship Scotland with England in a colonial reality. Consequently, his work had no place in a BBC that had fired two competent director generals for daring to ask for a better deal for Scottish broadcasting in budgets and UK transmission time.

The successor to *Brond* was *Jill Rips*, a dark, malevolent study of male violence on women. It has overtones of Jack the Ripper but is a female version. Men are discovered with genitals missing. It was published by Andre Deutsch who had Gore Vidal V.S. Naipal and John Updike in the files. I regard *Jill Rips* the best of his detective fiction. Fearlessly honest, it leaves a scar in the imagination. Lindsay's detective hunts the murderer of sex workers, scattered around districts of Glasgow. Each man in the plot is a version in degrees of male violence on women, from the cruelty of misogyny to the unfaithful husband, and on to the pimp with an iron bar up his sleeve. For a mild-mannered man, Lindsay was unflinching in his candour when describing violent crimes. He refused to use the genteel English *intercourse*. Fuck, screw, hard flesh into soft, are described unsparingly. *Intra*course means between at least two people, a gang bang, but that's the one sex act that doesn't feature in *Jill Rips*, though one can imagine the chief sleaze merchant in it, a wealthy construction boss, indulging in a bout to compromise the politicians in his pocket. In fact, the character has all the manipulative skills of the sleazy Jeffrey Epstein who was operating his little blackmailing hobby at the same time as Lindsay was writing the novel.

Confronting the sexually available young widow of his murdered brother, private eye Murray, a prude at heart, is treated to a lashing from her tongue.

"Someone like you doesn't have to talk like this."

Unexpectedly, she laughed. The noise grated on him like the squeal of a cat. "I don't understand you," she said. "I haven't understood anything about you since the day I met you. What kind of detective are you? What do you do if a witness says "fuck"? What about "Fuck"? How do you feel about "fuck", Murray?

"I do my job."

"Do you put your hand over your ears? She closed her ears with the tip of each forefinger, very gently in mockery.

Baited, he swung his head from side to side. "I can do my job."

"But you're no good at it. If you were any good at it Frances would still be alive—"

"I can do my job!" he said again, clinging to that. "Half the cops in the city are—"

"I'm talking about you." She reached out and struck him softly on the chest." If you were any good, you would have known by this time who killed Merchant and the others!"

"Maybe I didn't want to know."

He shouted into her face, all the pain and weariness forcing it out of him. And then in the silence, he listened to what he had said.

"I've solved you, Murray. Inside you're a mummy's boy—"

In an aside discussing the history of whoredom, Lindsay sticks to his chosen brief. In this passage Murray is talking to crime reporter Tommy Beltrane in the Crusader Bar:

> "The Romans did their whoring differently," Tommy Beltrane said. "Like everything they touched they made it sinister and grotesque. The whores of Rome, the bustuariae, believed, were persuaded to believe, they were the servants of Gods of the Dead. They practiced their trade in the cemeteries of Rome and received their lovers lying on the graves that had not yet been filled in."
>
> "I met one like that back there," Murray said. She looked as if she might have been buried and dug up."

It wouldn't do for the stained sheets of Lindsay's *Jill Rips* to mention how the Romans turned wild hedonistic couplings into magnificent mosaics on house floors and paintings on walls, more open about sex than any modern adolescent with his centre fold from *Playboy* on his bedroom wall, or a poster of a female tennis player scratching her bare arse to teach him sodomy.

For an American film version, his private detective became a gumshoe. This lifted the protagonist from an ordinary television police office to the archetypical loner on a mission. Unfortunately, the American producer was a copy of his scumbag construction boss. Looking for a fast buck, he picked up the 20 page storyline and had a hack chop out an ugly script, throwing it out to the marketplace as a cheap thriller. I think Lindsay was greatly relieved when the DVD disappeared from the bottom shelves of a bankrupt Blockbuster chain. Five years later the producer was given a jail sentence for corrupt financial practices.

Lindsay and I corresponded regularly while I was domiciled in Hollywood, me regaling him with experiences and anecdotes of Tinsel Town, he keeping me up to date with Westminster's shenanigans. I have those e-mails still. One told him of the clash Thomas Harris was having with the director of *Hannibal*, the last in a trilogy of the flesh-eating serial killer. Lindsay read *Hannibal* and replied:

"Not surprised to hear they butted heads – I can't see how that ending can be filmed, not because of the eating brains stuff, you can write around that. No, because you can't in a film take the battle of good and evil, as embodied in Clarice and Lecter, and have her *made over to* his *taste – he can't be Hannibal the Cannibal and Svengali. Even today audiences expect good winning out in the end in the same way a concert audience waits for the final chord to be resolved in the major key. I know there are counter examples, but usually there's a redeeming feature. None in* Hannibal, *none in the novel. Harris gives him a wee sister who was eaten by an animal, reducing him from mythic monster to another product of a hard luck childhood."*

Lindsay served on literature committees, was actively involved with PEN and the Society of Authors, attended his local SNP group, and also wrote for theatre and radio. Moreover, I don't recall him ever getting a bad review. We shared an admiration for Gore Vidal's scarifying polemic. I'm pleased I gifted him my signed copy of Vidal's *Palimpsest* shortly before he died.

I found Lindsay tremendously knowledgeable company, literate, wise, good humoured, and a damn stubborn cuss to deal with when it came to buying the rights to his books. His integrity was unassailable, his belief in his worth unshakeable. As for any reader planning to catch up on the best of Scottish authors, his novels are still available on Amazon; I recommend them all, some hardback covers reproduced among this essay. In 1975 he published a paperback of poems *And be a Nation Again*. He would have a lot of trouble coming to terms with the SNP of today from the one he knew.

Just before his death he was approached by a producer to write the screenplay for former British ambassador and human rights activist Craig Murray's forthright account of torture and British complicity *Murder in Samarkand*. A great pity it was not produced and released. It was a good match.

Death cheated Lindsay out of his independence vote by a year, but then Scotland's liberty delayed another decade, perhaps it was better he didn't have confirmation of how craven are his fellow Scots.

Writers of pulp detective fiction are expected to produce a book a year. With Lindsay, the time lapse between novels, the thought and research that went into them, was too long, but when those three hundred plus pages arrived in hardback they were worth the wait. Assuming there is no nuclear power stations or electricity and therefore no computers in Heaven, I hope Frederic has paper and pencil.

4
CIVIL DISOBEDIENCE

I joined a few sit-down protests and marches in my day, mostly CND, anti-nuclear related gatherings, only to witness my photograph taken by Special Branch officers perched on the top of buildings, their colleague in the street offering a copy of the *Morning Star*, the paper of the Communist Party of Great Britain. "Take a copy, comrade." "No thanks. Marxist dogma isn't applicable today. Anyhow, your colleague up there top of that block already has my photograph." The special branch coppers operating these days do not wear their hair regimentally short or a pair of police boots. They present themselves are ordinary guys to seduce unwary female protesters into illicit relationships so that they can spy on their organisation. When I was a youth they were less subtle and a lot more obvious.

Civil disobedience is not about principles. It is about tactics, should we do this, or should we do that? And if we do that, what are the consequences? Once you ask that question the morality of your actions come into play. I hoped to bring awareness and understanding to the political injustice I and my group were highlighting. We wanted change for the better, to end the manufacture of nuclear weapons. We did not get involved to antagonise others or denounce individuals because that would be the wrong tactic. We assumed people would respond to peaceful protest and be repulsed by intolerance.

The police tended to react with intolerance if instructed by the government of the day. Their violent responses to the closure of coal pits by the Thatcher regime, for example, are on record. The media showed such events safe from behind police lines. In the Battle of Orgreave in June, 1984, the media gave the impression police offers were being attacked by angry out-of-control miners' pickets when the polar opposite was true, the miners were attacked by police charging them on horseback, and swinging truncheons.

Another example, after the 2014 independence referendum downhearted supporters congregated in Glasgow's George Square. They were viciously attacked by gangs of right-wing thugs. The media, the BBC and Scottish press in this instance, portrayed the clashes as pro versus anti supporters in fist fights though it was plain to see democracy supporters defended themselves from injury. What chance is there for change for the better when reality is deliberately distorted to suit the status quo?

The first thing one has to plan is how to get one's message across in the way you want it understood, not the way the British State wants it understood. The secondary concern is to watch out for a protesting group's steering committee amassing power for itself beyond that given by the group it represents. We make choices, we delegate authority, but we have to check on what we are doing and why.

Matters become complicated when one's country is being subsumed into another, civil rights removed, one's entire way of life, principles, values and mode of governance usurped. If a protesting group becomes powerful, is able to attract a lot of media attention and sympathy from the public for its arguments, the controlling state will infiltrate its governing body or committee to receive warnings of plans, events and organised civil disobedience. In Westminster's case, it can even go to the length of having married police spies cohabit with women demonstrators by fooling them into a relationship.

One of the best examples of civil disobedience in Scotland saw two long-time residents of Glasgow's Pollokshields district rescued from repatriation by UK immigration enforcement officials in a dawn raid. They had not renewed their visas in time. Hundreds of local people surrounded the detention van to protect the two men who had served their community for years from their local shop. The state handlers were instructed by London, and the crowd took exception to incomers forcibly removing an individual from their midst, and doing it without recourse to the courts. The collective action was peaceable, determined and altered an inhuman policy. The authorities departed empty-handed. Campaigners hailed their victory for solidarity telling the UK Home Office "you messed with the wrong city". (The same event happened in Edinburgh in May, 2022.)

No one should be surprised that Glaswegians rose up to block an injustice. Looked at dispassionately, the poor and the downtrodden of Glasgow, and Dundee too, voted overwhelmingly 'Yes' to improve their lives in an independent Scotland. They had nothing to lose. Decades of Labour party and patchy Tory rule had not altered their circumstances one iota. The well-off and the highly influential voted 'No' and won, thus effectively enslaving the poor and the downtrodden. This has been the way of it ever since 1707, the year we rioted in the streets and the English government moved regiments into Scotland to keep the populace controlled. It was also the method of iron rod rule in other countries where rebellion was the only method to release men and women from enslavement.

When the French revolution began, it began by releasing the prisoners in the Bastille, many incarcerated on trumped up political 'crimes'. In Scotland, our juries, our peers, good men and women in the community, are still in charge – just. They decide guilt or freedom, as they did in Tommy Sheridan's first case against a lying British newspaper, and spectacularly in Alex Salmond MP's trial. Good people in the right places can alter society for the better. There was no jury of his peers for human rights activist Craig Murray which saw him jailed for eight months. Society has to have checks and balances in what it does with power.

Before feelings of complacency overtake common sense, I ought to take stock; almost every person who has been outspoken in the cause of Scotland's liberty, both pre-and-post Referendum 2014, has been attacked in various ways, smeared, condemned by the press, faced court action, jailed, or driven out of politics to the sidelines, this in Scotland's supposed *free* enlightened society. Watching colonial masters manage to see jailed an advocate of liberty tells us we have lost our innocence. Scots who wanted to govern their own nation have been persecuted down the decades and to a great extent still are, their elected representatives treated as lepers and shunned. This situation is taken to its greatest degree by Westminster hellbent on circumventing law and Treaty, emasculating Scotland's elected government.

History, they say, is written by the victor, truer to say history is written by historians who rarely talk to ordinary people, or bother to find out what ordinary people feel, how they fought, won or lost, how they were defeated, how they suffered the consequences. Historians talk of 'the people' and 'public opinion' but that is not where they gather their facts. They get their facts from official records, but above all, from newspapers, British newspapers, purveyors of the status quo and the rule of law. One can lie outright about the past and about circumstances. Or one can omit facts that will lead people to conclusions one dislikes. Admitting the executions of Sir William Wallace and Mary, Queen of Scots was officially sanctioned assassination, murders after Culloden and Glencoe and decades of clearing people off their land is genocide, is welcome. What is not acceptable is speaking of truth quickly and moving on. What happened yesterday affects what we think today. For those reasons, for those violent events, the right to exercise civil disobedience is justified.

Happily, the methods of communication are much swifter today. The ability of the general public to be their own newspaper, their own mini-documentary, is real progress unknown to our forbearers. Capitalising on the existence of Internet platforms to pass news and opinion to others based on events that are not word of mouth or Chinese whispers, is unique in the annals of historical record. This facility breaks the monopoly of the power elite.

Internet political protest is valid activism, albeit the sedentary kind, but cerebral activism nonetheless, in extreme instances an obligatory daily exercise. In time, this mode of instant communication brings groups together to debate, to warn, and when truly riled to leave the safety of their home to join marches and rally around political champions, and do it in defiance of authority. Internet activism is resistance by digital magic. It works even for those people who are not natural heroes.

There is down-side to too regular physical protest. If a rally meeting at a national monument or a green area such as a local park, with no discernable target the public sees and understands, protest can lose appeal as news. The point of the protest is lost to onlookers. If the organisers are not careful to couch their protest in peaceful terms, authority and the malicious can interpret the call to physical dissent as a subtle call for violence.

A big political issue, pushed by the public via the Internet, can motive academics, writers and journalists to get out into the streets to demonstrate in acts of civil disobedience against state policy. Being symbolic figureheads, they risk imprisonment, not an unknown punishment in what we like to think of as an enlightened Scotland. Jailing a person of no great public reputation might attract scorn from their peers and be local news for a few days, press cover slight, ignored by the media in general. This tactic helps to convey a serious injustice is of no great domestic impact. A well-known respected personality jailed gets everybody's attention for a long period.

In ancient Greece, the cradle of democracy, 'having your say' was done every weekend by standing on a large, specially fashioned series of stone steps, there for the purpose, to make your protest about this or that to an assembled crowd or anybody who would listen. The topic could be the price of goats, or cheese, a neighbour straying onto your land, or a corrupt official. The Pnyx is a hill in central Athens. Regular use of this earliest of open democracy platforms began somewhere around the 5th century. As its popularity grew, it hosted assemblies as well as individual speakers. By this point community officials were expected to attend the weekly 'speaker's corner' by law and to act upon any unjust matter as described and supported by the people of Athens. Officials could be disgruntled by what they heard if they happened to be the subject of the speaker's anger. This did not mean they were free to ignore the issue at stake. They were expected to fix things. Local council authorities are today's method of complaint, not used enough because we are too busy getting on with our responsibilities to attend to the concerns of others. To get around inertia, petitions are devised signed by members of the community and presented to town councils.

In contemporary times, authority has learned how to defuse anger and legitimate protest, to devise 'cooling off' periods, doing it by enquiry reports, and the like, that take time to compile and published when the public gaze is elsewhere. Systems can release pressures or cause more frustration. Something has to give. Eventually, people are pushed to use the courts to attain change, but that route is an expensive path and can be further thwarted by the government taking a counter-case to the court. As I write there are moves afoot by the British government to transfer key constitutional matters and human rights issues to the House of Lords, none elected, to circumvent courts. Justice Lord Neuberger, president of the UK Supreme Court until 2017, put it succinctly: an act that withdraws the right of a person to challenge the government through the courts, "turns democracy into a dictatorship, a tyranny". A tyranny is how one can describe England's governance of Scotland since 1707 from the mass of evidence available. And therein lies Scotland's predicament, how to throw off a more powerful colonial neighbour.

Civil disobedience is a topic one sees appearing with regularity in social sites. It ought to be a salutary warning to too comfy politicians – if our elected representatives will do nothing, the people must do something. The Tory party plans to reduce Scotland to a vassal province, its inhabitants effectively slaves of a power and profit-orientated regime, one with no regard for the semblance of a democracy.

In 1849, the American essayist and philosopher Henry David Thoreau wrote that individuals should not allow governments to overrule their consciences, and that they have a duty to avoid allowing their fears and meekness to enable governments to make them the agents of injustice. Thoreau was motivated in part by his disgust with slavery and the (1846–1848) Mexican–American War. Thoreau hated the war and denounced it. In rebellion, he refused to pay his poll tax, a classic tactic of civil disobedience by an individual. That was all the excuse the authorities needed to throw a vexatious objector in prison. He was jailed, as are men of principle on these occasions. His friend, the poet Ralph Waldo Emerson, visited him in prison. "What are *you* doing *in* there?" said Emerson, shaking his head and what he considered stubbornness. "No! What are *you* doing *out* there?" replied Thoreau, shocked that Emerson's anti-war sentiment did not motivate him sufficiently to following his beliefs to their logical conclusion, a jail term.

What does civil disobedience mean in practice? As Thoreau demonstrates, it can mean small or big sacrifices, boycotting newspapers, institutions, branded goods, shops, and corporate organisations. Anything causing corporate entities fear of losing profits, sufficiently to demand the government of the day meet public demands is a good thing. Withholding taxes is a good thing, but requires a lot of co-ordination and courage to stay the course, to stay united, while a few confederates are picked out by the authorities for an appearance in court. However, if enough defy core taxation courts cannot cope with the numbers referred to it. Throwing crates of tea into a harbour as a protest over imposed taxes made by a colonial government was a great idea. American secessionists knew what civil disobedience meant, they knew it worked well when you attacked businesses that supported the British government, but *did not* affect their own communities negatively.

Setting up his Committee of 100, a force to release Britain from amassing weapons of mass extinction, philosopher and mathematician Bertrand Russell said:

> "There is a very widespread feeling that the individual is impotent against governments, and that, however bad their policies may be, there is nothing effective that private people can do about it. This is a complete mistake. If all those who disapprove of government policy were to join in

massive demonstrations of civil disobedience, they could render governmental folly impossible and compel the so-called statesmen to acquiesce in measures that would make human survival possible."

Political activist and linguistic philosopher, Professor Noam Chomsky feels civil disobedience effective insofar as it achieves its objectives, that is, alters government policy. He suggests civil disobedience in modern western societies can be effective under two conditions: when the issue at stake is "a marginal class interest of the ruling class which will be conducted if the costs aren't too high at home"; and where "a large part of the population understands that the policy in question is morally wrong".

"In these circumstances, civil disobedience can mobilise the large part of the population who see the policy as objectionable, and this mobilisation can raise the costs of the policy to the point where people who run the society will decide that it's not worth pursuing it."

Talk is easy, action harder. We can tie ourselves up in arid debate about what is morally justifiable, or we can unite to regain Scotland and its wealth for its people. To my mind, civil *dis*obedience is not the real issue. The real issue is civil *obedience*.

In over three hundred years Scotland has tried various ways to rebel against unwanted colonial invasion, but only since it regained its parliament has it been able to exercise profound dissent by democratic means. This in turn has caused our colonial usurpers to threaten removal of constitutional powers and our parliament. Do they mean we return to the sword and the musket? If anything is guaranteed to vanquish civilised dissent, removal of a nation's right to exist is the breaking point. Stagnant passivity and smug complacency allow injustice to flourish.

There are moments in a nation's history when people need to act instead of relying on movement leaders. Leaders are often flawed beings. Whatever actions one can take – whether it's engaging in discussion with family or work friends, lobbying your MP, using

Internet social sites to exchange ideas and opinions, making donations to activists and organizations, or taking to the streets in protest or acts of civil disobedience – it all makes a difference. The small actions add up to big, co-ordinated social movements for justice; the women who chained themselves to railings to gain the right to vote knew that basic truth.

5

THE INFAMOUS LEDGER

The United Kingdom is a collection of nations yet people fall into the trap of talking about the entire British Isles as 'England.' The English do it as a matter of course. What they see on a map, England, Scotland and Wales, they see as one country. Foreigners, from tourist to politicians and onward to president, we are England. Strangely, I have never heard a Russian president or politician call Scotland anything but Scotland. They know it is a distinct entity from its neighbour. Celebrities successful in their chosen field and politically aware are careful to acknowledge Scotland as Scotland. As for the rest, Britain is identified as *England*. The rot is endemic, for those who ought to know better, a recurrent howler, a manifestation of lingering colonial rule. Amusingly, some leeway is given to Orkney and Shetland, islands uncoupled from the mainland gives the impression of separateness. Perhaps what Scotland needs is a large body of water between it and England, such as a wide canal fit for ships of a wide berth.

The source of this repetitive insult to the nations in the UK has its roots in the British Empire. It did not matter whether the new territory invaded was short-lived, chronically unstable, or secured long-term, nor governed by an Englishman, Irishman, or a Scot, the land and its wealth belonged to the Crown, and the Crown was represented by the 'Queen of England'. Not for nothing does India's Kohinoor diamond sit smack in the middle of the British Crown jewels, centre front.

To understand why people think Scotland is the Highlands of England, or the huntin', shootin' and fishin' playground, one studies the way England controlled its territories. The indigenous people of an invaded country soon find their language overridden by the English language. Allegiance is given to the English King or Queen.

When the empire was at its pinnacle, during the latter part of Queen Victoria's reign, and the composer Edward Elgar dutifully producing patriotic music for overblown pomp and circumstance royal ceremonies, England held complete sovereignty over all its international territories and dominions. There was general peace and stability. Internal colonies were not a problem. England had already annexed Wales centuries earlier (1536) – only English speaking Welshmen could hold office in Wales, effectively robbing it of sovereignty. As for Scotland, after military threats, extended trade blockades and bribes, England managed to gain full political control of Scotland in 1707, though not control of our legal system or Presbyterian Church. It did not manage to corral or Education Act of 1872, either, but by then we taught in English with a Scots accent. Scholarly and clannish, we were of an independent mind, and with centuries of history behind us, our links to European culture strong, this was a trilogy not easily broken down. Scots were hard to 'tame'.

The way to control Scotland was to denigrate the local culture and impose an English culture, and bit by bit, infiltrate the thinking of Scots to colonise their minds. To a great extent colonialism by stealth worked well, but there was always a residue of resistance, people questioning why Scotland was unable to make economic and social progress, yet had so much natural talent and wealth, a great deal of it put to work for the Empire. This is a long way of saying the colonies are not on record demanding independence from Scotland. England and the English Crown were the dominant features. No one should be surprised Scotland is so often spoken of as a part of England.

The Union of Ireland (1801) dissolved the Irish Parliament and robbed Ireland of developing its economy and industry in competition with England. The outcome of controlling Celtic nations was to deny their people the right to determine their own future, make their own decisions, and their own foreign policies. Whenever England felt in a good mood, faced by political hostility, we were apt to be given token resolutions. Those devious conditions survive to this day, the last regarding Scotland in the now discredited 2016 Smith Commission. When it seemed likely Scotland would regain its autonomy, England promised greater powers, only to have ninety percent blocked in subsequent negotiations that involved unionist parties in the proceedings. From 2018, the Tory government began clawing back powers, including taking Scotland out of the European Union, against its promise to stay in if Scotland remained in the Union. The 'Union of Equals' so often bandied around by English politicians and House Jocks as if saintly altruism, is a nasty joke. English power is all consuming. There are no exceptions when conquering a colony.

English speak with pride of *their* country, and have every right to express self-worth, but they are not stating delight in the nations or territories of Great Britain. Scotland, Wales and Northern Ireland are not included in their thinking, Gibraltar a protectorate is forgotten. At the root of the colonial mentality is racism, a characteristic of English 'exceptionalism'. England is as much an interdependent state as any other, but it does not see itself in that light. It sees itself as extraordinary, the mother land governing the other nations, keeping them solvent.

If Lord Nelson can get it wrong, "*England* expects every man to do his duty," signalled the naval flags at the start of the Battle of Trafalgar, others will make the same egregious error. Five ships were captained by Scots, Nelson's crews consisting of Scots, Welsh and Irish.

The Great War poet Rupert Brooke refers to a corner of a foreign field that will be 'forever England'. He does not write "forever United Kingdom," and not because it will not scan with his verse. He draws attention to his Englishness. It is precious to him. The poem is standard curriculum fare when discussing the millions who died in the mud of the trenches. Tens of thousands of Scots died in the First World War. Apparently we inherited nothingness. Brooke goes on to talk of 'a richer' soil beneath the foreign soil. Presumably, shedding Scots blood nourishes damn all, nor Welsh, nor Irish blood. How marvellous to exude pride in one's heritage, to be patriotic, quite another to think your country so superior to other countries you demote them, or forget they exist.

Residents are Brits, imbued with that abstract, nebulous thing called 'Britishness', but exactly what is a "Brit?" For Scots, the question is arid, the argument circular. Again, we can trace back this racism to the decades after the Union was signed by three percent of Scotland's earls and clergy. Scots were 'permitted' to send a delegation to London for debates and votes, but one so small in number it was completely insufficient to influence or overturn decisions taken regarding Scotland. Scots were scorned in the corridors of power. Naturally, resentment grew incrementally as Scots felt reduced in status, our institutions downgraded.

Where are we now? The confusion begins with what to call the United Kingdom without demoting England's place in it, England the imperial power. English are subsumed, lost into Britishness: Britain, Britannia, Great Britain, British Isles, the United Kingdom, 'this Sceptre'd isle', or if drunk on patriotism, Albion. If there is a simple method by which a nation can be demoted, made to feel inferior to others, giving it a generic title is the way to do it. England has outwitted itself. The answer is to refer to it as if it is the whole United Kingdom.

Some years ago I began casually collecting instances where Scotland was referred to as England or a region of England. Sometimes it was done out of ignorance, sometimes out of a state of mind. I listed the round-up in an imaginary book, *The Infamous Ledger*, a suitable title for the disgraceful racist slurs from colonials and pitiful Scots who want to be English, viewing their own culture cringe-worthy. The list stretched to the moon and back. In the end, I gave up. There were too many to handle.

Here are a few everyday examples. Prepare to be vexed.

"I do not want Scotland to leave *the rest* of England." *Ed Davey, Lib-Dem party, exhibiting an ingrained colonial mentality.*

"We're going to take a look at the best in *British* culinary, from Newcastle to Suffolk." *Television chef Tom Norrington-Davies.*

"Written in 1215, which British document in its Clause 39 guaranteed trial by jury?" *Game show host Ben Shephard. Britain did* not *exist in 1215.*

"I think that England is an island. I think that England should be England. I think that we should keep that." *Ian Botham, cricketer and foot massage salesman.*

"Where's England? What's happening with England?" *Donald Trump on that place where lives the "very lovely Queen of England".*

"The referendum in England was about Britain, about England leaving the EU, nothing to do with Scotland." *A confused Tony on Twitter.*

"David Douglas was a great English botanist and explorer." *Biography of Scotland's famous plant hunters. He was born in Scone. The Douglas Fir is one of his discoveries.*

"Remember, England depends on you!" *English captain to Scots battalion in WW1 trenches.*

"The Prime Minister has cojones of steel and is putting in a punishing degree of effort to deliver for our country. *Tory Ruth Davidson, on a prime minister who ignored Scotland.*

"British policing faces crisis: Crime soars as police numbers drop to lowest in 37 years." *Peter Stefanovic. Scotland has its own police force.*

"90 Portraits of Eminent British Women." *National Gallery, London. None Scots; all English, one 'Brit' a hundred percent Irish republican.*

"*This England* (1941)": *IMDB, the only recorded instance of a title change inside Britain. The film was titled* Our Heritage *for release in Scotland.*

"For too long people have been sneered at for loving our country, and believing that we can prosper beyond EU borders. I love our Country, and truly believe in Global Britain." *Andrea Jenkyns Tory MP, muddled and emotional about England's empire.*

"I have received the email from you regarding your order and I am able to inform you that the National Scottish Referendum has taken place and the majority of Scotland decided that the lovely country of Scotland would belong in, and stay within, the UK, and will be a part of the country known as England." *Marks and Spencer customer service.*

"And now, the national anthem of England." *Announcer, Rugby League World Cup final on "God Save The Queen", a dirge that is not and has never been an anthem.*

"But in our English parliament …" *Janet Street Porter talking about the UK Parliament.*

"Great to see Last Night of the Proms a celebration of English tradition and patriotism, only spoiled by the morons waving EU tatty flags." *A musically illiterate tweet from somebody called Malcolm Wood, one hopes not a descendant of Sir Henry Wood. The orchestra of the BBC Proms plays music from composers around the world.*

"Take a look at the British engineering triumph." *SKY News describing the inauguration of Scotland's Queensferry Bridge over the River Forth, built with Chinese steel and not a penny from the UK Treasury.*

"Who speaks for England? – and by 'England' we mean the United Kingdom." *Paul Dacre, former right-wing editor-in-chief of the right-wing* Daily Mail. *Who is 'we'?*

"The SNP is tantamount to an illegal occupation by a foreign power." *Simon Heffer in* The Telegraph *reminds us England rules the UK.*

"The SNP is playing political games with *our* country." *Theresa May, Former UK Prime Minister; England owns the United Kingdom.*

"Britain is a nation with the right to rule itself… faced with the contemporary resurgence of regional or tribal uprisings…" *Bilge from Melanie Philips writing in the* Times.

"Those who love their country would never seek to divide it!" *Jeremy Corbyn, former leader of the Labour party confusing England with Scotland.*

"Murray is England's Best Hope in the Games." *Daily Express headline on Scotland's tennis great, Andy Murray. When Murray won Wimbledon, the First Minister of Scotland seated in the crown, waved the Scottish Saltire and was roundly hammered by the British media.*

"You have a wonderful British accent." *American interviewer to actor Hugh Grant. Grant has Scottish grandparents who were wealthy ship builders.*

"David Cameron will have to resign if there's a Yes win. He can't say, "But I can keep my job?" He will be told, "No, you lost the country we are supposed to control." *Fraser Nelson, editor of* The Spectator, *a Scot better known disparagingly as a House Jock.*

"Heathrow is the airport for the capital city of our country! Be proud of it." *Piers Morgan, opinionist and blowhard on BBC's* Question Time.

"We must promote British values in our schools!" *Michael Gove, MP, a Scot who wants to be English, talking about English schools in an English educational system.*

"It was Churchill's genius to find the words that spoke for England." *BBC presenter Jeremy Paxman wiping out Scotland's blood sacrifice in World War II.*

"A Bulldog, the national dog of Great Britain." *Peter Purves, co-presenter at Crufts Dog Show. Scots have no national dog, but the Border Collie is generally seen one of many breeds purely Scots.*

"And now, welcome Ed Miliband, the next prime minister of England!" *Delia Smith, cook, wrongly introducing a man who had never held a job in his life.*

"We can look forward to a rousing match England versus Australia." *Sue Barker making the classic sporting faux pas – it's Great Britain versus 'separatist' Australia.*

"Wales and Scotland are smaller than other parts of England." *Kezia Dugdale, a Scottish politician proving Scotland can produce dullards same as other nations.*

"The things I do for England." *Spoken by James Bond in too many 007 films.*

"The Scots no longer think it worthwhile belonging to England." *Peregrine Worsthorne, journalist, in a New Statesman interview being proprietorial.*

"I believe in England, and I believe we shall go forward." *Etonian, novelist and essayist George Orwell demonstrating in 1941 how conscientious intellectuals can get it wrong.*

"I read the news today, oh boy. The English army had just won the war." *From the Beatles* Sergeant Pepper's *album, lyrics in the song "A Day in the Life".*

"Today the *Mail* asks a question of profound significance to our destiny as a sovereign nation and the fate of our children and grandchildren. Who will speak for England?" *An editorial from the UK tabloid's far-right editor, Paul Dacre.*

"To shoot grouse you have to be exceedingly rich: it costs around £7,000 per person per day. Owners of grouse moors … justify these fees by having vast numbers of birds to shoot. This requires, across great tracts of our uplands, elimination of almost everything else." *'Our uplands', possessive shorthand description of the Scottish Highlands, a phrase from the normally precise environmentalist George Monbiot who supports Scotland's autonomy.*

"A Yacht Voyage Around England." *Travel book by W.G.H. Kingston. There is no way 'around' England without sailing around Scotland and Wales.*

"The UK and Spain have been partners and allies for over 500 years." *A delusional fabrication tweeted by the UK Foreign Office. The acronym UK only came into use in 1801, and there is the small matter of the Spanish Armada (1588), Battle of Trafalgar (1805), and Gibraltar in England's long antagonistic history with Spain.*

"Britain is unique among modern developed economies in sucking the creative juices from the provinces to the capital." *Simon Jenkins in the* Guardian *reducing Scotland to a province.*

"I don't feel British. I am French. I don't have that association with England." *Nicole Farhi, former dress designer turned sculptor, actually getting it more right than wrong.*

"Nicola Sturgeon is leader of a regional government…" *Presenter on BBC Radio 4 reminding us that the voice of British colonialism is the British Broadcasting Corporation.*

"Murray England's Best Hope in Games." *An insulting* Daily Express *headline on Scotland's tennis great Andy Murray playing for Great Britain.*

"Scotland has every right to call a referendum, but we Brits see things differently." *Lord Heseltine, Tory grandee on BBC radio lets us know Scots are Scots, but by god, sir,* Brits are English *through and through! This defines precisely the ambiguity for all, answering my question in the Preface, "What is a Brit?" A Brit is an Englishman!*

Even the Welsh get it in the neck.

"The rail strike is cutting Wales off from the rest of England." *Kate Burley, news journalist, laying bare the colonial-minded bias of the British media.*

6

AN ARTS POLICY FOR SCOTLAND

It took weeks to get my head around a paper propounding a philosophy of art for all, what should be reformed, what should be encouraged. I believe participation in the arts ought to be available to all, from young children to elderly adults, not merely as audience. Talented youth deserve the best facilities to develop and flourish. This last tenet is sometimes rejected out of hand as elitist which is counter-factual. A nation has a responsibility to identify outstanding ability at an early age and nurture it. How to retain talent in Scotland is the big challenge, not see the best go elsewhere to make a living. This wants careful consideration. Actors, directors and playwrights head south; the best painters tend to regard Scotland and its unique light as their natural home but know London critics and galleries exalt artists; musicians are itinerant; writers tend to stay here, but the very successful such as novelist Alistair MacLean toddle off to tax exiles.

One could subtitle this paper, 'Not a proper job'. The Scottish Diaspora includes philistines who think the arts for the work shy, a cop-out, no way to make an honest living. The same get angry to learn a painter or a theatre group receives state funds in subsidy. We can find the lazy in any professions, like the office worker who has perfected the act of seeming to be at work when talking into a telephone. Freezing to death at 6am on a winter's morning in Lanarkshire, waiting for the crew to set up for a drama scene shot outside a rural pub, I was holding a paper cup of coffee for warmth when a passing lorry driver shouted, "Why don't you wankers get a proper job?!" Vulgarians are everywhere. Moaning about there being too many arts festivals is a Scottish hobby. Edinburgh folk keen on isolationism are apt to grumble at the world coming to their city every year for the International Arts Festival.

I suggest we should have a celebration of Scotland's greats, let the world know who our best are, rather than hoping the non-Scottish director of the Edinburgh International Festival might include a few 'local' productions in the August extravaganza if we doff our cap. That aside, I would rather see a permanent new gallery devoted to Scottish inventions and achievements down the centuries. I would like to see it designed by a Scottish architect.

The Palaeolithic cave paintings in Lascaux are every bit as great as any of Pablo Picasso. The palm print on the cave wall tells us the artist existed, just as we place our palm in the earth with art to show we exist. The epidemic of graffiti that disfigures fine buildings is an unknown doing the same thing, letting us know they want to be heard, seriously annoying and costly to clean off as it is. Although ninety percent of graffiti is balloon lettering, local authorities who install walls for the specific use of graffiti work are enlightened. Occasionally a truly original illustrator emerges, such as Keith Haring, but people like him are the exception.

In publishing my thoughts on what should be nurtured, what we have worth cherishing, what we need to enrich our culture, I add that I am reduced to exercising my intellect these days, others do the hard work. While I can publish an outline of principles on art and people know who wrote it, others get no recognition for their physical effort. I offer principles not rigid policies.

A fable taught when a child was the story of the grasshopper and the ants. The grasshopper plays sweet fiddle music all summer for the enjoyment of a colony of industrious ants storing food and building homes. When winter's hardships arrive he is refused food and shelter only to be lectured about the virtue of hard work prepares us for tomorrow. That is how our society treats the arts when budgets tighten. Other nations *increase* support. They acknowledge the arts bring pleasure and happiness, *and they know the arts heal.* Great art is an ambassador for a nation's culture. It fosters global friendships.

To begin at the beginning: Education is prone to churn out conformity; rather we should cultivate the best instincts in human kind. I am sure this is conceded by most thinking people. One begins with the inalienable right of every individual to develop from opportunity offered. To confine learning to existing job opportunities, education as a sausage factory, is the state at the mercy of capital. The arts can create well-adjusted personalities, confident, articulate and imaginative, the very essence of human progress. The arts motivate people to enquire, to experiment, to question and in participating, find new ways of seeing and communicating. The arts can challenge beliefs, push aside shibboleths and aid understanding.

Primary Education: Everything begins at the primary level, everything. Inculcating an adventurous spirit in children, exploring by creativity, and co-operating with a friend or group, eradicates the fear of failure. The joys of construction are shared. There should be no such thing as failure, only *experimentation.* (The Montessori Method excels at this.) Failure teaches the child he or she is of less worth than their peers, that they are of limited ability.

Infant schools include art, dance, music and storytelling. Children should explore their indigenous culture and that of other societies, concepts that connect people the world over. (I include Gaelic culture.) Primary teachers usually key in work to the cycle of the seasons, but it is vital children make connections with the world immediately around them, the one that exists every day.

Take art as an example. Primary teachers are excellent as all-round teachers; however, few have any specific expertise in aesthetics. A peripatetic specialist is needed for that task. Bringing in a secondary art student is an answer. Let them teach lessons in the principles of art, why art is all around them, from colour and pattern, through design, to architecture. Teach children how aesthetics are important in everyday life, knowledge imparted *without being over-complicated.* At an early age, through play and games, children are expert in imagining themselves as adults, pirates, ballet dancers, bus drivers, tigers, movie characters, and the like; the origins of theatre are there to develop. Exposure to arts and crafts is paramount if an individual is to see power not as superiority over others, but as learning by artistic creation or scientific discovery.

Children of this age are information sponges, they absorb without bias. Teaching without children knowing *why* they do it, is useless.

Secondary Education: The arts are, by their nature, anarchic and free flowing, like youth itself. The pioneering work of dominie A.S. Neil and his Summerhill School and his disciples John and Morag Aitkenhead with Kilquhanity House in Castle Douglas, ought to be in greater practice, a renaissance, where young adults are freed of adult coercion over subjects suppressed by rigid curricula. Free will spurs self-motivation.

In secondary education we should follow the same line of curiosity as primary education ditching the rigid lines of learning. Truth is important but imagination comes first. Leonardo da Vinci would have a lot of trouble adjusting to strict educational categories of subject matter. To him science and art were one and the same. Therefore, in the fourth or fifth year of secondary school study a pupil ought to be free to specialise.

To know who plotted the death of David Rizzio, Mary Queen of Scots favoured musician, is of no great application. We should know our history, of course, but look for more than plain facts. Much better to understand the male psyche to give insight into human nature. The aggressive youth may find pleasure in the armed services as an adult, but utilising the arts as a means of exploration can illicit others skills that will bring as much satisfaction as an adult than military drills and adventures in wars.

Music must remain a staple of an education system. Venezuela provides the triumphant example of school students, individuals from *poor income backgrounds* have group effort consummate in youth's enthusiasm to participate as a team in playing orchestral music. The renowned Simón Bolívar Symphony Orchestra, often under the baton of Gustavo Dudamel, is the best example of its kind. For a short time, we had a similar experiment gaining praise in Lanarkshire. A nationwide echo of their principles is the way forward to create Music Scotland. Let no one be put off by fear of scale.

How good are the arts in education? Drama classes boost language and communication skills; music classes boost an understanding of mathematics and foster team work; dance exhilarates and is physically beneficial and teaches grace in movement, modern dance innovates, painting, print making and sculpture teach the science of colour, design, creative use of earth's materials, enhancing imagination. Russian-American abstract painter Mark Rothko's intense colour-field canvasses taught us colours trigger emotions. The designers of Edinburgh buses learned a lesson from Rothko's experiments. Bus passengers got nauseas when riding in the city's battleship grey and maroon transport double-deckers, two hues that cause sickness placed side-by-side in quantity. Subsequent bus designs saw their seat colours altered to dark blue. The bus example tells us the arts free us to discover things we did not know or see, they offer other possibilities.

Filmed drama and documentary: The moving image is *the* form of storytelling of the modern age. The novelist and writer, the auteur, cinematographer, designer, composer, musician, digital magician and animator come together through filmed drama and documentary. Alas, Scotland is locked into the British film industry, to a great extent the English film industry. Understandably, England's output chiefly promotes English culture. The bosses of the British film industry are known to reject Scottish subject matter, allegedly because it is 'not commercial'. This leaves Scots filmmakers at an acute disadvantage, subordinate, forced out of Scotland to find work. Moreover, it keeps Scotland's activity at the level of a cottage industry. We remain a country more often used as a backdrop for films of other nations, than one making movies.

One has to give thought to the amount of financial benefit a community accrues when a film is made in its boundaries. As well as hotels, and police security, a film's budget pays for staff, catering, street hire, goods from shops, and ultimately will bring in tourists who have seen and liked the film's content. Local councils and newspapers like to boast about American productions shot in their area, but this alone reduces Scottish films to also-rans. Foreign productions, for that is what they are, use Scotland merely as a backdrop, sometimes clothing it to look like somewhere else. They do little or nothing to promote Scottish culture, values or life. And it has to be said, profits from foreign films made in Scotland are not the possession of Scotland.

The Norwegian model is one to study. The Norwegian government gives an annual tranche of money to existing film production houses, and a large portion of cinema ticket profits go straight to the production company. Income and government funds are conjoined and recycled. This is a standard Scotland would do well to implement. By this method Norway, a small country like Scotland, is able to produce a dozen films a year without worrying about international sales or subtitles. Producer's films find an audience on Norwegian television, paid for the right to have their work broadcast to Nordic countries. Scotland does not have a broadcaster actively involved in encouraging movie making. If writers, directors and producers want to see their work shown in the UK or abroad, we require a body devoted to it that includes a resident expert in international sales, with local cinemas *guaranteeing* exhibition of home grown material. Scotland could easily emulate the Norwegian model, our stories expressed in Gaelic, dialect, or in Scots-English.

The Appurtenances: Creative Scotland, the body devoted to financing the arts, labours under a faux commercial role, which is essentially, anti-experimentation and risk. It dominates those that cannot survive without subsidy, and new talent looking for start-up funds. The decisions it makes are hit and miss. Some decisions are inexplicable. Sitting in an office dishing out rules and application papers is bureaucratic. The old Scottish Arts Council had a policy where an arts officer turned up at a client's door or event, *unannounced*. There is need of an 'Academy of Arts' that dispenses funds, and also *elevates* its practitioners, no London critics needed to decide on standards or values. Creative Scotland is a stop gap that wants a rethink.

Corporate sponsorship is a dragon consuming all before it. Big business reduces creativity to consumerism. A new Scotland can discipline corporate ownership of the arts. Ditch pick-the-popular sponsorship in favour of a national accumulated fund – sponsors duly thanked and publicised. Take a modest portion of mandatory tax from businesses. Together with a wholly Scottish Lottery Fund (still a *reserved* fund), a 'National Fund' rids us of the mendicant culture where only the strongest survive. Let arts activity free itself from stifling commercial imposition, wary of radicalism.

Art colleges moved to *installation* work some years ago, 'concepts', encouraged by second-rate UK prizes. (An installation caused the first fire in Glasgow's Mackintosh building!) Art schools exploit this fashion to save on painting and drawing materials. Art students are graduating who cannot draw or paint. They know nothing of the process of artistic creation. The pendulum has swung too far one way. The principles of art are sacrosanct; those skills take years to acquire. Nurture the gifted, not the lazy keen to become an 'artist' on the back of shallow concepts. And in that regard, we should see stronger support than now for the guardian of Scottish art, the Royal Scottish Academy. In addition, the Scottish government should consider removing the Edinburgh College of Art from the suffocating confines of Edinburgh University, and give it the freedoms and ethos its needs to flourish once again.

In Summation: Education is the province of the political charlatan. Opponents of Scotland's rights carp and bite at the edges of education, from primary to higher education knowing there is never enough money to alter things, their moans and groans are safe. The proposals set out here for the arts in education and the community are *not* expensive. Above all, a government that embraces the arts embraces human aspiration, a place where we gain a sense of ourselves as a great civilisation. A spirit of adventure and liberty will bear fruit in an atmosphere of consistent and sustained national support of the arts. The arts are critical to developing an independent mind, not an easy thing to accomplish, but a necessary thing if we are to create a better society. Scotland, be bold!

7

THE ROAD TO CRIEFF

For a number of years I had occasion to visit relatives in Crieff, Perthshire, a pleasant drive from Edinburgh on a sunny day, part motorway, part A-road, part B-road. Like most drivers, my attention was on the road ahead and not the scenery either side. When it came to my last visit, relatives moved on or passed on, I took a slow tour to Crieff stopping to see the sights and marvel at what lay either side of my wing mirrors, in villages and over the hedges, a journey worth sharing to remind ourselves of over a thousand years of Scotland's history we take for granted, history that lies only a short walk away. I enjoy driving if a car is enjoyable to drive, if it has character, but normally long journeys are boring.

Unfamiliar with the leitmotifs of the genre I claim no skill as a travel writer, a specialist craft, so I shall stick to the historical aspects to be found on the journey. Travel writing is for the inveterate or accidental traveller, the restless who have to see the next town and the one after that. I am a home loving guy. Walking too far anywhere has always put me off the journey. I have never been much of a walker. Only once have I been known to run for fun, in Spain, momentarily free of worldly responsibilities, I shot off down a country road in bare feet, elated at the sheer pleasure of being alive, like a dog let off the leash in a grassy field. Torn skin on the soles of my feet took several sticking plasters to heal. If a castle or garden is worth a visit, the car park better be a close stroll. Stopping, parking, expected to reach a distant point on foot is a big decision. There to look at and soak in the ambience, I leave photographs to my travelling companion. There are people who rarely take iPhones from off their face reducing the parameter of their vision; everything in front of them becomes a potential composition for a snapshot. I never take photographs of anything, neither panorama nor ubiquitous selfie, preferring to commit to memory sights, sounds and smells.

Once you swing off the M90 motorway, driving between a long drystane dyke once the pride of the village, the stone from the same quarry that built Braco, you begin to get annoyed at all the gaps in its architecture, the wall cannibalised in too many places by locals destroying its fine build and history. Braco is one of the earliest villages the car traveller passes on their way to reach Crieff. Few stop to linger. The road cuts through the middle of it, and its contraction over time makes for a sombre narrative.

The place first appears as a village in 1815, a new settlement to attract agricultural workers and the trades they needed to do their work, the blacksmith, the drystane dyker, the farrier, the woodsman, the miller and the grocer. Back then, it had 385 inhabitants, now about 515. It has gained a staggering fifteen new inhabitants since my last visit, probably births. We must find that woman and stop her!

Villages in fertile places prompt the feeling there's room for expansion in a modern Scotland. Lots of our villages could accept sympathetic development one way or another. All our villages can boast at least one resident that left to make their name. Past residents of Braco have included the founder of the Football League, William McGregor, computer game designer, Chris Sawyer and artist Ronald Forbes.

As for Braco's notable history, there are two churches, one the driver is apt to miss because it is reduced to its clock tower, Ardoch Free Church. The other, plain Ardoch Church has an interesting history. It was built in 1707, sparing local inhabitants miles of a trek to Muthill further north. Although riotous living is not recorded, it was a happy band until righteous morality entered its portal. The church saw a mutiny. Rather than allow the local landowner to choose the minister, the congregation were encouraged to walk away led by their preferred minister, a follow-your-leader departure. To show his new-found authority he created the United Free Church, though it was anything but spiritually 'free'. His action was a clear case of self-preservation that replicated itself throughout Scotland among other angst-ridden clergy, like rabbits in a warren. History is one person makes a stand and others of a like-mind follow, or no mind, content to have it made for them.

In 1442 over thirty pieces of land were confirmed to Michael Ochiltree, the Bishop of Dunblane, by King James II of Scotland. These included the Braco estate, which at the time was known as Brecache. "Breac Achadh" means "Spotted Field" in Gaelic, a field partly cleared of bracken.

As you leave Braco to take a hard right turn, you cross a two packhorse-wide bridge lying across the River Knaik. The guide books have it there since 1743. Knowing the history of that one area you can understand how the earls and ministers managed to sell Scotland so easily and swiftly in 1707 for English gold when the majority of Scots lived off the land, not in sophisticated towns like Edinburgh, too long a horse and cart distance to berate Scotland's mercenary parliamentarians.

There is little evidence of agricultural industrialism today that used to make Braco a village of hustle and bustle, a market place of distinction, the place to go for produce and trade. You can still see the foundations of the two mills that were in use, on the River Knaik, and the other near the Keir Burn. I recall reading there was a threshing mill there too, although I can find no mention of it and on the day my legs did not take me far enough to check the lay of the land.

As everywhere in Perth and Kinross there are Roman remains to explore, here conveniently lying above and along the side of the road. Why Roman habitation is described as *undiscovered* is a puzzle. It probably refers to reluctant explorers like me. Obviously the existence of ruins is known otherwise it would not be recorded and publicised. Roman occupation on the Gask Ridge, stretching across Scotland, included the Roman Fort of Ardoch located to the north of Braco. The ramparts and ditches of the Roman camp are still visible as grassy knolls and ditches; the site now designated a scheduled monument.

The law of averages reminds us there must be Roman treasure buried in Scotland, mosaic floors, coins, glass and jewellery, as yet never unearthed in an archaeological dig. The fort at Ardoch has survived so well largely thanks to the landowner in the late 1700s, Sir William Stirling. He enclosed the remains to prevent their being ploughed, a process that, as so often happened elsewhere, would have resulted in the ditches and ramparts obliterated altogether. Late in the 19th century, the Society of Antiquaries of Scotland excavated parts of the fort. They uncovered evidence of a complex sequence of buildings and walls. The Romans first seem to have built a series of large marching camps in the area, perhaps during the initial campaign in northern Scotland led by Julius Agricola in AD83. This would have helped support the line of Roman defences that ran north-east along the Gask Ridge, intended to protect the Roman area of occupation from the marauding attacks of hit-and-run indigenous tribes. Within this first fort were a series of wooden buildings.

Defeated by a combination of constant forays made by local groups who used the land to their advantage to attack lightning fashion, and disappear just as swiftly, swarms of biting midges and the cold, wet weather's effects on hot bloodied Mediterranean types, the Romans pulled back in AD105 to what later became Hadrian's Wall. Not learning the lesson of how midges keep a wilderness wild, the Romans tried to conquer Scotland a second time, returning in AD139 and found life just as miserable. If only the English had taken a lesson from them.

Emperor Hadrian died in AD 138 and his successor, Antoninus Pius, not content to leave the Roman frontier on the line Solway to the Tyne moved back into Scotland. Even after decades of retrenchment, the Roman policy of *emperium sine fine* – empire without limits – was a popular concept. The Romans advanced back to the

Clyde and Forth isthmus and built the Antonine Wall. According to the records and some supposition, the second fort at Ardoch, built in stone not wood, was occupied in the decades either side of AD150, about the same time as the Roman's established the 1,000-strong legion encampment and a harbour on the Cramond estuary, just outside Edinburgh, on the River Forth. The barracks has always been interpreted as the feeder port for Roman incursion into the 'north lands'.

Taking a wander up the slope to the fort – aided by a stout stick – what you find on the ground at the top might seem a little disappointing to the untutored eye. There is a series of very well defined ditches and earth ramparts. The outlines of the southern and eastern edges are fairly nondescript, but the northern half of the eastern ramparts have as many of six distinct lines of ditches and ramparts. They are easily seen. The northern edge of the fort is still more complex, comprising eight or nine distinct lines of ditches. They extend either side of what was once an access road. Written guides tell of faint traces of a building within the fort, all that remains of a medieval chapel. Roman marching camps were used by the army as a means of penetrating deep into hostile territory. Roman tactical thinking assumed that an enemy could be defeated in the field by the superior training and equipment of the Legionaries, they just did not reckon on the cleverness or the ferocity of Scots and Picts using the cover of darkness to attack guerrilla-fashion. The defence to this sporadic warfare was the 'marching camp' – a makeshift fortification that could be dug by the soldiers in a few hours at the end of a day's march. I can imagine the groans from solider told to dig ditches having marched twenty miles. A ditch, perhaps only one metre deep and two metres wide, provided spoil for a rampart. This was topped with wooden pointed stakes – the Legionary marching equipment included two stakes per soldier – were lashed together to form caltrops. A significant gap between ramparts and the tents enabled a mustering area and ensured the soldier's accommodation was out of range of any projectiles thrown over the ramparts such as large stones. According to archaeologists, there were no gateways.

Open entrances to the camp – presumably to allow quick access of egress of legionaries and horses – were protected by an additional ditch and rampart earthwork.

As you travel on along the road to Crieff, you pass vast agricultural wealth, landowners keener on London rule than Scottish. They consider themselves businessmen who vote for the business party even if they like to popularise their worth as farmers to give the impression of hard working folk of the soil. In reality, they derive their wealth from arable farming, livestock breeding, and areas reserved for shooting sports. It isn't for nothing the green welly brigade holds annual game fairs in Perthshire, exhibiting an assortment of the expected and the über-niche into rows of marquees to sell their produce or merchandise: kilts, leather belts, burdock wine brewers, gin dabblers, honey bottlers, craft and jewellery maker, the good, the bad and the truly kitsch.

Braco Castle is still there but not Ardoch's magnificent Georgian mansion demolished late last century, leaving behind rolling hills of exotic trees and shrubbery and rabbits.

Twisting one way and then another, the road passes white painted farmsteads, barns and corrugated iron steadings, and then opens up into a panorama of grazing fields for sheep and cattle, and wheat fields, sitting high on your right, sweeping down and away on your left. Those on the left of the road get flooded in winter's heavy rains, creating mini lochs. The flooding leaves stranded beasts bewildered, soggy hooves, until rescued by the farmer on his tractor. The view across Strathallan to the Ochils is magnificent on a sunny day, contentment to the eye, a stretch of rural Scotland that has you feeling good to be alive.

Further on, overlooked by copses of fir trees, sits the tiny village of Muthill, there longer than Braco. It held a monastery in early times, a pretty fundamentalist, live off the land, prayers ten times a day, refuge for men of the sackcloth and no spirit of adventure. You can still see the bell tower that was attached to the medieval building. The village itself grew in fits and starts from the 1770s, perfectly placed to embrace the Agricultural Revolution that began in the

1600s and gather speed and intensity in the 1800s. At this point on the road the careful driver has to stop viewing the scenery and drop speed dramatically to negotiate the zigzag ninety degree bends and head for Crieff. On the way, a pair of wrought iron gates catch your attention, not far behind through a double guard of beech trees, stands Drummond Castle.

The castle has a chequered history, impoverished when the Earl of Perth, James Drummond, chose the wrong side in the Jacobite Rebellion in 1715. (How different Scotland might have been had his side won.) Drummond was one of two active lieutenant-generals of the Jacobite Army, though past historiography of the rising has tended to minimise his role. Drummond met Prince Charles at the town of Perth accompanied by around two hundred tenants from Crieff who were formed into the Duke of Perth's Regiment. Penalties imposed by the English authorities on the area after the 1715 rising, Drummond had difficulty raising men to arms, the recruits fewer than he hoped. Despite concerns over his practical military knowledge, Drummond was well-liked. James Maxwell of Kirkconnell (who wrote an excellent account of the '45 Rising when he settled in St Germain) said that Drummond was "much beloved and esteemed even by those who did not wish to see him at the head of an army".

Following the defeat at Culloden he sought safety in the 'Auld Alliance'. He and several others boarded a French boat at Borrowdale, a small hamlet on the Isle of Skye. Drummond was said to have had a delicate constitution following a childhood accident; the campaign had taken a high physical toll on him and unwell was carried by retainers. He died during the voyage and buried at sea. His death was something of local disaster for he was keen on improving arable land and sharing it equitably with his tenants. Most interesting of all, he never bothered to learn more than a smattering of English but "invariably used broad Scots" which endeared him to many in the social ranks, and annoyed the writer and Whig politician Horatio Walpole who dismissed him in typical English style as 'that silly horse-racing boy!" Drummond was known for breeding race horses. By the end of the 18th century the castle had fallen into disrepair, but the gardens were saved and replanted in the 19th century, causing Queen Victoria on a visit to purchase a piece of what she considered England's empire as, "really very fine, with terraces like a French garden".

From Drummond Castle the chimney tops of Crieff beckon. Entering the town you pass Victorian and Edwardian mansions sitting stolidly in large walled gardens, homes too big to heat without a large bank account, but a lot cheaper to buy than counterparts in Edinburgh. Crieff was once a bustling, important market town. There is an air of time standing still in the musty store window displays, the modern street furniture at odds with the old buildings. The Drummond Arms Hotel stands on the square empty, dilapidated, sandstone facade stained from cascading rain water out of broken gutters, the inevitable shrubbery growing, roots gripping down into stone cracks.

Crieff was already well established as a town by the time the River Earn was bridged in about 1690. The following year it became the site of Scotland's first public lending library. The town's growth and wealth benefitted from its communication links to the Highlands and the Lowlands. By 1700 vast herds of highland cattle from across northern and western Scotland were driven along the traditional drove roads to the trysts, or cattle markets. Each year up to 30,000 cattle arrived on foot for sale in the town. Crieff gained a reputation for wildness, cattle owners whooping it up in the local drinking dens. Highland drovers far from home enjoyed the fruits of their efforts after the sales. With the exception of how people dressed and the American long horn breed, the town's streets must have looked much like Chicago when it was a cattle market and Glasgow emigrant Allan Pinkerton was pitching his new detective agency amid rutted mud and cow dung.

By the 1770s cattle increasingly tended to head to markets in Falkirk rather than Crieff. Scots always able to adapt, Crieff reinvented itself as a resort, mainly on the basis of its famous Hydro Hotel – a sprawling Victorian pile – a stay there once considered a status symbol by the bourgeoisie of Edinburgh. It became popular with the rich and famous of the day and still was when I was young, that and a good employer of local people. Fair to say the Hydro is no longer the number one Mecca for lowlanders looking for a health spa and 'taking the waters'. The original swimming pool used peaty brown unfiltered water, making emersion a bit like bathing in thinned Bovril. The Hydro was the largest temperance hotel in Scotland at one time. They gave big discounts to the clergy to pack them in. Day's ablutions over, ministers tripped down into town to the nearest licensed hotel, The Murray Park, or ran liquor bars in their room. The Hydro was helped by the arrival of the railway in Crieff in 1857. Sadly, Crieff is dominated not by its history but by the motor car as unwanted incomer, my own included. There are few places to park, the streets too narrow. The tendency is to give up and drive on. This is shame because Crieff has its own identity. What it can boast is Morrison's Academy, one of the leading independent schools in Perthshire.

The town of Crieff has one lasting association for me. James Rae my father-in-law was Provost for many years, and well liked by the citizenry. When he was there the place had liveliness about it. Crieff is in dire need of central government investment and a new vision to return it to a functioning dynamic town and not just a tractor halt for a farmer's Subway sandwich.

If the old fashioned window dressing of the main shops is off-putting, the motivation is to drive on and aim for the village of Comrie, a place to park, and a place to eat at the Royal Hotel, a bunch of free newspapers to read while you wait for your meal to be served.

The road to Comrie takes you through verdant field and wood, and new-built holiday homes until you arrive at the Glenturret Distillery, licensed in 1775, home of the Famous Grouse (no relative), a clever marketing ploy. Less clever was the distillery's insistence to announce it backed a No vote in Scotland's independence referendum, a serious retrograde step for an industry that has since suffered the predicted repercussions. Taken out of the European Union by a predominately English vote – 53%, Scotland voted to remain – removed protection of whisky at a stroke as a unique Scottish brand. It takes some understanding to fathom why a Scottish distillery could make that gargantuan error of judgement. The distillery markets itself "Scotland's oldest". One feels like adding "and stupidest". In any event, many a glen held illegal stills in the Highlands before 1775, but Glen Turret was probably the first legal, commercial distillery.

A few miles down the windy road you arrive in the sleepy village of Comrie, the busiest place is the charity shop. The Charles Rennie Mackintosh's building on the corner is an early project he helped design in 1903 while working for the architect firm of Honeyman and Keppie, in Glasgow. It was commissioned by a local draper and ironmonger as a shop with a flat above and workrooms in the attics. Mackintosh's intention to exploit Scotland's baronial style is evident in the projecting turret. The first floor flat with spacious, airy rooms shows his tentative touches of design flair. It can be rented for holiday visits. Across the road is a vast white church, the scale a surprise in such a small village. Graveyard enthusiasts and history buffs will appreciate the ancient carved headstones.

If you approach Crieff from the west through country roads, by the A822, you might encounter the Parish on Monzie, the estate and Monzie Castle. The original was built around 1600, and later larger additions gutted by a fire in 1908, rebuilt by renowned architect, Robert Lorimer. Monzie is associated with witchcraft, the ghost of a wretched women falsely accused, exploiting spells for her protection. One such was Kate (Catherine) McNiven, a nurse who served the House of Inchbrakie in the Parish of Monzie. The date of her death is disputed, the way of word-of-mouth stories. No authentic record of Kate's death exists. The story has caused endless discussion and argument, but is worth the telling.

According to local legend, Kate McNiven was a witch who lived in a cave in Monzie. She had served as nursemaid to the Laird of Inchbrakie when he was young. She was a healer and, in one version of the story, was rumoured to take the form of a bee. Bumblebee or honey bee is not known. I cannot find either if she sold pots of honey. Found guilty of witchcraft, she was sentenced to die by strangling and burning on the Knock of Crieff, near her cave. Exactly what sort of witchcraft she was accused of is lost in the Monzie mist of time but fear of the unknown and the spiritual was enough to see the locals retaliate. The Laird, a non-believer of wizardly powers, attempted to stop the execution but failed. As she died, Kate cursed the local town of Monzie and its officials so that they would never grow or prosper. One has to suppose she made her curse before the ligature was placed around her neck and tightened. However, she spat out a small blue stone – a "moonstone sapphire" – in some versions, this was pulled from a necklace she was wearing – and gave it to the Laird of Inchbrakie. She promised him that as long as he and his descendants kept it on their land they would always have heirs to hold the property. Not long after the stone was lost the property was sold. Careless or what?

Monzie is where my day's visit to Scotland's Middle Earth ends. As you sink into the winged armchair of Comrie's Royal Hotel to enjoy haggis and chips and a glass of malt, considering the history of the land through which you've just travelled, you are left with mixed feelings. For one thing there is Union spy and pamphleteer Daniel Defoe's advice that "middle Scotland wants for a revolution in its agricultural practices", a reference to farm poverty he never actually saw. When Scotland has settled down to its independence they will miss the largesse gifted by the European Union. The towns and villages of Perthshire are long overdue their own revolution.

8

COLLABORATORS

There is a lot of clearing up to be done when a nation throws off its colonial masters, banishing traces, the detritus, the odour of the old order, removing the regressive from indigenous institutions, reopening old mysteries to find answers, firing the inept. It ought to be done *before* Independence Day, sweep away colonial pawns who hold Scotland back now, the civil servants, the chiefs of broadcasting, the advisers of government policy, otherwise they will do their best to derail and upset the new order. That's what they were once paid to do, halt progress. Collaborators think of themselves as liberators. They are bringing 'civilisation' to the natives.

What is it collaborators do? As well as reporting to their masters what is happening in their area, they keep order. They receive praise and reward for their loyalty. Their skills were needed and put to good use. It has been this way down the centuries in country after country. Authoritarian order has to be sustained and if eroded, reconstructed. How is that done? Collaborators follow dominant government dogma to the letter. Business must be dominant, tax relief, local and national grants handed to big business and not placed on welfare, hospitals or education, labour split and weakened, and the burden of taxes placed squarely on the shoulders of the working classes and the poor. In extreme cases it can mean keeping a district or an area under-funded or causing economic collapse so that the dominant power can enhance influence and move in with draconian laws to reorganise society to the new order. Democratic ideals are unwanted.

In Scotland the major thing standing in the way of colonial power is the independence movement, a high voltage electric fence blocking the extraction of wealth from the country at cheap rates or next to no cost. Self-determination is the main target for attack, the strategy is frustrate, encourage alien culture and values, impose rules, resist local power, disrupt, split old alliances, cause divisions in homogenous groups, break unions, create political distractions and diversions, using tactics that will suppress free will and free speech. In short, a collaborator is a corrupt individual. If they mess up or tire they are shifted upwards and taken home again, usually elevated to the House of Lords.

Who are to be considered *collaborators*? They are identified in various ways, those who live in Scotland or own property or land in Scotland and did all they could to keep Scotland a colonial territory. Those who headed large companies or institutions that barely served the indigenous population though that was the sole reason for the institution's existence. I imagine none consider themselves as anything other than loyal British patriots. That helps to keep their conscience clean. If they look in the mirror each morning they don't wonder why they do what they do to subvert their country. None would arrive at work if they had a conscience. The smart up and die before the day of reckoning, such as the Labour MP George Cunningham – Labour, the party of the people – who turned democracy on its head by introducing his amendment demanding a minimum of 40% of the populace vote for Scottish devolution, a tally that included the dead. For perverting the course of democracy, he remained unrepentant until the moment of his final breath in 2018.

How do we deal with collaborators? One among many tasks is to rid our institutions of colonial employees. Many will leave of their own volition taking their wealth with them some of which will have been grants from the Scottish government, a fact our laws should be ready to sanction. Others will sit tight refusing to show shame. Being of a colonial mind ought to see them demoted, removed from influence, their privileges cancelled, and their civil rights abbreviated for a given period of time. Should they continue to give Scotland the finger, and refuse better education not based on race or indigenous inferiority, their rights remain *ex custodies semota* – out of reach. The counter-argument is a reasonable one. It will come from those who do not understand the usefulness of truth commissions. They say let bygones be bygones. Forget the past, don't dig it up; let us move on. They have a point, but only can we know our present and where we are going if we know our past.

On the day the Scotland's national party gained a majority of seats in the Holyrood parliament and in many local councils, one English wag announced on Twitter in disgust that he was leave bonnie Scotland because he could not abide living in a "one-party state," forgetting Scotland had been governed by the Labour party for over thirty years without any real opposition, and the inescapable fact that Scotland was governed by people they had never elected. If he feels so disgusted by the advent of an elected government he is not the person we look to for the renaissance of a new Scotland.

The other way, and the fruit of this essay, is to purge individual and national guilt in public interview and answer sessions, and do it without jailing thousands of people who betrayed a nation's humanity for personal enhancement. Those in other countries emerging out of decades of hell called them Truth and Reconciliation Commissions, *conciliation* being as important as speaking truth unto the people.

There are good reasons for mounting truth sessions: open, public hearings place quislings, betrayers and flaky placemen into the light, the worst inoculated and neutralised, motivation depleted, unable to gather new recruits to undermine the constitution of a liberated Scotland. The process can get rid of unwanted cargo. A truth commission stops the unscrupulous blackmailing turncoats who have committed crimes while in office, from shredding vital evidence or squirreling away public funds. Public hearings protect the guilty from themselves and from others. The reasoning of hearings is *not* to denounce and jail, Nuremburg Trials style, but to help people unburden themselves of shame and offer to follow a better life for the common good.

Nelson Mandela is the most obvious champion to advocate public confessionals as a means of allowing those who had committed atrocities or lesser crimes such as theft from the public purse, given the chance to enunciate their mistakes and become free men and women again. They were called '*Truth and Reconciliation*' groups. Members of the South African Bureau for State Security, Afrikaans Buro vir Staatsveiligheid – also known as the Bureau of State Security (BOSS) – lined up to confess heinous crimes, people who had indulged in torture and assassination on behalf of the state. Until that time falling out of a police station window was a common cause of death. They were followed by the former president of South Africa, F. W. de Klerk. Frederik Willem de Klerk, OMG DMS. While the tide of history would probably have made the change inevitable, it was De Klerk who accelerated the pace of reform. Essentially a right-wing conservative by nature, the last president of a segregated nation came to believe that white-minority rule was not sustainable. His ending of the ban on the African National Congress and freeing of Nelson Mandela were the steps that signalled the move to majority rule. As he neared death he took it upon himself to make a statement of his guilt to the world's press. Some might say it was safe to do so by then, but he had the choice of keeping his legacy of reform void of any involvement in the dark things that had happened before he renounced oppression as a means of control. De Klerk did not throw off his apartheid beliefs altogether. In 2015 he waded into the row at Oxford University, criticising the demand of activists that a statue of Cecil Rhodes at Oriel College should be removed. "Students," he said, "have always been full of sound and fury signifying nothing."

Writing about Mandela and the anti-apartheid fighters brings back vivid memories of De Klerk's predecessor, the unwavering hardliner PW Botha and the day he stood reluctantly before a court, unapologetic, angry and insistent he had done no wrong. Botha sputtered and bellowed, waffled and snorted, sweating profusely in the glare of a South African courtroom. "Die groot krokodil" (Afrikaans for "The Great Crocodile") had been trapped by the laws of a country he never wished to see. He'd spent his entire life, like generations of his people before him, with his proverbial boot on the neck of South Africa's black majority. But that day in 1998, he faced a black judge, in a land ruled by a black president, Nelson Mandela. The world was watching him. Though his charge was a minor one – contempt of court for defying a subpoena from South Africa's Truth and Reconciliation Commission – he became the only apartheid-era political leader to be prosecuted after apartheid's end. Botha would not explain himself, not to a "bunch of bliddy blacks". That's all the commission wanted. It isolated Botha as an unreconstructed white supremacist, or truer to say, he did that himself, and the new South Africa removed his rights one of which was he was not allowed to vote in elections.

The comparison of South Africa's experience with Scotland is bound to be dismissed by the unreasonable but racism is racism irrespective if both sides are a shade of white. Colonialism is racism. Colonialism is the practice of one nation depicting the people of another nation as inferior, less intelligent, and incapable of making reasonable decisions. Just because no one has amassed a list of who has been removed from work, lost their livelihood for supporting Scotland's freedoms, or assassinated – I can think of the naval officer, lawyer and SNP chairman Willie McRae and his demise on a lonely Highland road – does not mean that the British State has clean hands. The informed will direct people to the tactics of the British State in Northern Ireland during the years of 'the Troubles'.

Mandela's truth sessions were predated by President Samora Machel of Mozambique, one of the first African leaders to utilise this humane process, once he had overthrown his country's Portuguese invaders, a man greatly admired by Mandela. Machel was an extremely astute leader on top of being the nemesis who drove the Portuguese out of his country. My cousin, the journalist Iain Christie, was his biographer. He wrote this of Machel:

> *"Beyond the usual attributes of statesmanship, his greatness was expressed in very human qualities – a great breadth of vision, a compulsive honesty, determination, and a zest for live and human contact. He had vibrancy, panache, and a self-confidence that broke down barriers of language and ideology."*

It takes a person of tested integrity and statesmanship to organise confess-and-shame confrontations and conduct them with dignity. Leaders of the character of Machel are trusted to supervise honesty sessions, as he did personally. His people knew he would handle tricky moments with great care. Machel included university students in his truth commissions. They were paid by Portuguese infiltrators to spy on other students and report what fellow undergraduates said about their colonial invaders. In return, the recruit had their university fees paid and given back-pocket money. Machel brought betrayed graduates to the session to face their accuser, those in the 'dock' asked to apologise to them. There is film of one such event, the shamed student eventually saying "I am sorry".

Before baleful unionists point out we are not at war with England as Mozambique was with Portugal, and sensitive Scottish nationalists throw their hands up in horror at what they *think* I mean, treating what I write with deep suspicion, I have news for them. We *are* at war, we have been since 1705. If this assertion sounds outrageous made in the modern age, I agree, it *is* outrageous, but it is also true. These days there are subtle ways of demeaning and demoralising a country without bombing it. Why destroy a territory when careful entrapment enlarges your power base and helps fill your treasury coffers?

Of truth sessions, I *do not* mean we revert to the reprisals we saw carried out all over Europe against Nazi collaborators. Unfortunate people, some women who had struck up a relationship with a German soldier, dragged into the street by ugly mobs had their hair shorn from their heads, their faces spat upon, their clothes torn off their backs, men and women urinate on their naked, kicked and beaten bodies. Nor am I talking about the barbarity of tarring and feathering that was the practice in English colonies such as America.

What I mean is this: I would like to see a *humanitarian system* put in place where people are asked to step forward and confess what they did was disreputable, repugnant, venal, unlawful – whatever they and we feel to be the case – knowing that it caused people hardship, loss of earnings, livelihoods, loss of civil rights, or even death. In the system I propose there is *no threat of punishment,* other than those named who *avoid* telling the truth are sanctioned for allotted lengths of time. I propose a system of forgiveness.

Absolution is the motivating force behind confessional exercises. There are two ways to accomplish this task. Both require a degree of voluntary involvement. Those refusing to attend can be sanction in ways I have already mentioned. Our elected administration can call bigwigs to the table to admit their wrong doings, press and television cameras present to record their deliverance. The second is for local councils to do the same for miscreants in their area. Better still, sessions can be held in workplaces, bosses called to account. If we are genuinely agitating to create a better society, weeding out the betrayers and collaborators to give them a chance to right wrongs a good beginning.

Without realising it, the SNP touched upon the idea when Jim Sillars warned the bullies of big business to stop leaning on their workers, demanding their staff vote against their constitutional rights. (An action illegal is some countries.) He was then deputy leader of the SNP. With days to go before the 2014 vote, Yes–No apparently neck and neck, the unionist press true to form called Sillars' statement an "act of revenge". What was his crime? Sillars cautioned company CEOs with a "day of reckoning", a pretty mild reproach considering some company bosses had acted like dictators and blackmailed staff.

Readers who feel we live in a highly civilised society where public confessionals are not necessary are kidding themselves. The United Kingdom is one of the most corrupt nations on the planet. London is recognised as the money laundry capital of the world. Scotland is infected by association. Collaborators allow tax evasion as a legal activity; approve shonky companies dumping workers on the dole for boss and investor profit; drawing down of pension funds, signed PPI deals putting Scotland in hock for decades, placing police as moles into protest groups, employing private companies to remove welfare rights from the poor, the sick and the vulnerable, turn a blind eye to religious groups molesting children, allow the purchase of democracy, the poor imprisoned, the rich go free.

I want to see sessions deal with people in a humanitarian way, dignity the watchword, allowing defendants to speak openly and honestly, and be pardoned. Those invited to take part who exhibit arrogance or defiance, the facts staring them in the face, should not expect forgiveness. If they deny culpability, shout down questions, those around them can judge the depth of their principles and know what their real standing should be in a new Scotland.

Who would I like to see clear their conscience? Here are a few at national level.

Sir Ian Wood: Multi-millionaire, wealth made from North Sea Oil. What was he hoping to achieve telling the nation our oil reserves were running out when he knew it untrue? Why does he then turn around to glory in new oil fields discovered? Why did he want to own the centre of Aberdeen and refashion it?

Gavin McCrone: McCrone argues he did nothing to suppress his official Report for thirty years that explained how the oil bonanza would make Scotland a wealthy nation and give a huge boost to the nationalist movement. He compounded his felony with a book on why he feels Scotland too poor to be independent. Does he relate it to the theft of Scotland's oil?

Murray Foote: As editor of the scumbag *Scottish Daily Record* he placed the illegal, phony 'Vow' on the front page that diverted many to vote 'No' in the referendum. Now a reformed man he still needs to confess why he conspired to defraud a nation of its rights.

JK Rowling: the world renowned children's author uses her vast wealth and influence to block the civil and constitutional rights of the nation that adopted her.

Sir Nicholas MacPherson: Former permanent secretary to the UK Treasury; he is supposed to remain impartial, but he chose to enter the public fray over independence by publishing his advice to the cabinet stating independence would not be good for 'the markets'. He also forgot to mention his family's land investments in Wester Ross.

Kate Watson: A former Better Together boss with links to the 77th Brigade, a military propaganda unit of the British Army, a branch now operating in Scotland. Political candidates with Union connections should be barred from standing for election.

Gordon Brown: Hard to know where to start: for financing the illegal Iraq war; never visited the Scottish parliament; bag man to crooked banks; continues to lie about Scotland as a super-federal state; the pitiful 'Vow', and so on, *ad nauseam*.

Blair McDougall: For a litany of lies and fabrication sustained in the face of glaring facts to the contrary, uttered without embarrassment prior to the 2014 Referendum and after.

Muriel Gray: As chairperson of the Glasgow School of Art board of governors, why did she endorse the whitewash of a Report on the first fire, and take no moral responsibility for the fire as guardian of the institution, nor for the second fire? And please, where is the millions of pounds donated to rebuild the Mackintosh building out of the first disaster?

Brian Spanner: Not his real name, an odious snivelling Internet creep protected by the British press; his associations with the Orange Order, who finances him; why did he feel able to be close to the fragrant J.K. Rowling?

Jill Stephenson: Better known as 'History Woman'; a neurotic harpy who berates the SNP at every turn with blatant lies and Nazi slurs; called a female SNP MP a 'slut', yet continues to describe herself as an academic. She owes Edinburgh University an apology.

Ian Lang: Baron Lang of Monkton; Tory former Secretary of State, for the dog's breakfast that is GERs, designed to confuse political opponents but specifically, "the SNP" – his words – from knowing the real economy of Scotland.

David Mundell: 'Fluffy' Mundell, another secretary of state working on behalf of the British State against Scotland's interests, wanted for mendacity, blocking Scotland's progress, doing more turns than a whirling Dervish.

Nicola Sturgeon: Encouraging the hunt of an innocent man who could have been jailed for the rest of his life and delaying independence by ignoring mandates provided by the will of the electorate. There is a litany of other colonial accommodations but that one is enough.

There are lots of others to add to the list, academics, students, SNP youth, and journalists moonlighting for espionage reasons, 'patriotic' civil servants and BBC bosses.

Nobody's perfect, everybody makes mistakes. The difference is people with power and influence can make serious errors of judgement that have repercussions for years. The excuse we will hear in truth and reconciliation sessions is how they only followed orders. They will evoke the 'patriot' defence – the, I am as much a patriot as you, argument, forgetting they were servants of an alien, colonial government.

If we believe we want independence to see the beginning of a better society, among all the other necessities we shall have to attend to, one of the most important is to help cleanse the walking wounded of gangrene.

There are those among us who are morally obliged to explain why they betrayed the democratic principle. If they wish to take their place in Scottish society, an explanation of their behaviour is the least they owe us. What was good enough for Nelson Mandela is damn well good enough for Scotland.

9

THE FOLLY OF NUCLEAR WAR

Westminster is determined to spend billions of taxpayer's money on upgrading Trident, a weapon of mass destruction. Are we to continue entrusting our lives to men without sympathy or empathy, who have nothing to recommend them but methodical hatred?

Humankind is faced with the perfect storm of two dynamic forces, terrifying climate change and nuclear war, yet our leaders ask for more money to build more submarines to carry more deadly weapons of annihilation. To be conciliatory in any dispute we argue with lethal logic, we must first threaten to go to war and then pull back. The creed of extermination; men who think humankind hates humankind, their minds have never risen beyond the contest of diabolical power.

Trident is the armament of nuclear submarines. The British State berths the submarines in Scotland, in docks at Faslane on Gare Loch, a bay near the village of Garelochhead. It has four submarines: HMS Vengeance, Vanguard, Vigilant and Victorious. The British State retains delusions of grandeur. It thinks England rules the waves. Billions are to be spent on bombs, not billions spent keeping people alive, fed, educated and happy. No wonder we question the sanity of our elected representatives.

If ever we decide to fire our parcels of death we have a choice, for according to our leaders our enemies alter by the week, one week nasty Russians, then Iranians, the next the North Koreans.

The country that actually unleashed destruction, the USA, is our best friend. Lots of countries have nuclear weapons. It might be Pakistan that unleashes Armageddon, or our supposed ally Israel, a nation that secretly developed its own bomb with some clandestine help from the USA. Why worry about a submarine as a launch pad when it could be a Moslem with a small nuclear device in an Asda shopping bag strolling down our High Street? There are moments of horror I wonder if life on Earth would be better if we did not exist. Our stupidity, our cruelty, knows no limits.

The only country to have accidents with weapons of mass destruction, losing two off the coast of Spain, and exploding two deliberately on another nation, is our ally the United States of Amnesia. Hit by a first strike, politicians never talk of an *accidental* incident, or of being unable to retaliate because we will be dead, survivors disorientated. Nor do they mention Strontium-90, radiation lingering for centuries blistering our skin, thinning our bones, until our teeth fall out and we waste away. They talk of us as winners.

Dropping one atomic bomb on Hiroshima could be argued necessary to stop Japan from participating longer than it did in the Second World War, but another on Nagasaki? How do we justify dropping two bombs? The first was an experiment to see how many people were killed and to measure the extent of the devastation. The second was an act of vengeance. "Oh the pity of it," says Othello, just before he kills Desdemona.

To sit at a top table with the 'big boys,' so we are told, we must have weapons of mass carnage and death. It is sound military thinking. But there is a catch. We dare not press the button to release Armageddon because neither NATO nor England has that authority. The decision lies with the USA. So why have WMD? To quote an infamous betrayer of socialist principles, Aeurin Bevan, our representatives "do not want to go naked into the conference chamber".

Let me get one thing out of the way. Though I use Russia as a convenient 'enemy' for the purposes of this analysis, Russia has no WMDs on any western nation's border, but we have moved hundreds of ours up close to *their* border. No wonder Russians are jumpy. Think about that in reverse, a scenario in which Russia has surrounded us with nuclear rockets. Pontificating about controlling Russian ambitions takes a brass neck. Russia has far fewer weapons than the West. We are determined to multiply them; stockpile death, the poor and the working class can go to Hell.

In the 1960s President Kennedy was ready to nuke Cuba and Russia and start a third world war if the Russians delivered rockets to Cuba, a legitimate request considering the USA was planning invasion of that beleaguered, illegally blockaded island and assassination of their elected president, Fidel Castro. Nevertheless, this is what we like to call 'the balance of terror.' We don't like Russians for protecting their borders by annexing the Crimea in 2014, and after the USA backed a coup in Ukraine in 2014, we detest them for retaliating, committing a war crime, although it's quite acceptable and legitimate for them to invest in England's bankrupt football teams, and buy expensive London properties without paying proper tax.

Politicians in the West are terminally addicted to cold war politics and yet a modern thermonuclear war is full of chilling uncertainties. A first strike carries with it disastrous failure issuing from partial success. The chance of a first strike going awry is so great decision makers shy from taking it. The only reason to go to war is when it is *less* risky not to go to war. This leaves aggressive nations with the problem of safety valves.

Early warning systems have to maintain some sort of super-alert eye in the sky. Supposedly remaining on guard continuously day and night helps us react quickly. But if nations are in peace talks when do we turn it off? What is our litmus test? Do we relax immediately we have a partial or a full and final negotiated settlement and the other side backs off? Hanging around on high alert duty is costly.

Enemy missiles target specific threats. Trident on the Clyde is only one. There are many hidden bases of administrative decision making to wipe out: government bunkers, planes that carry WMDs, communication systems, silos with intercontinental missiles, strategic airfields, radar centres, centre of finance, plane making factories, and more. How many buttons do you have to push at once to wipe out the lot in one go, ten, twenty, fifty, a hundred? The last official estimate was the West would need to fire at least seventy-five missiles at Russia to make the slightest dent in their capability to retaliate. And the missiles have to be fired in closely coordinated fashion which will take at least one hour or more to complete, allowing time for our enemy to send the same amount of missiles back at us. Mutual destruction is the aim. A blind man can discern the massive flaw in this philosophy.

Let us keep Russia as the big bogeyman for the sake of illustrating another example. Russia is a vast continent. It has *eleven* time zones. We have one, two if you blame Scotland for wanting some daylight in winter. Even without Scotland as part of the United Kingdom, unwilling to do what England wants, Great Britain is a very small country in comparison to Russia. For Russian's part, they will retreat to the Great Central Plain, Outer Mongolia, or Murmansk, and still have room to rebuild a few football stadiums. Keep in mind not so long ago Russian territory was hit by a very large meteor but hardly anybody noticed. And they had a nuclear reactor go into meltdown, Chernobyl. Russia is still around to tell the story. Had Chernobyl been in England, in say, Hambleton, Rutland, England's smallest county, over three hundred miles around the nuclear reactor would be a dead zone for a hundred years effectively paralysing England. What food could be grown by farmers is another question, as is, how long it will take for radiation contamination to reach the furthest terrain and enter the body.

What if we attack a small country that we think has nuclear weapons, about to use them and we do it on an unreliable informant? On our side we rely on having no intelligence leaks that give the enemy the advantage. With the Internet age absolute secrecy is impossibility. System can be hacked. The entire edifice of nuclear strikes depends on accurate data. No one can calculate an attack unless the data is a hundred per cent correct. Think of Prime Minister Tony Blair and his assertion a strike from Saddam Hussein on England was only "forty minutes away". American informants on the ground in Iraq told him so. In the event, it was totally false. Hussein's henchmen were keen to pretend Iraq was armed to the teeth. The commission of Inquiry sent to Iraq under United Nations protection said as much but their findings were distorted and dismissed. When men want to play brave generals on small countries they will go to war. This is entirely the wrong sort of courage to lead people from potential death to hope and peace.

We can discuss hypothetical situations and we can discuss actual situations. There are on record at last half a dozen instances when a reckless decision has moved the firing process up the line to one step away from pushing the button. In one famous case it was a flock of geese on a radar screen. The system called Fail Safe is supposed to ensure an accident cannot happen. It is a system implemented against human or mechanical error. As we know from movie plots, the system is, proceed toward your target for a fixed number of nautical miles and then turn back if at that moment you do not get coded orders to proceed to Doomsday. This has happened many times triggered by a false alarm, an alert created by a line of meteors, interference from high frequency transmitters, a flight of geese, or by the appearance of foreign objects. In one instance US aircraft carrying nuclear bombs turned home to their bases from halfway as soon as it became clear the alarm was false. These near accidents show humankind has been on the brink of a deadly war by the error of one technician, from carelessness, miscalculation, or faulty conclusion.

The deterioration of international relations inevitably results in calls for more weapons. This is when the 'money threat' is activated and spirals uncontrolled. The more the British government makes public an increased budget on armaments, the more the enemy has to calculate if it is willing to do the same in counter programmes. Aggression comes down to outspending each other. Renewing Trident accelerates the arms race; it does not slow it down. We are striving for overwhelming qualitative and quantative superiority over nations we think want to attack and destroy us. Our paranoia increases tension. We are our own worst enemy.

There is no alternative to arms control but ridding ourselves of weapons of mass death unilaterally. There was a time the West was going to intervene in China's upsurge of Maoist communism. Now we trade with them. Many British companies have manufacturing bases in China. We did not need to have nuclear weapons to reach this stage of friendly co-operation. The USA forgets it was attacked successfully by a few extremists armed with nail clippers who had learned to fly but not land an aeroplane. They had no knives, guns or hand grenades. No amount of stockpiled WMD deterred those mad men from destroying the New York's Twin Towers, and the lives of three thousand innocent people.

I don't believe we have unlimited time to rid ourselves of weapons of mass destruction. And I don't believe multi-lateral agreements are the answer. We live in an age of horrific contradictions, the double sledgehammer of environmental disaster and nuclear war, both man-made. And no politician likes to mention the extinction of our flora and fauna that did damn all to start a nuclear conflagration. But to keep your population in fear so they remain compliant to your aggressive foreign policy you must whip up tension constantly. Thus, we argue for costly submarines patrolling the oceans ready to fire nukes on command. No matter how preposterous and dangerous nuclear weapons are, bombs we won't use against an enemy that is not attacking us, we want more of them. To follow that route lays madness. Politicians who say they will push the button *are not sane people*. The only winner of a nuclear war is the last person standing.

The University of Chicago keeps a Doomsday clock. As tension mounts or abates somewhere in the world the hands of the clock are moved forward or back. The clock warns the public about how close we are to destroying our world with dangerous technologies of our own making. It is a metaphor, a reminder of the perils we must address if we are to survive on the planet. It was created by scientists seventy-five years ago. Midnight is the Armageddon hour. In my lifetime I have never known it to be less than five minutes to midnight except in 1991 when it was put back 17 minutes. This happened when with President Gorbachev's initiative, the United States and

Soviet Union signed the first Strategic Arms Reduction Treaty, and the Soviet Union dissolved to become Russia on December 26. This is the farthest from midnight the Clock has been since its inception. Now, with Climate Change upon us it is seconds away from midnight. There is no choice, leaders of the world must co-operate, or we must force them to make the right decisions.

A post script: The arms race sounds complicated to the uninformed. What it boils down to is common sense and humanity. My assessment is shared by many people. I listened and learned. The evidence to reach a conclusion lies around to be read. Unlike the United Kingdom which encourages censorship and secrecy, one positive of American society is the freedom to obtain access to documents and published books. There is any number warning of the dangers of all-out nuclear war. The curious wishing to make up their own mind, their own judgement and not accept my view need not be apprehensive of weighty study to gain enough knowledge. One or two books are enough. I found older books by rummaging, 1984's Winston Smith-like, in second-hand book shops. Here are a few on the subject.

In no special order: **On Thermonuclear War** – *Hermann Kahn*; **Security in Disarmament** – *Robert Barnet & Robert Falk*; **The Uses of Military Power in a Nuclear Age** – *Klaus Knorr*; **The War Potential of Nations** – *Klaus Knorr*; **Deterrence and Defence** – *Glenn H. Snyder*; **Power, A Social Analysis** – *Bertrand Russell*; **Limited Nuclear War in the 21st Century** – *Jeffrey A. Larsen*; **Command and Control** – *Eric Schlosser*; and one for children and adults, the illustrated **When the Wind Blows** – *Raymond Briggs*, a classic of its kind.

10
EMBARRASSMENT

Childhood was filled with surprises, on the learning side guilt, disappointment and stern rebuke but I do not recall ever suffering embarrassment. That arrived with a crash at the onset of adolescence, that horrible time when the individual turns hyper-self-conscious. Hormones begin whizzing around the body like loose pinballs, the result is pimples, or *zits*, as the American term the eruptions on our face. In Scots the word for a pimple is *plook*.

Plooks are a sign of over-activity of oil glands located at the base of hair follicles, especially on the face, back, chest, and shoulders. Some adolescents are plagued by them. Being a sallow skinned Mediterranean I was not too troubled by spots, but when one did arrive it appeared on the end of my nose, the one place I could not hide with face hair, a cap, or high collared shirt. On the day I planned to take a girlfriend to the pictures, or attend an important social function, I could guarantee the morning would be greeted with a plook on my snout as luminescent and as powerful as a lighthouse in a storm. It took strong willpower not to squeeze the puss-filled lump and make it worse.

Laughter from schoolmates could reduce a boy or a girl to a quivering mass of uncertainty, a bright red flush of colour to the cheeks made worse by the same tormentors pointing at it in fits of giggles and jeering, "Yuv gotta riddy!" The colloquialism in Glasgow is a 'beamer'. One positive quality of the human trait to be embarrassed is learning not to do the thing that caused the emotion, but there is not much one can do to arrest the development of other pimples and spots until the body's metabolism stops playing silly buggers. In my youth, before a boy reaches manhood, he had to get over the fear of ordering condoms in a chemist. The predicted shame was so great in my case I remained a virgin into my twenties, which is taking the art of delay to extremes.

My first experience of *acute* shyness was when caught among a gaggle of women. When they get together, out for fun, women have a way of ganging up on a guy and there's very little one can do to halt the verbal assault. Face on fire, they tripped me into a pained smile.

The next occasion was a mishap, meeting the parents of a girlfriend, one who had attached herself to my arm as I crossed a road – she came at me from behind – honestly, officer – and decided I was her boyfriend there and then. As she introduced me to her father and mother on the other side of the street, and I stuttered a few answers to their polite questions, the mother kept looking at the ground and the father glared at me as he spoke. This made my responses all the more confused. I kept recasting what I had said, letting sentences trail away into thin air. As we parted, and I agreed to dinner at her house, I looked down at my trousers half-hidden by my jersey. My fly zip was wide open, black shirt tail hanging out – the consequence of a rushed visit to a public toilet. Her father saw to it there was no place setting at the dinner table for me to sit. It was the cue to go home.

The second time my shyness got the better of me was a classic of its kind, one I learned many another shared. Late for work, I saw my bus taking on passengers at the bus stop, the last passenger boarding the platform. I ran like mad to catch it before it moved off into the mainstream of traffic. As I reached the bus stop the double-decker did just that, the driver turned the steering wheel and the bus moved off. I was so embarrassed at missing it that I kept running. I ran past the people waiting for a different bus, covering my awkwardness by pretending I was not running for a bus at all. I looked back, pleased to note no one saw my deliberate misdirection or looked puzzled at my odd actions. However, embarrassment was doubled at the next bus stop. I arrived out of breath as a second bus arrived minutes later. Only those who had not boarded the previous one were on the new one. They stared at me from their seats wondering why I had run two stops for a bus.

For the rest of us, the dinner table is a social disaster area: trying to cut that hard potato in half only to see it scud across the table onto the floor. Carrying the wedding cake and dropping it. Saying hello to a neighbour in the morning is fine, meeting them again at the shops less so, and seeing them a third time in the day a trial if running out of polite small talk. And what woman has not crumpled told a length of toilet paper is hanging from the back of her skirt? Breaking wind in public is a killer. (One woman's answer was to exclaim "Hark at me?") Who has not got stuck into bad mouthing an individual only to be told by the listener that the subject of the conversation is their wife or their best friend? We have all made the obligatory social *faux pas*.

I have not experienced mild or crippling embarrassment for years. Perhaps I have beaten my inner critic to a pulp, perhaps age defuses reaction. Or it could be that my day's activities are too full to allow me to fester over a mishap. Psychologists tell us that embarrassment is pretty easy to trigger. It is a powerful force. In my mind that raises more questions. Why are we so quick to feel an emotion that makes us so uncomfortable? What does a tendency toward mortification mean? Psychologists' research reveals embarrassment may repair social relationships and even advertise positive character traits, but at the same time, sheepishness could lead you to make poor decisions, you are plain scared to be seen by your peers making a mistake. I have retained a certain mild shyness all my life, the quiet observer in a group, blossoming when faced by an audience of students or adults there to hear what I have to say. Oddly enough, I am there to hear what I have to say. Solo musicians have a similar divergent response to the private and the public.

Unfortunately, I have never been sure how to help adults deal with the emotion of embarrassment, other than to boost their confidence as best as I can by emphasising the positive in them. For some

EMBARRASSMENT

people, it can become crippling — not just in a social setting, but in other situations as well, from making new friends to going on dates. Perhaps it might help to tell them not to be irrational. Others may not judge us as severely as we judge ourselves.

11

NEW ZEALAND CANNOT EXIST

According to Scotland's tormentors, we are too small a country to exist as a nation state. What size has to do with freedoms is never explained. There is any number of small independent nations, some republics. But I shall stick to New Zealand for the purpose of the brief comparison study. If Scotland is so mouse-like, it won't ever be a capybara, it follows New Zealand is similarly handicapped. And yet it thrives as an independent nation.

How does New Zealand compare to Scotland? A small country, it has a huge meandering coastline. The population is 4.5 million. It has topography similar to Scotland, lots of mountains and glens. It rains a lot. It has many generations of Scots emigrants. Some places are named after Scottish towns, such as Dunedin after Edinburgh. At one time, during the Highland Clearances, there were more sheep living off the land that Highland population. Today, New Zealand has ten sheep for every person, wool being one of the main industries.

It is a "primary" producer, mainly dairy products and wool. Tourism brings about 25% of it income. Tourists arrive to photograph cities and visit the mountains. Once upon a time its sole export market was the "mother land", the United Kingdom. Overnight, and against New Zealand's vociferous protests, Westminster decided it wanted to switch to European produce. It dumped New Zealand. England has since dumped the European Union taking an unwilling Scotland with it. New Zealand's people being hard working, resourceful people, soon adjusted. The country prospers.

It has a small army but no fighter jets and no submarines. The army is utilised for natural emergencies, earthquakes, security, rationing during emergencies. Their soldiers tend to be alive when leaving active service and not horizontal in a wooden box. It has no aircraft carriers. Nuclear weapons are banned from its land and nuclear carrying vessels banned from its waters. It has yet to be invaded, unless you categorise Maoris as non-indigenous. Maoris were the first people to colonise New Zealand, about 800 years ago. Scotland has human history going back at least 7,000 years.

12,000 New Zealanders who died during the Second World War might not seem like a large number by comparison to the 57,000 Scotland lost, but at the time New Zealand's population was under two million. 135,000 Scots were killed in the First World War. New Zealand saw 16,000 killed. (41,000 were wounded.) These comparisons may seem spurious, but they show how a country smaller in population than Scotland survives and renews itself.

Unlike Scotland with its near neighbours in Europe and the Nordic countries, its markets are 12,000 kilometres away over vast oceans. Yet the cost of living is not especially high, medical care free or private, pensions paid on time. It supports a welfare state.

New Zealand does not have gas reserves in substantial quantity. Agricultural products—principally meat, dairy products, and fruits and vegetables, are New Zealand's major exports; crude oil and wood and paper products are also significant.

In statistics supplied by the Organisation of Economic Co-operation and Development (OECD) on GDP per capita, New Zealand ranked only three places under the United Kingdom, seventeenth. Life expectancy is an average of 80.2 years, longer than the south of England. Life expectancy for males in Scotland in 2021 was an average of 76.8 years. Women managed 81.2 years. The average life expectancy in Scotland has fallen year by year, this in an unholy Union since 1707 that is supposed to benefit us.

I would say, in general New Zealand's politics and values are left of centre, though it has a few stalwarts addicted to hard capitalism. New Zealand is a representative democracy, that is, it has a Parliament consisting of members who represent voters who elected them. This is true of legislatures (parliaments) in all modern democracies except Scotland, where some politicians are not elected directly, first past the post, but by a convoluted system that can still see them given a place in Parliament. New Zealand has a complicated assortment of socialist causes and organisations. Several prominent political parties in New Zealand, such as the New Zealand Labour Party, have historical links to socialism but are not generally considered main socialist parties today. They accept a capitalist economy.

It has its own broadcasting system devoted to the nation's interests. And as everybody knows by now, it has a film industry brought to world attention by the director Peter Jackson, who follows a long line of distinguished New Zealand auteur filmmakers. Their films bring notice to the world of a dramatic land and a diverse culture, powerful enough to get Hollywood studios to agree to its contractual conditions. There is no colonial dominant nation through which they must process their art to see it promoted or rejected, or ignored.

New Zealand's international trade, political negotiations, meetings and obligations are not carried out by proxy, at the whim of a neighbour nation.

What Scotland does not share with New Zealand in Gaelic, Doric, or Lallands, is a town with an extremely long name: Llanfairpwllgwyngyllgogerychwyrndrobwllllantysiliogogogoch is a Welsh town, not Scots, hoping that one day it will grow up to be as big as the town of: Taumatawhakatangihangakoauauotamateaturipukakapikimaungahoronukupokaiwhenuakitanatahu.

The town of Taumata, for short, lies on the east coast of New Zealand, the Maori meaning is very roughly, "The place where Tamatea, the man on the big knees who slipped, climbed and swallowed mountains, known as the Land Eater, he played the flute to his loved one." However, elastic names aside, we can boast Gaelic is an official language the same as Maori.

The land of the 'long white cloud', New Zealand is famous for its lofty mountain peaks and glaciers to mesmerizing blue lakes. It's also known for its wine, Russell lupins, an invasive species, and multi-contest winning national rugby team, the All Blacks.

Opponents of Scotland aver New Zealand is a small, fractured, two-island country, unable to protect itself, a supposed 'bunch of backwoods farmers sheering sheep and milking cows'.

The proponents of colonialism are the same group that hope to keep Scotland ignorant and docile. So long as they argue Scotland is incapable of existence as a nation state, so long does the same argument apply to New Zealand – it cannot exist as an autonomous state. It is simply too small, too weak and too poor.

But it *does* exist. And it thrives. And it makes its voice heard internationally.

12

MELODY MAN

Everybody should try to befriend a composer once in their lifetime. Classical idiom, jazz, rock, it does not matter; the human mind fashioning music from thin air and sounds is a magical process. It civilises. It lifts the spirits.

I have known three composers; it could have been four if only someone had whisked me off to meet Jean Sibelius at Järvenpää, his home in Finland. When I was young he was still alive. In my teens I played his tone poem *Finlandia* over and over again, and his Karelia Suite to destruction. Of the three composers I actually did meet and befriend, one was Guy Woolfenden the music director of the Royal Shakespeare Company with whom I had the greatest pleasure of collaborating on a musical. He was an absolute gentleman. I learned to tell when he was annoyed for he never showed anger in his face. He tended to be annoyed by his own perceived errors. "My fault, dear boy. The ending is an anti-climax. Give me ten minutes. I'll fix it." And he did, in five. By the time I got to know him he had composed for the Shakespeare canon three times over in his term with the RSC. I enjoyed his finely tuned sense of humour.

Opera composer Thea Musgrave was much more introspective than Guy, less outgoing. She started off at Edinburgh University at medical school but was drawn to the music school, eventually switching career. She remains our most talented composer grossly undervalued. The Europeans appreciate her more than her homeland for they line up to premier her latest work. I met her in Los Angeles where she lives, but she was born where I now live, in a village on the edge of Edinburgh. In 2019 she celebrated her ninetieth birthday. Composing music seems to cultivate longevity.

Finally, and uppermost here, is the movie composer Patrick Doyle, for whom this essay is really an unashamed tribute. And how fitting to write of a composer in the same book of collected essays that includes a brief history of my musician grandfather, and they own fine Irish names. When I walked toward Patrick to shake his hand I knew he had not changed since we shared a hurried drink in a theatre bar decades earlier. ('Shared' as in one each!) The genial smile, the mischievous twinkle behind the spectacles, the bubbly personality, was not diminished by his years in the thick of a demanding professional career.

Patrick Doyle is always ready for a blether and joke, but as a composer I bet he could cut one to the quick if you mucked things up laying his music on a sound track. To know such a remarkable talent makes one feel expansive. I knew him when we were both working in theatre and as happens in the theatrical profession, lost contact for twenty years, until he made contact. That is the way of it; friendships are made easily and just as easily evaporate, but a few are deep enough in respect to endure.

There is a pleasing symmetry to these reminiscences. Patrick scored the remake of the Agatha Christie who-dunnit *Death on the Nile*, collaboration with director Kenneth Branagh, and also Christie's *Murder on the Orient Express*. Branagh directed the cast and played the moustachioed sleuth. The high level of actors playing marquee roles is enticing, but remakes are also high risk. How do you rewrite a winner to have it seem fresh from the first version, and still produce a winner, many like me having enjoyed the earlier one?

Tchaikovsky, Prokofiev and Berlioz all composed very successful versions of the Romeo and Juliet story, written in that order, none put off by the existence of their predecessor's version; so, innovative, memorable and new can be done. The risk lies in film versions being compared. On the positive side, Branagh is as adept as was Sydney

Lumet at drawing powerful performances from his seasoned actors. Critics did not warm to Branagh's *Orient Express*. For my part I found it heavy-handed, determined not to be too similar to Lumet's first version, the train not stuck in a snow drift as in the original and as described in the book, but caught in a snow-slide from a nearby mountain. The melodrama is heightened for no apparent reason. Everyone is taken out of their warm carriages where hot food and a samovar of tea are ready to be consumed. They are made to sit in the mouth of the cold railway tunnel in the front of the locomotive, rather like a montage of *The Last Supper* while Hercule Poirot makes a long speech.

Branagh looks younger than his age. His interpretation may have suffered from older actors who took on the role before him, in particular, the never-ending television portrayal by David Suchet, he always deadly serious, a detective who affords an occasional smile, who has petty habits and his gait a mincing walk. Were it not for Patrick's music, the main theme chugging of a steam engine counterpointed by the sweep of violins, only Branagh's outrageous moustache would stay in the mind. I am happy to add that Branagh rounded the character of Poirot in his remake of *Death on the Nile*, and in so doing made the part work for him.

The muscular engine is not a character in Branagh's story, which is a shame. Locomotives are a terrific attraction to all ages. Back in 1974 when I was still a sapling I interviewed Richard Rodney Bennet, composer to Lumet's adaptation, for an hour's worth of radio. Bennett's music was perfectly coupled to the locomotive, and Lumet made a feature of it as the engine pulled out of Paris's Gare de l'Est station.

Lumet had a low opinion of his effort, "a dumb train movie and I didn't get it right". I thought Lumet did a fine job, while Bennett's music raised it to another plain altogether. What grated was Albert Finney's stage caricature of Christie's detective, too theatrical to stand close scrutiny from a film camera. (Peter Ustinov got closest to the pomposity and seriousness of the Poirot in the novellas, but then Christie was terrible at constructing character and a genius at plots. Ustinov added the subtleties.) Christie was reluctant to hand over the rights to Lumet. Her first book filmed, *The Mysterious Affair at Styles*, she disliked intensely. It caused her to be cautious about the way the film industry reinterprets and markets a writer's work.

How best to categorise Patrick that isn't surface? His idiom is symphonic, his work tending to be attached to classical literature. Melodies slide out his head like eggs from a turtle, hatch, and make their way to the warm sea of his music. If I have it right his first film composition was *Henry V*. Branagh spotted his talents were well suited to film composing, and hired him to write the score for his adaptation of Shakespeare's rabble-rouser. Considering this is his first score, it's incredibly confident and must rank among Doyle's most memorable. On first hearing I was struck by how varied it was, the frenzied battle sequences compared with the quieter moments showed a composer on his way to becoming a fine orchestrator. His expert melodies carry the ebb and flow of pre-battle moments perfectly, they engage the emotions, and they just sound right, a 90-minute work almost operatic. He also appears in the film, a wee cameo, the first soldier to begin signing '*Non Nobis, Domine*' following the conflict of Agincourt. His underscore of Branagh's speech whipping up killing fervour on St Crispin's day is perfect, even if England's Henry is goading his men to die for England or live and be his best pal ever after, both a cheap promise easily made.

A composer seems to me a sort of wondrous sorcerer. They buoy our spirits. They evoke in us that rare state of being called pleasure. They don't all have to wander around in a thunderstorm as if maniacally depressed Beethoven straining for inspiration. They can look like bespectacled, good natured Patrick, almost cuddly, amenable. You can find him in the cosy cloister of his Shepperton Studio office, adding a dying seventh to a score that will catch our breath and tug at the heart strings. If Bennett was alive today he would be astonished at Patrick's output, and envy how much he is in demand by filmmakers at home and in the USA.

When I called to tell him I was about to publish an essay as biography he was on his way to accept an invitation to the International

Film Festival of Braunschweig (Brunswick), Germany. The city feted him, making him their first recipient of their *White Lion* Lifetime Achievement Award for Music in Film. He can add that to his Scottish BAFTA Lifetime Achievement Award, his PRS Lifetime Achievement Award, and many others. He also has Oscar, Golden Globe, César nominations, and a BAFTA nomination to his credit, as well as a Los Angeles Film Critics Award. Lifetime awards sound as if people presume your work is over. Not so Patrick. Multifarious awards are evidence a Scottish-born composer can achieve international status. In the past too many European composers led an impoverished existence: no CD or DVD sales, television episodes for theme tunes, or radio stations to fill impecunious periods with welcome royalties. Today, a composer can specialize in one genre or another and make a decent living. For Patrick it was the dramatic combined with the descriptive.

I knew Patrick in my youthful theatre days, he usually seen clutching a sheaf of music sheets and staying close to a piano. I have an abiding picture in my mind of him playing wee Hector in John Byrne's *Slab Boys*, and later at a party playing lively tunes on an old Joanna, always happy, always smiling, always composing snippets of music. Speaking to him after an interval of thirty years confirms his sense of humour remains intact. The interview was peppered with hilarious anecdotes of people encountered.

Patrick's childhood haunt was the west of Scotland, Uddingston to be exact, nurtured by a caring family.

> *"I had tunes going around in my head; I could hear the orchestra play them but I had no understanding of how to construct them. When I was six or seven I was given a Glockenspiel and began externalising harmonies on it. In school, I found a piano in the Assembly Hall, and lifting the heavy lid with a bang, I sussed that the keyboard was similar to the Glockenspiel. I started to play 'Catch a Falling Star'.* [Crooner Perry Como's big hit.] *Hardly a few bars into it and the janitor appeared bellowing, "Shut that lid, boy!"*

Despite the philistine intervention Patrick found the experience "scintillating." From that moment on his future was mapped out, a vocation cushioned by red carpet premiers. First comes the hard bit, music academy. The best movie composers are classically trained. Patrick studied at the Royal Scottish Academy of Music, now the Conservatoire of Scotland, to give it its more recent pretentious name. There he wrote a trio for piano, cello and violin. His student colleagues couldn't believe he was the author, a case of undervaluing ability too close to perceive.

Working in draughty theatre music pits, playing at Glasgow's Fountain restaurant, to sustain wife, mortgage, body and soul is an arduous business. A peripatetic lifestyle takes its toll on a musician.

There's an assortment of fates awaiting the unwary: employers who delay fees, non-payers, crooked agents, gigs closing down, and kudos stolen from you. Patrick avoided the bear traps. It was a stealth attack of acute myeloid leukaemia that dealt him a deathly card. To deal with a life-threatening cancer in a few short paragraphs, an illness that drags courage to the brink of extinction cannot begin to convey the pain and despair endured. Nurses napalm your blood with chemotherapy. Bed ridden, immobile, you're a useless body watching consultants discuss your condition. Patrick's treatment lasted six months.

> "The ominous signs were mysterious bruising on my skin and bleeding gums. When the doctor called me with the news I dropped the phone in shock. At that moment somebody knocked at my front door, a policeman searching the district for a criminal. "Do you mind if I look out of your top window?" he asked. It was a truly bizarre moment."

Faced with an answer to life's biggest question, a man wonders if it is time to swear allegiance to a higher being. The smallest moment is experienced in the sharpest terms. Bird song outside a window so often ignored takes on a haunting quality; youth's bloom assumes a spectre all of its own. Spirit assaulted, Patrick managed to complete a score for the children's animated project *Quest for Camelot*, a Herculean task. That was 1998. Happily, the disease was diagnosed early. He made a full recovery. "*I have nothing but praise for the NHS,*" he says, a compliment to their life saving skills. Profound illness beaten is guaranteed to harden resolve in an exceptional talent. It is no surprise Branagh was there to help Patrick, together with a brace of film actor friends, stage a charity concert at the Royal Albert Hall, *Music from the Movies*, in aid of Leukaemia Research UK.

Though Patrick has worked with many outstanding directors, the British film business tends to place Patrick's music in association with Branagh above all others. The collaboration produced a string of pearls: *Henry V* (1989), *Much Ado About Nothing* (1993), *Mary Shelly's Frankenstein* (1994), *Hamlet* (1996), *Love Labour's Lost* (2000), and *As You Like It* (2006). Naturally, Doyle speaks of his mentor with affection.

> "*We first met to discuss the music for his new Renaissance Theatre company's production of* Twelfth Night *at the Riverside Studios in Hammersmith in the late 90s. We hit it off immediately. Richard Byres played Malvolio. I think that Branagh and I being Celts helped a lot. It was refreshing to meet someone with no pretensions; with a clear vision of what his ideas were for the play. The play produced was exactly as he described it would be, in every detail. I thought he was a class act and still do. Incidentally, he never asked to hear a note of my music in advance.*"

Patrick was nominated for an Academy Award for his *Hamlet* score. Among all his compositions for the Bard's canon, to my mind Doyle's theme for *Henry V* stands out. It got him an Ivor Novello Award. He teamed up with Branagh again for Marvel Comics *Thor* premiered in 2011. His score is suitably percussive, hard metal bashing anvils and crashing crescendos, full of ostinato phrases and rhythms. I found that a good compensation for a fantasy character dragging a heaving mallet around. (The designer of Volvo cars has fashioned the hammer shape to fit into Volvo headlights.)

Regular moviegoers get familiar with a composer's style, their orchestral voice. Ennio Morricone's innovative western themes are a good example, and John Williams' insistent Wagnerian stormtrooper riffs another. As soon as you hear them you perk up because you know you're in for a good time. I am never quite sure what I will hear when Patrick has written the score. He is the musical equivalent of a chameleon, so adept is he at suiting scores to a movie's topography. To my mind, when he employs choral work he is easier to identify, yet even smart musicologists can misjudge his work. They view with mixed feelings his score for *Much Ado about Nothing*. Nobody can deny it's bright, sunny, energetic and optimistic. It radiates happiness, the very essence of Shakespeare's comedy.

Patrick's film oeuvre is impressive in idioms it encompasses. *Rise of the Planet of the Apes, Carlito's Way, Sleuth, Eregon, Bridget Jones's Diary*, and Scotland's own Pixar cartoon *Brave*, guild the lily of a prodigious output. Those films are testament to his ability to collaborate with the world's most accomplished and demanding movie directors. Working with Ang Lee on *Sense and Sensibility* is one thing, a huge compliment when Mike Newell calls you back after *Into the West* (1992) to score *Donnie Brasco* (1997) and *Harry Potter and the Goblet of Fire* (2005), all extremely successful movies. Directors have a way of sticking with a winner. He has scored six films for Régis Wargnier. Among my favourites Doyle scores are those for Robert Altman's *Gosford Park*, and Alphonso Cuaron's contemporary interpretation of *Great Expectations* (1998) set in New York. There is a gracefulness in them. I could go on but there is too many works to fit into this essay.

When we met I was keen to hear of Patrick's work with the youth orchestra he founded, its genesis an invited talk to high school students in Strathaven, Lanarkshire. There are plans afoot to perform at major venues. Details of the Patrick Doyle Arts in Film Youth Orchestra will have to wait until announced. However, he told me he had a "sensational" time galvanising young people from different social backgrounds towards creative endeavour. Music has much to teach the young, team work, interpretation, mathematics, timing, the expressiveness of sounds, and a shared exaltation in applause. Playing in an orchestra is a great discipline.

A kaleidoscope of composition has flowed under a fiddle's bridge since Patrick's days in the Royal Scottish Conservatoire, including a few pieces for the concert hall. If you listen to his early work through to current scores you can detect the stages where his music grows more and more abstract and transcendental. In Los Angeles, thinking us an ocean and a sea apart, I recommended Patrick to my producer as composer for the film I was working on but idiotically failed to seek him out. He was working in the City of Angels. Perhaps it was a good thing; we're still friends, not collaborating on a project means we have not fallen out because half his score is on the cutting room floor.

Listening to Patrick reminisce about tribulations and treble clefs of musical hard graft is listening to a globe-trotting life lived fruitfully with meaning. We should cherish Patrick Doyle for the creative being that he is, and celebrate him whenever we can by buying and listening to his music. I am privileged to have heard some of his work scored to his grandmother's unaccompanied sublime Gaelic singing. He may very well be our national composer. If we want for a national anthem, he should be top of the list.

I finish as I began; every person should try to befriend a composer. They are good for the soul. Film scores are too often characterised as sub-classical, descriptive music representing mood, character and scene, subservient to the will of the director and the editor, but in the 21st century this aspect of a film is the one most recalled by a film's fans before a line of dialogue is remembered. The sound track is what we buy, rarely the published screenplay. With all the intricacies, the notational mathematics involved in composition, and then in the playing of it, music is science made audible.

My affection is inexhaustible for Patrick Doyle and his melodies. I am envious of his talent.

13

THE IRISH EXPERIENCE

Hearing Mary Lou Macdonald – leader of the Irish social democratic party Sinn Féin (Irish for 'We Ourselves') – in a television interview, I was struck by how unselfconsciously she used the term *English* nationalist, rather than *British* nationalist. She was not, after all, referring to Welsh or Scot. If the term is used in Scotland it meets with inane cries of 'racism' from colonials who, by the very nature of their creed are racist.

In the Republic, English nationalism is familiar to Irish from centuries of brutal colonial rule. In Scotland we prefer to blank out similar suppression of our rights, attempts at genocide, and forced immigration, crimes littering 300 years of London rule. Far too many Scots suppose life in modern Scotland is free of tyranny imposed on us by a neighbour state. What is there to worry about? We enjoy unfettered freedoms and full democracy. We can buy what we want, travel where we like, marry who we wish, we just do not get the government and policies we vote for, a small sacrifice. But exactly the opposite is true. Our lives are blighted by alien policies that take no note of Scotland's needs.

Decades rejecting Tory policies at the ballot box result in decades of Tory policies inflicting on us, as if a punishment for exercising our democratic rights. We are not thanked for voting for an English-orientated party, no gift of largesse comes our way to keep our loyalty, like a shop offering discount coupons to customers on their next purchase. We see our cost of living rise, our taxes increase, state pension withdrawn until we reach seventy, and the Treasury keep billions we earn. What good is there in staying attached to a thief and a bully?

But the blind lead the blind who see no evil. We see no Stasi agents arresting dissenters, the victim hustled off the street into an unmarked van, disappearing into the night. We know there are agents of the Crown among us, special branch officers, we know MI5 infiltrates the very fabric of our society to undermine hopes and liberalisation, but why worry? They go about their work without being too obvious. All is fine. Or so we think, for the most part.

The more adventurous among us look for historical parallels in an attempt to understand Scotland's situation. We can do no better than study Ireland's bloody struggle which I undertake here with a great deal of trepidation lest I anger my Irish republican confederates by misinterpreting political events. We have a lot to learn from Ireland's past turbulence.

For the curious a good starting point is to follow Winston Churchill's wake. If anybody stood for the imposition of Imperial rule, he did. He was its champion. Anything less, a concession here or there, he considered appeasement or humiliating defeat. There are plenty of modern-day English nationalists slopping around who express the same hostility to any suggestion of Scottish hegemony no matter how mild. Scotland gets too much democracy. It must be curbed.

In 1922, before he crossed the floor of the House of Commons to join the Tory party, Churchill was still a Liberal working in the War Office under the party's then leader David Lloyd George. Together, they had had to come to terms with the 1917 Bolshevik revolution in Russia. It dawned on them it was not a one week skirmish, it was there to stay. Shock at the rise of radical socialism surged out across Europe like capillary ripples from a boulder thrown into a pond. Revolutions made British politicians jittery. They sensed the old world order was in for a kicking and altered irrevocably. It did not help to be reminded that Sinn Féin was a democratically-driven republican socialist party.

As the Russian Revolution became a fixture on the world's political map, Churchill gave up shouting 'Down with Ruskies!' and got his head immersed in work. How did Churchill's restless, impulsive nature cope with the reality of violent revolution? At first he contemplated overthrowing Lenin before sanity got the better of wild ambition. Churchill's proposal alarmed his colleagues. For his part, Lloyd George considered Churchill 'an obsessive' and politically unsubtle. Blanked by Lloyd George, Churchill turned his ire on Ireland. He was no less antagonistic when discussions alighted on Ireland's liberty.

Although the Easter Rising in 1916 barely altered the Liberal party's attitude to a united Ireland, Churchill was perturbed by the growing rebellion and thought it should be "put down" if the need arose. His solution to most anti-Westminster dissent was to jail or shoot. Churchill's *sturm und drang* was wasted emotion. His colleagues refused to take the bait. Meanwhile, IRA guerrilla attacks continued unabated. The only solution was to allow an election to take place in Southern Ireland – Ulster being protected from any fallout – and see what happens. There was talk of a truce, but as far as can be gleaned from historical reports, this passive tactic relied on lots of *anti*-republican candidates standing for election.

Had Churchill been able to commandeer the slogan 'Sinn Féin is *not* Ireland' to paraphrase the inane counter-democratic Tory coinage 'The SNP is *not* Scotland,' he would have used it. Back then, 'Ireland is British' was good enough. Mad as bat with one wing pinned down, he said, "If necessary, we can break up the Irish parliament and resort to coercion." (*David Brynmor Jones Diary – Vol 3.*)

Lloyd George grew tired of Churchill's sabre rattling. It was 1918. War saw disillusioned wounded arrive home from the blood and mud spattered trenches of the Dardanelles, the Somme and Passchendaele. Men who had previously lined up to serve King and Country had grown cynical of incompetent generals and mass slaughter. The British government realised invading Ireland was not a priority. They chose caution and immediately after the Armistice with Germany was signed called a general election.

Churchill, planning for a wipe-out of the republicans, had his feet clawed from under him. The executions of many of the leaders of the Easter uprising of 1916, the news of brutal force-feeding of those imprisoned for their part in the uprising, and the Conscription Crisis of 1918, all served to alienate Irish Catholic opinion from the United Kingdom. To Churchill's anger, and groans from his Empire loyalist followers, the election resulted in a walk-over for Sinn Féin. Moderate Irish nationalists of the Irish Parliamentary Party, ready to accept Home Rule under British conditions, were swept away. Sinn Féin secured 73 seats.

The Irish sent the British a warning; they would take no more colonial claptrap. No Irish was longing to be English. Sinn Féin, who vowed in their manifesto to establish an independent Irish Republic were as good as their word. They formed a breakaway government and declared Irish independence. Apparently the wide sphere of Earth was not England.

It was the first general election to be held after enactment of the *1918, Representation of the People Act*, allowing women over the age of 30 to vote, and all men over the age of 21. Previously, women and many impoverished men had been excluded, the assumption being, poverty and a poor education dulls the mind undermining good decision-making. Many women had voted for Sinn Féin, the first time they could demonstrate free will at the ballot box. Ballots cast by soldiers serving overseas were not included in the tallies until they were home. It made no difference. Sinn Féin was now the elected government of Ireland.

Churchill was frustrated by his colleagues acceptance of the Irish situation, they somewhat mollified by Sinn Féin's policy of not taking their seats at Westminster although they continued to lobby Westminster for their constituents, a tactic they sustain to this day. Lloyd George, his government still in coalition with the Conservative party, was in a flap. Liberals who did not back the coalition lost their seats. Irish Republicans saw a British parliament in disarray, tired, and at its weakest. The moment was right to strike a new bargain, Ireland for the Irish, England for the English. The British government had no strategy to stop the march of Irish nationalism. The only voice heard was Churchill and his 'shoot 'em up' solution to everything.

Politicians in the Ulster Parliament watched events unfolding with increasing alarm and resorted to putting pressure on Westminster behind the scenes to gain favour. With Churchill banging his fist on the cabinet table, the alternative was to adopt martial law in all the Irish counties and govern unelected, or do a deal with Sinn Féin. The former idea was a logistical and costly nightmare, the latter initially unthinkable.

In keeping with English colonial habit, the British government did what it had always done, refused to talk to elected 'upstarts', and instead imposed martial law, backed by the infamous imported regiments of Black and Tans that Churchill declared "were getting to the root of the matter quicker than the military".

Whenever the question of Ireland was brought up, Churchill's view was the same as when at the War Office, he advocated suppressing rebellion with fiscal and trade coercion or if that failed, armed force. Always perceptive of where his support lay, he recognised his policy of reprisal was not winning the hearts or minds of his colleagues or the British public. His colleagues argued on the balance of probabilities, military force was destined to fail. They opened negotiations with Éamon de Valera, Michael Collins and writer-editor Arthur Griffith who founded Sinn Féin, to negotiate a hand-over of powers which resulted in the *1921 Anglo-Irish Treaty*. It was a good time to make their move. Lloyd George was busy selling the First World War as a great victory, and the general election opened to voters to decide what terms to offer the defeated.

An interesting fact: Churchill was *not* given a place on Lloyd George's Irish Negotiating Committee – the mechanism by which a leader delegates important matters of state and make recommendations. Churchill was distrusted by his own party and by the Tory party he was soon to rejoin, with whom he had a lot in common. His absence from the discussion table presented a caring, benign face to the disconsolate Irish. In Churchill's absence, the committee looked at the implications of stomping all over a nation they had let starve during devastating potato famines. Instead, they made conciliatory offers of a truce. Churchill never liked the word, a quirk that came to his rescue when facing Nazism. He felt, justifiably, a truce gave kudos to IRA tactics. Outnumbered by colleagues, he accepted his hard-line and often criminal approach to contain Irish dissent had not succeeded – *for the moment*. The British government was no longer masters of all-Ireland. Acceding to a truce left Republicans in charge of the Irish Parliament and most of southern Ireland.

Lloyd George packed his bags and organised successive meetings with the Republican leader Èamon de Valera, the first task to agree upon the basics for full-scale negotiations. The Irish wanted a republic, no half-measures. The British hit on a strategy of protracted talks. They wanted negotiations to stretch endlessly and tire out Irish to weaken their demands in the hope Republicans would accept *dominion* status – no better than a colony or a protectorate. Lloyd George wanted the Republican movement to split into soft and hard factions, and with luck and infiltration, start an internal war. The British way of control has never varied, generation after generation, divide and rule, and if uncontrolled disorder arises, step in as the saviour of law and order. Churchill, ever the war monger, calculated partitioning Ireland would inflame the all-Ireland Republican Party, which it did, internal conflict a certainty.

At this point, I am obliged to digress for a moment to pre-empt alarmists among readers by stating the obvious. I am not advocating violent insurrection. I do not use the term, the code phrase 'whatever is necessary' to attain Scotland's civil rights. Scots do not die for their country; they die for other people's countries. What I suggest is when Scotland achieves a landslide victory, as we have on two occasions, seeing the Tory and Labour parties down to one lone, lost representative and a tomato stained Union Jack emblazoned waistcoat, the Scottish government should use that mandate to declare Scotland independent again, and open talks.

There are two caveats attached to this all-too obvious democratic move. A nationalist government has to have prepared a new Accord to place before their English counterparts as the basis of handing-over powers. We are ill-prepared if not stupid entering talks without a carefully nuanced counter offer. For another thing, the question arises, who in Scotland's nationalist movement has the statesmanship and courage to raise the Saltire high and declare the day won but for the detail?

The British Tory party, by warlike history and its exceptionalism, knows sewing violent discord helps wins the day for the colonial power. In Ireland's case, the intention was to offer a settlement, spurred by Churchill breathing fire and brimstone, allowing *limited* Republican rule but keep Ireland as a state within the Empire. Excessive authority can be stamped on a disorderly society with impunity if a portion of society is compliant. Authoritarian regimes know enough of the bourgeoisie will welcome tough action if it helps them get to work on time. People are content to see anti-war and environmental demonstrators dragged off roads and taken to police stations, even if they support the reason for the protest, so long as inconvenience happens to the other guy. The strong arm approach has a down-side. Strict control is expensive to maintain over a long period. It drains the Treasury coffers. It upsets the social order. Eventually, the authority is *forced* to negotiate. The British Treasury started to count the cost of brute force. Lloyd George ordered dialogue not rifles and night raids.

It is hard not to see Scottish devolution as a significant parallel, a parliament offered in diminutive form, an 'executive', with hobbled powers, a gift on loan like a hedge trimmer, please return it, its teeth sharpened. Freedoms limited artificially call for group action to allow people to exercise free will. In Ireland's case, after cabinet discussion, the British offered unconditional talks to the Republicans, Churchill having preferred to restart war.

Lloyd George, as unionist as any Scotsman on the make, and in common with today's English politicians, chose a one-sided, largely unionist negotiating team to brow beat the Irish down to a free tram pass and a latch key to live in their own country. Scotland should expect the same treatment when its time comes.

Churchill chaired the defence side of the negotiations. Contemptuously he dismissed justified Irish calls that they be responsible for their own defence, had their own army, dispensed with a navy, and wished to be neutral in conflicts involving the British government. For the initial talks, Churchill was sidelined a second time, watching in annoyance as Lloyd George saw to the detail of the settlement. By any standard it was a case of the invader demanding restitution for things he had actually stolen. Churchill wanted full control of strategic ports in Ireland, a condition that had de Valera's team scoff in disbelief. From this one can see Westminster demand retention of Faslane Dockyard to house Trident in a future Scottish settlement. I suggest the counter offer; they rent it for £5 billion a year for a maximum of 5 years, and pay dearly to clear up any toxic mess left behind.

Of interest are the conditions the British wanted for a free Ireland. It reads like a duke's list of what he wants in taxes and tithes from the commoners tilling his land. In no special order: members of Ireland's parliament, the Dáil, must take an oath offering loyalty to the British King; respect for the Crown to be accepted in the new state, including hereditary land; recognising the Ulster Parliament together with a Northern Ireland boundary, partition – a 'boundary', that old problem again! – Ulster kept as a separate province; no fiscal autonomy; and Britain to decide which countries Ireland could and could not make a treaty. British enemies must *ipso facto*, be Irish enemies. Finally, trade had to be with England before all others. Behind those conditions was Lloyd George and Churchill's determination to keep Ulster Unionists happy, as the Tory party does now with billion pound bungs from the public purse for DUP support.

Lloyd George managed to have de Valera sign an outline agreement which virtually reduced Ireland to dominion status, one of the key issues that opened wide the schism between de Valera and Michael Collins. For de Valera's part, capitulation to British demands troubled him deeply. His subsequent *volte face*, rejecting the Agreement, was to have tragic consequences. To his credit, for it effectively created the Republic, Churchill stood by the Agreement and expected to implement those sections under his brief, but in later months he is recorded belittling the accord as 'wicked'. He remained pig-headed and dogmatic; he thought the war against Sinn Féin should have been continued until they were truly broken.

The Irish knew how to capitalise on principles to encourage adherents to the cause. Collins, Minister of Finance, and Griffiths leading the delegation, handled negotiations, de Valera staying in Ireland to allow the plenipotentiaries to refer back to him without being pressured into any agreements. "To me, the task is a loathsome one," Collins wrote. "I go in the spirit of a soldier who acts against his best judgment at the orders of his superior." In a letter he wrote that he had "signed my death warrant". He was right to be on his guard. De Valera suddenly rejected the Agreement because it involved the partition of Ireland and *did not* create an independent republic. In Griffiths and Collins in particular, de Valera had found scapegoats. To the crushing disappointment of Collins the revolutionary, de Valera reverted to war to achieve a genuine, self-reliant, obsequious to no nation, republic. Because of the Oath to the King, he and his followers could never, ever, vote for the Treaty. Collins thought it a paltry excuse, something not worthy of breaking an acceptable deal. De Valera was heavily castigated for his alleged deviousness and vanity. Nothing less than a true republic would do.

I think de Valera, a master politician, recognised his place in history. He understood he was a symbol of Ireland's struggle for independence. De Valera had been jailed and then released because of his American-born status (he was born in New York); otherwise he might have been placed up against a wall and executed like some of his less fortunate collaborators. But it was Collins who had fought and beaten the British to the negotiation table by his brilliance for intelligence work and by the way he harried English troops and second-guessed English tactical politics. He wanted to remain faceless, to advise from the sidelines, but de Valera shoved him into the limelight as a negotiator.

As Colonial Secretary, Churchill took on the role of handing powers over to Ireland but went out of his way to make the process a tangled web. There is scholarly disagreement he did so deliberately to gain advantage. By January 1922 a provisional government was established with Michael Collins and Arthur Griffiths drafting a constitution. Churchill put his trust in Collins and Griffiths to deliver the dominion state negotiated, which they did with great reluctance. Like Scotland's devolution, to them it was only the beginning of things. Churchill was shocked at de Valera's renunciation, Churchill the quintessential Englishman who did not understand the passions that motivate revolutionaries.

Churchill retaliated by submitting a bill to the Westminster parliament asking for support for an invasion force. In April 1922 Churchill approved the *Special Powers Act* that suspended *habeas corpus*, removed civil rights, including detention without trial, legalised street searches and house raids without warrant, and instituted imprisonment for refusal to comply. By the next election, people fearing conflict, the Provisional Government achieved a win for the pro-Treaty side, and Churchill used that to drive a wedge between Irishman and Irishman.

Churchill gave his *full support* to Ulster Unionists. Churchill had no fear of Catholics fighting Protestants, they were too few back then, he guessed correctly Protestants would be hostile to Catholics. Today, the Protestant community finds itself in the minority compared to the growing numbers of Catholics and consequent support for Sinn Féin's political candidates, something Churchill never foresaw. A Catholic majority is more inclined to vote for a united Ireland.

Once more, England's departure from a territory it governed resulted in partition and prolonged violence. De Valera was the man who did what Churchill wanted done, cause dissent among confederates. Despite Churchill's many attempts to derail the Irish Agreement ("a sane chauffeur who suddenly drives you over a cliff"), it came to pass without his Machiavellian intervention.

At this point this brief history of Ireland's struggle ends, chiefly because the well informed know the rest of Ireland's tortured history, a war that lasted until the end of the 20th century.

Zealots and soldiers all grow old. What we see now is a proud, confident, independent nation state, recovering quickly from the financial crash of 2008, still belittled by a jingoistic England, ironically prospering at the expense of England's grand folly – the dumping of European co-operation.

Over time, Ireland removed the remnants of dominion status and, with a new Constitution in 1937, became fully independent. It took blood, sweat, poetry, stage plays, bombs and murder to rid Ireland of its colonial leg irons. Scotland need not encounter any of those crimes and betrayals wreaked on Ireland because it will not be isolated.

In abjuring Scots to follow their own course to self-determination, Scotland's leaders can take solace knowing England made a catastrophic error dumping Europe. Ireland is a member of the European Union. If the British government tries to strangle Scotland by withholding powers or funds it is due, they will come to Scotland's aid and outlaw England as a renegade nation.

Next time a unionist dullard decries the possibility of a border between an independent Scotland and England, remind him it was the British government under Lloyd George and Churchill that demanded a border be stuck between Ireland and Ulster. Now excuse me while I fill in an application for an Irish passport.

14

THE MAN WITH THE WALRUS MOUSTACHE

He had a habit of chewing it. He would stick out his bottom lip on one side of his mouth, and with his lower incisor teeth, drag in hairs from his impressively luxuriant lip appendage and bite down on them. Like an unkempt, uncut hedge, it was not trimmed. Every now and then he ran his fingers down its length to smooth it flat. The moustache doubled as an extra sook of beer when he lifted a glass to his mouth and left foam on its edge. Tomato sauce probably had the same affect but I only ever saw him eat once, and that was breakfast.

He was proud of his walrus moustache. He reminded me of a nonsense poem I once adapted.

> *On Glasgow Bridge a Scotsman stood*
> *Chewing his beard for lack of food.*
> *"This beard," said he, "Is no fun to eat,*
> *But it's a damn sight better than Shredded Wheat".*

I couldn't understand why he let it grow so long only to get hairs in his food, until I noticed it hid a small mouth. In middle age, his head hair was thin, the mullet keeping the nape of his neck warm. "Ah dinnae comb it in case it faws oot."

He was a year younger than me but looked twenty years older. His eyes were deep set under a Neanderthal brow. He had a cracked, rasping voice from years of heavy duty smoking and boozing. He smoked roll-up cigarettes, an hourly ritual he had perfected, licking the Rizla paper, a lizard licking its lips. Walrus rolled the sausage packet of tobacco from a tin in his pocket between thumb and forefinger. Not difficult to wonder when cancer would get his throat and booze destroy his liver. He perfected a hard man image but drinking undid that, turning him into a legless man.

His boozer's way of dropping a crass remark aimed at whoever was standing nearby did not endear him to passing admirers. He could seduce by giving you the impression you were his best friend, buddy for life, while bad mouthing you behind your back. A drunk blames his problems on those around; the problem is never the drunk. They have a way of showing remorse, an over-generous gift, or in the case of Walrus, a visit next morning with an invitation for a shake hands and make-up a gargle. Drunks are great company for the first hour of chatter and jokes and anecdotes, a nightmare if you hang around too long. You are liable to get arrested as an accessory to the fact when he or she throws a punch at a stranger, or you end the evening as the mug paying a taxi driver to take him home, the first two driving off soon as they spot your pal is legless. If you managed to pile Walrus inside a taxi he was liable to instruct the driver to take him to a bar as soon as the taxi door closed. He did not want to go home to his wife. He was a born barfly.

You never knew how much of his tough guy stories or his adventures in movie land were true or embellished or plain fictitious. He did a lot of boasting. He cannibalised experiences from people he met and recycled them as if his personal experience. He gave off an air of fearlessness faced by authority, or anybody wearing a suit. His conversations were peppered with profanities. "I told those fucking Suits tae fuck right off wi' their memos," he would claim. "That's their entire BBC joab, takin' memos fae one fuckin' department tae another!"

If you drank with him too often you tended to hear the same stories repeated, his memory forgetful who he had told, precision of their telling a sign they were well polished. He used hangers on as sounding boards. His friendship was the duration of a drink. A judge might describe him as unreliable. A friend could say the same thing. He knew he looked a tough guy, and he went out of his way to cultivate the macho man appearance, creating his own fame, an acquired image, as his brand. I thought him a pale copy of the screenwriter Alan Sharp in whom he shared a great many characteristics, booze, women, lost days and deadlines, derelict dawns, even a walrus moustache. Sharp could drive a campervan, lived in one a time to and from a World Cup football match, and pilot a small boat to his New Zealand hideaway. Walrus did not own a car and I never saw him drive one. Other than snobbishness for English orientated material things – "This is a *real* Norfolk jaiket, pal. It's no crap aff the peg" – he stayed true to his origins when it came to his literary subject matter, he wrote about Scots poor, the no hopers, the downtrodden. He never became conservative because he had nothing to conserve.

Listening to his stories of women he met, I asked a close friend what she thought of him, a smart woman who knew men and how their brains and balls work in synchronisation. "He's an animal" she said, without hesitating. She was right, a full-blown keep your cap on, wallop it up them misogynist. Then again, I am assuming his tales of sword play without a sword were true. The hangers-on who gathered around him were similar in disposition, or wanted to be like him, the West of Scotland's Brendan Behan. In fact, like Behan, he had been locked in a toilet by an irate BBC schools television producer, told to finish the script. In the archaic language of old school cliché, he was a lovable rogue.

What he wanted to be but would never be – you do not ever see the best from an alcoholic – was the novelist William MacIlvanney. Aye, for all his bawdy behaviour he needed a father figure.

His last partner was at least a decade older than him. His many faults personal and contractual were offset by a child-like set of twinkling eyes when he made joke and enjoyed its effect. He could charm a venomous snake, a quality to ensnare unwary women. A loving woman thinks she can change a drunk's madness for the better, their compulsion, a crazy, romantic delusion. Alcoholics need professional help. They need to admit what the problem is to help them beat it. Otherwise they make life for those around them miserable.

By the time I met him Walrus was living off past glories. His earliest work had won a prestigious award. He was unperturbed. He got on with drinking and smoking until work came to him. His London agent saw to that. He did not appear to plot out his television plays, they stuttered from him. If inspiration failed to write the next few pages, it was time to visit his favourite pub. All human life congregated in a pub, he said, his excuse for a drink. His later work failed to catch the public's imagination like his first but all of it was honest. He did not write about kings or queens or dispossessed aristocracy giving it meaning for the masses. He wrote about life in the low-end of town long before Irvine Welsh painted Leith as a society full of toilet bowl gagging disillusioned drug addicts.

When I got to know Walrus he was still a name. He announced himself frequently as an "unschooled" man. I think that was the true in part, but he was not illiterate. He had good literary skills especially for working class dialogue of the kind heard in beer bars. If you met him he was not easy to forget. My reason to meet him was to see if the playwright in him would write a stage play for my theatre company. On hindsight, it was a stupid thing to do. Stage plays do not command television-sized fees. I thought it worth a try. He might be down on his luck. Anyway, Glasgow tough guy stories were all the rage and he was the epitome of the tough guy writer. I noticed his central characters were young, footloose adolescents or just in a job they did not like. My theatre cast were all of the same age; maybe there was a fit.

I called on him at his London home early night. It was a cold place. I think I walked in on a heated argument between him and his then wife. It was not a venue to talk business. I upped and left. Around the corner, looking at items in a bright shop window, my sheepskin collar pulled up to ward off the cold wind, he suddenly bounded into sight. "Sorry about that, pal. Didnae mean tae insult yi, or anything. I'll gie yer offer serious thought." I told him no offence was taken, nor mentioned I had paid for the wasted journey out of my own pocket. The man with the walrus moustache shook my hand and agreed to meet again.

The next meeting took place in his Scottish hometown. "Let's go for a pint and talk," he said, and off we strolled yapping and joking to his nearest watering hole.

"So, where are we going?

"A special place. Yi dinnae need to ask for a specific brewed pint. There's only two kinds, light or dark. When the shipyards emptied oan lousin' time whistle, rows o' light and dark pints were ready for them oan the bar. Yi jist piled in an' grabbed whit yi wanted."

There was nothing to commend the place. The painted brown ceiling, the varnished, grease-stain wood from thousands of dirt encrusted hands steadying themselves as they staggered to the bar or toilet, or tried to stand up out of their seat, made the place one to walk past. Rough unmopped floorboards and the cheap patched Edwardian bar said a cleaner was not wanted. It was indistinguishable from any other drinking den in a working class district where regulars are not expected to look for interesting decoration or historic elements. It was a bar you would never find in Dublin. The pubs in Dublin are shrines to the city's outstanding literary past and present. Walrus's pub would never have a plaque on the wall saying he drank there, or it was Billy Connolly's first for stand up jokes and a ukulele tune.

I have never understood why some men feel they can open up about how many women they have slept with and what intimate act they did in bed or were allowed to do on each occasion. If married and describing a night's illicit affair, it puts one in a difficult position, how to face his wife next time we meet. What do I say if she asks me if her husband is cheating on her? What kind of person does it make me if I stay silent? Walrus joins the list of men I know who assume they have bragging rights, treat you as a Father Confessor. Walrus did it all the time. To him, porn was love stories with all the boring bits taken out. His conquests were for the telling.

"So I'm in Los Angeles oan a jaunt fir a studio tae dae rewrites oan a movie, and Ah've met up with this great lookin' woman who just loves mah Scottish rough ways. Oh man, in bed she lets me dae it all." His rasping tone is reminiscent of a car exhaust from an idling engine.

> "Efter, we did it, she lights a fag and says she loves me and wants tae keep in touch. So Ah says, Ah'll phone her when I get back tae Scotland. But she disnae wait. She writes me a letter and sends it to mah hoose an' ma bliddy wife opens it. She wis livid. Got the silent treatment fir weeks. Next back in Los Angeles, smokin' another fag, I tell her no tae write letters tha' ma wife will open. "How do I keep in touch with you?" she asks, in that way a woman pleads after thinking she loves ye. Ah had tae think fast. "Ah'll gie yi mah agent's address. Write tae him. Okay?" Well, she writes tae him but afore I get back tae change planes in London, ma agent sends the fuckin' letter tae ma wife ma hoos an' ma wife opens it. AH'M OAN MA LAST CHANCE, fer fuck's sake!"

Three hours later we were still the 'Light An' Dark' pub, talk of a stage play reduced to ten disjointed minutes with no outcome, interspersed with him licking his Rizla roll-up paper and lighting the end a dozen times. Those emaciated slices of paper with a sticky slip side sell in over one hundred countries, and have been on the go for over two hundred years, a small-time family company handed down generations. I have yet to see one perfect roll-up, smooth top to bottom, no baccy hanging out the ends. You get three decent puffs out of them.

"Ah'll have the same again, Big Boy," he says. My turn to buy a round. I rarely get served quickly by bartenders. I don't have a boozer's face. I can stand at a bar counter waving a wad of money and still be ignored. On this occasion I prayed the length of time it took me to order a round put him off another drink. But no, there was another Rizla paper to lick and another self-deprecating story to tell of his writing adventures, often repeated, a sign of an addled brain. "Gie me a Talasker this time, Gareth!"

My youngest brother was a barman for a time in a franchised pub. He was instructed by the corporate owners to dilute each quality bottle of malt whisky with a third from a cheap whisky called Cluny, on the assumption a drunk has no subtlety of taste. When a customer asked for a specific malt whisky they were given a diluted volume but charged the price of the quality whisky. On the other hand, if a customer ordered a glass of Cluny my brother would ask, "Talasker, Highland Park, Jura, Laphroaig, Glengoyne, Glenfiddich?" and so on, and so forth. He swore blind no drinker ever complained, they all thought he was joking.

Walrus always had money for a round, never for a meal. Buy Walrus a pint and whisky chaser and he returned the gesture ignoring stern refusals. I drink whisky late evenings, one glass. His back turned, or off to the toilet, I poured my whiskies into his glass. I quench a thirst, boozers feed a habit. My car journey a hundred miles home required a clear head. In a few quarters of Scotland you rank as a mature man if brain frazzled and legless, Scotland's disease that will stay until we run our own country again, the usurpers banished from it.

"Ah'm bored here. Let's go someplace else," said Walrus, stubbing out his umpteenth skinny roll-up. My relief at the change of atmosphere was dashed to discover 'someplace else' was another pub further down the street. Drink dependent folk expect you to starve.

By the fourth pub, one where pints are actually pulled, and you can buy bottled beer, I was itching to make my excuses to go home. The pub's lights were out, candles lit in saucers on tables and granite bar top. In entered Tanza, an old pal of Walrus. He was overweight, and had one eye. He screwed up his seeing socket and surveyed the half-darkness.

"Whits up wi' the lights?" he asked Walrus.

"Nae idea, Tanza. Some kind o' power failure."

"Away yi go!" he shouted back. "The lights are still oan in the buses."

I met the writer one last time, at a movie wrap party. He fed me an insult. It was motivated by envy. By then he was not worth the trouble. It was my film and he had gate crashed it. I remembered he had taken an anecdote I had told him about my childhood, and used it in a television play to help unblock his inability to move the scene on. That's what television writers do, borrow from anybody near enough. Writers do that. What irked was a humorous anecdote I told of my unhappy short stay in the Boy Scouts which he handed to a comedian who then used it as his own in a television interview. And dealing with his London agent unearthed a posse of cowboys. One asked for £40,000 to commission a client with the condition if he failed to meet the deadline he kept the money. He thought I was a hick from the sticks.

There is one more meeting to tell. Earlier in our association Walrus promised to arrive at my home to discuss the subject matter of the play I had suggested. Instead he disappeared with a barmaid and arrived next morning, bedraggled, slept in his clothes, shivering, nowhere to stay. I fried up a plate of sausage, eggs and bacon – "nae gin in the hoose?" Handling a massive hangover he looked at the sausages as if he expected them massaged briskly to increase their size. Finished, plate licked, thanks given, he produced an expensive Mont Blanc pen and small leather bound journal out of his Norfolk jacket pocket and began writing an apology in near perfect copper-plate script. "This is fir yer wife."

"*Please tick the appropriate statement:*

1. *I do not like what you are doing.*
2. *You're leading my husband astray.*
3. *It's criminal, if I'm no' confused about things.*
4. *Maybe its Garath's (sic) fault.*
5. *One would think he'd a chip on his shoulder.*
6. *The more I think about it, the more it's him.*
7. *That boy is up from London, Garath should know better.*
8. *To be honest, I don't like the way he treats me either.*
9. *And here's me working all day too.*
10. *Christ! Soon's I see him, I'm gonnae batter'm!"*

I never got a stage play out of him. Many years later Walrus Moustache wrote three short dramas for a 'Play and a Pint', pub. Fortunate is the man who can combine his work with pleasure, if you catch my drift.

15

NATIONALISM AND NAZIS

Every so often one will come across a provocative insult in the press or social media claiming the founders of Scotland's national party were Nazi sympathisers. A brazen lie, of course, one concocted by the far-right – closer to fascism and racism than any Scottish nationalist.

A superficial glance can lead the reader to think repetition of the inflammatory claim proves it plausible if not quite true. The SNP came to public notice in the 1930s. Attempts to attach the SNP to the rise of Nazism are a lazy insult oblivious of the photographs that exist showing English aristocracy, including the young future Queen Eliabeth, practising Nazi salutes in admiration of Hitler's discipline of the masses. It is also oblivious of Sir Oswald Mosley – self-appointed leader of the British Union of Fascists – emulating the Nazi Party, practising wee boy scout soldiers in London's streets with his ragbag of Blackshirt comic goose steppers. The great humanitarian, holocaust survivor and writer, Primo Levi, predicted the resurgence of fascism, nosed its acrid odour, he knew what it looked and sounded like. He would not have used it as freely as some do against individuals, were he alive today.

Before pointing out the differences between fascism and Nazism, it is worth understanding why we should not describe right-wing views automatically *fascist*. I have seen supposedly intelligent people in Scotland's government call peaceful street protestors, fascists. We should be very careful about bandying the word. The rise of authoritarian populist figures around the world, intent on strict control of their citizens, is a remarkable feature of the 20st century. This development *does* have similarities to the fascists of Mussolini's Italy.

Fascism and Nazism are usually miles apart. Fascism holds to a set of authoritarian principles, Nazism was a totalitarian ideology. Lines become blurred when Nazi ideology is applied to societies using neo-fascist principles. What they share are charismatic leaders. Both encourage a culture of leader worship and vainglorious national pomp.

A primary aim of the controlling Nazi leadership was the *destruction* of any organizational threat that might challenge the attainment of "state" ends. Race and religion were viewed as enemies of the state. Jews, gypsies, rebellious clergy, were round up, herded into ghettos and millions exterminated in gas chambers. Unions, students, professional organizations, anything that looked remotely subversive, especially political parties, were infiltrated, harassed, destroyed, or brought under state control. One can argue the British State's uses of state security policy to infiltrate unions and legitimate protest groups is a manifestation of fascism. The Scottish Government's ban on all dissident assembly around Scotland's parliament building in 2021 was authoritarian, intimidating and alienating, but not fascism. It betrayed the free, open society promised by its nationalist government, but one trusts the regulation will be revoked when independence arrives.

Nazism was exported to South American countries when the worst officials fled the defeat of Adolf Hitler; hence we witnessed how Nazi refugees helped South American governments, often backed by the United States, to keep political control and the indigenous poor written off, their land possessed by government forces for the exploitation of big business. We do not think of the USA as having adopted Nazi tactics, yet it has rained death on defenceless smaller agrarian nations solely for their political outlook, Vietnam a prime example. The USA has committed war crimes to a far greater and deadly degree than any country that has committed terrorist acts on the West.

NATIONALISM AND NAZIS

When people use the word *fascist* I think of the European model, of Benito Mussolini first and then Franco, dictator of Spain. General Franco enjoyed full patronage by his people and by world leaders as Spain's leader for life. We toddled off for our fortnight's package holiday to Spain uncaring of his history in league with Nazi Germany, or bought property there without knowing the next door neighbour or local tapas bar owner adored Franco's policies. Informed people visit the Picasso museum in Barcelona to marvel at his remarkable image of the bombing of Guernica, shake their heads and think it all in the bad past, but fascism is still around, detectable in the backs streets of Spain among the elderly who lived by Franco's rural policies. The Spanish judicial system and some aspects of government are tainted by Francophiles. His disciples still exercise considerable influence in the running of Spain and the crushing of Catalonia's political hopes. Fascism resists new ideas.

The genesis of Scotland's main nationalist party, the Scottish National Party (SNP), has not the slightest association with European fascism or German Nazism though a few have tried to smear it with excreta. The obnoxious faux academic David Starkey lost his job, and put an end to his television career, and his wits, describing Scotland's national party as akin to "Nazis". He maintained the two political parties were "strikingly similar". He uttered the preposterous remarks in a newspaper interview. Digging his grave faster than a ferret chases a rabbit down a burrow, he said the SNP's emblem of a thistle is like the swastika, and compared the SNP's view of the English to Adolf Hitler's hatred of Jews. One presumes he did not consider Scots as Jewish.

I have never thought much of the SNP's logo, not at all inspiring, but in that brief brain fart was Starkey's ignorance of abstract illustration, and the Scots detestation of colonial English arrogance of his bitchy kind. The brutal rule with a smile and a game of cricket of the British Empire was not part of his historical studies. Not realising he was ending his well paid celebrity days as a pompous lover of gout-ridden and woman hating Henry VIII, the poor fellow went on to say the kilt was reminiscent of the traditional dress of

Germany, inadvertently making us aware of Scotland's long association with European universities, and his association with sane judgement remote.

Pitching the nascent SNP next to Nazism arrives on Internet social sites and in the press in another ugly disguise. Arthur Donaldson was a leader of the SNP, an assistant registrar of birth deaths and marriages by early trade. His name pops up on the Internet whenever a far-right thug tries to besmirch Scotland's attempts to achieve social justice. His home and others of the SNP was raided when he joined the Scottish Neutrality League in the Thirties, an organisation established at the start of the Second World War by conscientious objectors. He was arrested on the hearsay evidence of a third party, the trumped up charge he might be about to set up an interim government in Scotland if the Germans managed to invade England.

Here is an extract from a typical piece of black propaganda fabricated by a dyed-in-the-wool agent of the British State, the *Scottish Daily Express*, owned by Lord Beaverbrook who, like Hitler, felt "The Jews may drive us into another war."

> "Mr Donaldson, leader of the SNP between 1960 and 1969, was investigated by MI5 for plotting to set-up a Nazi government in Scotland. The wartime spy report released in 2005 claims that the former SNP leader conspired to set up a Vichy-style government with himself as a 'Scottish Quisling' in the event of Adolf Hitler's widely-anticipated invasion. In 1941, Mr Donaldson allegedly told a close confidant – who was also a British agent – that a network of Nazi sympathisers were planning to undermine the war effort."

On the basis of an accusation made without written verification or witness, Donaldson was thrown in a police cell for six weeks and then released. Not much study is required to see the accusation carries no evidence whatsoever. Nor is there any truth in the charge he had a branch of the Nazi party in mind. The smear makes an appearance half-a-dozen times a year, easily dismissed.

This brings me to the greater evidence of why the Nazi's would never be attracted to a little known politician from an obscure wee 'eccentric' Scottish political party to help them take over Britain's infrastructure and be nice to Scotland in reward. Nazis preferred the aristocracy. Why else did they loot so many great works of art from national galleries and private collections? They wanted to raise their status and ancestry, people the Arian masses could look up to and admire. Nazis identified with the old German elite not with the obscure Scottish champions of the working classes. The British Royal family knew that and duly responded. Sir Oswald Mosley could not get his black shirt, contrasting tie and belted Hitler jodhpurs on fast enough. John Reith, then Director General of the British Broadcasting Corporation, later Lord Reith, heard from the British cabinet office that Hermann Göring had been invited to a week's shooting party at an earl's country estate. He wrote to Göring's secretary, "Tell him I will be happy to fly the Nazi Swastika from Alexandra Palace flagpole as a welcome if he consents to an interview."

Adolf Hitler was extremely adept at networking, ingratiating himself with the great and the good of German society. His earliest sponsors were the Bechstein family, famous makers of arguably the best grand pianos in the world. He was invited to their home, their parties, and they showered him with gifts, including an expensive Mercedes saloon. High society women were entranced with the slightly uncouth adventurer who regaled them with his ambitions for a great Germany.

The Nazi movement went out of its way to acquire friends in high places, the social elite of their day, while their henchmen were beating up union members and socialists in dimly lit back alleys. Prince August Wilhelm of Prussia was a confirmed devotee of Nazism and joined the Stormtroopers in 1930. Through him Hermann Göring got access to Prince Wilhelm. Himmler got in the act of sucking up to German nobility, no doubt certain in his belief they were the pinnacle of the selective breeding he espoused in his SS principles. By the time the Nazi were well embedded in the top levels of power about a fifth of SS officers were titled noblemen.

It is not difficult to see how adoration of Hitler's totalitarian doctrine made its way to the British aristocracy. Duke Carl Eduard von Sachsen-Coburg und Gotha was a grandson of Queen Victoria, born 'Prince of Great Britain and Ireland'. He joined the Nazi party in 1933 and by 1936 became an SA-Gruppenführer (group leader). From his example flowed a stampede of aristocratic enthusiasts, members of the Hohen-Lohes and from the House of Hesse. More nobility than you could curtsey to in a week flocked to the cause of the Third Reich. Princes would have made the biggest group of Nazis anywhere. The scene in the early part of the musical *Cabaret*, based on Christopher Isherwood's semi-autobiographical *The Berlin Stories*, when the camera swings a hundred and eighty degrees from stage to audience reveals it full of German officers at the tables, where before were lower class workers. The Germans enjoying debauched entertainment were not ordinary soldiers but the elite of Himmler's SS squad in their trademark black uniforms.

The belief Nazism was the tumble of downwardly moving petty bourgeois, teachers, shopkeepers, minor officials, the unemployed, is quickly dispelled when one looks closely at those at the top echelons of the Nazi movement. From there, the princes and the dukes passed their enthusiasm of the Nazi creed by word of mouth, letter or newspaper article to their relations in the English aristocracy, and they in turn packed their suitcases and very English umbrellas to visit Herr Hitler, Chancellor of Germany, in droves and mingle with his power elite. The photograph of the British Royal family giving Seig Heil salutes suddenly makes sense. The nobility may not have been big enough as a social stratum to elect Hitler, but they were happy to entrust Hitler with high office. They provided the example to the masses. It did not take long for the Nazi hierarchy to invite bigger and bigger families of the aristocracy to their parties and weddings. From there it was a short step to British politicians and celebrities from the worlds of theatre, film and concert performance and sport. Automobile tournaments and horse racing especially were favourite sports for elite gatherings, after all. Like England's Ascot races, they were all about the best breeds, horse *and* human. The press cameras flashed sending pictures of those glittering occasions all over the world. Arthur Donaldson, leader of the Scottish National Party, was not invited to those events.

The UK government and the US thought Mussolini a fine chap; UK politicians thought his methods got results. They admired the way he coerced and motivated Italians. Mussolini's Italy was the new model to follow, an extremist party with extremist policies dominated by a charismatic, all-powerful leader. Adolf Hitler, hiding an inferiority complex, together with his head of communications and propaganda, Joseph Goebbels, thought Mussolini a great man that is, until they met him, and thereupon decided he was a fool.

Mussolini declared the fascist ideology of fear and omertà, a kind of 'wheest for Benito", 'the summation and unity of all values'. He felt everything existed in the state, nothing outside. There had to be no other party but the Fascist Party. In Berlin, the Nazi's garlanded their walls with Degas, Utrillo, Bonnard and Monet, Dürer and Boucher, to give their power base that touch of class. I have no idea what Arthur Donaldson put on his Ayrshire poultry farm walls, most probably a photograph of a prize cockerel.

The rise of fascist groups this century is ominous. It has its roots in America, where the Republican Party studied the methods of the ideology. In the 1950's American right-wing, third-rate scholars such as Zbigniew Brzezinski noted how the structures of fascism managed the concentration of power, free to impose, free to terrorise. Imagined enemies were conjured on a regular basis to keep the populace fixated on some existential fear giving the Fascist party greater and greater control of the economy and the lines of communication. Perhaps without knowing it, the SNP exercises what French philosopher Michel Foucault calls the "individual as both an effect of power and the element of its articulation: the individual which power has constituted is at the same time its vehicle".

All parties enjoying political power too long eventually do what they can to consolidate power to use to extend their powers and their administrative life. Power not given by the electorate is taken by any means possible to use against the electorate when necessary.

The most excessive misuse of power employed by the SNP leadership has been the hunting of the former First Minister, the Right Honourable Alex Salmond MP, a feverish chase as baying hounds run down a fox, aided and abetted by the corrupted stewardship of the Scottish Crown Office. The sole reason for the chase was to ensure he did not return to politics and become a threat to the British State. Were it not for a High Court jury determined to keep a tight hold of natural justice, Alex Salmond would be languishing in jail for years to come. For all its flaws, judged by your peers remains the best way of righting wrongs.

Fascism crushes the human spirit, Nazism crushes human skulls, but Scotland's nationalist parties should exist to kindle pride in one's country and culture, never for any reason of superiority only to remind us what is possible rather than what is *not* possible.

The German philosopher Frederich Hegel wrote:

> "The essential being is the union of the subjective with the rational will [that is, our unerring ability to fit reality to suit or prejudices]; it is the moral Whole, the State, which is that form of reality in which the individual has and enjoys his freedom; but on condition of recognising, believing in and willing that which is common to the Whole ... the state is the existing, realised moral life. The morality (sittlichkeit) of the State is not of that ethical (moralische), reflective kind, the true morality is based on the principles of abiding by one's duty to the State at large."

The state tends to look for loyalty of allegiance, your country right or wrong. Independence of judgement becomes taboo, errant, marking out a person as deviant. The last thing Scotland needs in the middle of a new Enlightenment is docile, uncritical citizens, blindly serving party dogma.

Colonial-minded individuals who want to see Scotland locked into an abusive relationship with England act as if the State itself. They are masochists. Conformity is the death of independent thought and political progress. Vitality is smothered.

NATIONALISM AND NAZIS

As for the absurd claim that the SNP is a full-blooded Nazi variant, it is far too inept to lace up a pair of jackboots let alone goose-step down Glasgow's streets like the Orange Order banging big bass drums. Frivolity aside, it does not mean fascism is not on the rise again. It most certainly is.

16

THE PROFESSOR'S PERVERSION

Let me call him Dapper Dan for reasons that will become clear. He was always dressed elegantly, his appearance enhanced by a trim, dapper figure and attention to detail, his face shaven not scraped, hair brushed back, immaculate black suede brothel creepers, a conservative cut suit, contrasting waistcoat with pocket watch and silver chain, shirt collar never out always in, and a flowery kipper tie. The man of reserved nature had a flashy side. I say 'had' because he upped and died just after the subject of this story received an acceptable ending.

A straight back, a sprightly walk, an elderly gentleman's charm, and a wide smile added to the overall effect of a sound education and studied courtesy. When I got to know him he was retired and in his mid-seventies. I had heard from others he had a dark side, a surgery in his basement painted in battleship grey like a dungeon, but the couple who told me he had caused them grief were contradicted when Dapper Dan retaliated with the tale *they* had been 'appalling' to *him*, a threat to the institution of which he was a guardian.

He wanted to be a painter by recognised his limitations and instead collected modern works of art, the rewards of a well paid university post. Art was a lifelong passion. He had toyed with the idea of becoming an artist – his words – before committing himself to a career in medicine. In an interview, he said: "There was a woman who worked with Christie's, the auction house in London, who used to bring classes to homes and show them the collections of private collectors. She regularly came to our house and on one occasion said to her class, 'And all on an academic salary'. My wife kicked my shin surreptitiously, and said under her breath, '*Two* academic salaries'."

What I liked about him was his acute intelligence, but having a psychiatrist as a friend leaves one with troubling doubts. One might over-stretch the friendship by confessing personal anxieties which unbalance the relationship, as one might in an incautious moment discuss with a doctor, who is a close friend, a skin tag on your scrotum, an intimacy too far. With most friends advice carries no forfeit, no price, no loss of face, or deference. A man who analysis the mind is altogether different. Listening to your concerns, a psychiatrist might decide you are not the rock solid character he befriended. Or he might decide to suggest listening followed by therapy and bandages is a professional service and feel obliged to charge a fee. The second issue is the uncomfortable feeling to know a psychiatrist is to feel one is in for a day's psychoanalysis from the moment you say good morning.

Cautious, but attracted by his learning that some of it might brush off on me; I entered into a friendship by letter. I found we had one subject in common, a safe one, we both loved movies. Our friendship began with an email from him to say he had read my film reviews, liked them, and liked films I enjoyed. What film should he go to see at the weekend? I recommended a new film by Martin Scorsese, *Hugo*, a children's story set in Paris, a lively story of an orphaned boy that is not another of Scorsese's studies of Mafia thuggery he has made his own. I found it lovingly made and to look at but not in the least memorable, not a genre Scorsese was likely to visit again. "That is exactly my summation, Gareth," he wrote in response, "And yet a story that held you until the telling was told".

And so it went on, back and forth for some months, our correspondence always warm, pleasant, both keen to agree with each other's opinion, each adding an insight the other missed.

One day, something puzzling occurred. His letter began "You used *effect* when you meant *affect*. Ha-ha-ha!" Literary friends do not send crass gibes like that; they couch a correction in diplomatic terms. "*Effect*? Did you mean to write *affect*?" thus giving you honourable room to answer without making a grovelling apology. His riposte had stinging barbs on it.

The confusion is a common error. "The weather definitely can **effect** funeral scenes." The correct word, of course, is *affect*. One thing *affects* (verb) another thing, but cannot have an *affect* (noun) on another thing. It was a rare slip, a genuine typo, but the potty professor was insinuating it was a Freudian slip; he was implying subconsciously I had no confidence in my grasp of grammar. There is some truth in his perception. I am mainly self-taught. I believe being autodidactic frees me to coin new phrases, and new ways of saying old phrases because I am not hidebound by literary tradition. The psychiatrist in him was subverting the friendship. I always remember which to use because in my head is 'special *effects*' used in filmmaking. *Effect* usually serves only as a noun. There are occasions where it serves as a verb: 'the company gave their workers their P45 unemployed slips in order to *effect* savings'. In that sentence *effect* means, to produce. A conscientious writer soon learns sloppy habits will *affect* meaning.

Professor-pupil relationship established in his mind, from then on I was a lot slower in sending my film reviews to him before the general public had a chance to digest them and comment. If he took exception to a critique I was able to show a majority of the public felt as I did. "Don't try to tell me what to think!" he protested, on another occasion. That remark had me permanently on guard.

My next meeting with him was an invitation to afternoon tea in his garden, preserve of the rich and wealthy with time on their hands to gather around a table indoors or outdoors in the garden watching the gardeners at work. I began the soiree with a wonderful joke of a gardener pleading to the laird owner of the palatial house for a new barrow. "What is the problem with it, Jock?" asked the laird. "The wheel is old and rusty. It goes squeak… squeak… squeak…

squeak." The expression on the laird's face dropped. "I ought to fire you," he said. "Why?" asked the astonished gardener, "I have tried oil, sir, and it doesn't work". "Because," said the laird, "The wheel should be going squeak-squeak-squeak-squeak-squeak!"

Drinking tea in the 19th century was considered precious and kept out of the reach of stick-fingered servants in locked serpentine-fronted cherry wood tea caddies, accompanied by cakes piled high on a tier of plates. Biscuits on the move are my staple mid-afternoon snack taken with a glass of orange juice 'with bits' in it. I once ate an entire packet of digestives unthinking while deep in creative activity, something I call a *snaccident*. I cannot drink coffee after 11am, and never drink tea. My stepfather drank tea with oodles of milk out of a jam jar in the days when crockery was a luxury. The smell lingers in my nostrils. The subtleties of Chinese tea were unknown; tea bags still to be invented.

Afternoon tea it was and at Dapper Dan's house, a long low breeze block built property, with expensive art work on the walls. He entered smiling from his galley kitchen holding aloft a tray of warmed madeleines to make the soiree swing.

A Madeleine – the French give it a capital letter as a noun – is a traditional small sponge cake originating from Commercy and Liverdun, communes of the Lorraine region in north-eastern France. Some are made with finely ground nuts, some with lemon zest. They are fine eaten on their own, better with jam or honey. No one quite knows who invented madeleines, most probably a pastry cook who wife, girlfriend, mistress, or daughter was named Madeleine and he had a mould fashioned to shape them. Whatever the source, the madeleine became the staple of the diet of the French bourgeoisie, and Dapper Dan was right in line for that epithet.

Those 'baked' by Dapper Dan were out of a packet from Sainsbury's. The rogue claimed to have cooked them himself. The perfect factory baked shell pattern on them told me he was telling a big fat lie, a strange thing to try on someone with a sharp eye for detail.

I joined in the professor's light-hearted exaggerations. "These are delicious," I said, "And you baked them yourself, how clever." I added

"I am no cook," in deference and to put him at his ease. He smiled the smile of a successful chancer who had just conned a mark.

"Have you read Proust's homage to the humble madeleine" he asked while buttering one nonchalantly as if I should know the book intimately, *À La Recherché du Temps Perdu* – or *In Search of Lost Time*. I knew the passage he referred to, a few lines of it, where a moment in the childhood of Proust's narrator is kindled by the taste of a madeleine dipped in tea.

Valentin Louis Georges Eugène Marcel Proust, novelist and essayist; I began to recite what I could remember from the passage, "No sooner had the warm liquid with crumbs touched my palate than a shudder ran through me and I stopped…" I hesitated. Quicker than a chameleon can flick out it tongue onto a passing cricket and devour it whole, the professor completed the sentence. "…intent upon the extraordinary thing that was happening to me. An exquisite pleasure had invaded my senses, something isolated, detached, with no sense of its origins." He was letting me know he knew the passage off by heart, and I did not. The insinuating game of professor and pupil status had begun.

Invited to afternoon bites and a chinwag, I had not expected to get involved in a parlour game of 'Who's the Biggest Literary Snob?' He sat back in his chair; top end of the table, of course, placed his thumb in his fob watch pocket, and munched his madeleine held with the other hand. It was time to play my only ace card.

"Proust never began that piece with a madeleine," I offered, reaching for a second from his plate of Bonne Maman's pur beurre best.

"Is that relevant?" he asked.

"In my opinion, because Proust could choose anything that was the McGuffin for his butter luxuriant anecdote, his McGuffin, the device he needed to…" My sentence trailed away.

"I know what a McGuffin is. Hitchcock made it his own creation."

He sounded mildly annoyed. I turn over my ace card, face up. "The original draft has Proust chewing a biscotto', a hard biscuit, like an American cookie."

"Really?"

"And I think it was his third draft."

"Still not relevant, Gareth."

"My point being," I carried on speaking as if he had not made a remark, "Proust decided a *madeleine* dipped in tea more poetic than a biscuit, the calmative syllables of it more comfortable to sit in a pleasant memory, 'madeleine', like summoning a mother's name."

"I see you can be poetic yourself when the moment calls for it," he said, eyes swivelled up to the sky, beaten, and swallowed down the last swig of his Ceylon tea packaged in Scotland, banging the cup back into its saucer.

He pulled out his pocket watch to check the time. I used the moment to remind him I had a meeting to attend in an hour. "Ah, work. When retired from academic life," he said, referring to his self, "any chore is a welcome challenge".

He stood up and asked me to join him in a quick look at his art collection. I am sure he felt this would impress me though his knowledge of Proust did not. And it did. There were quite a few Scottish artists among the small paintings dotted about his house, but the large framed posters in the long corridor to his study caught my attention most of all.

The large posters in black frames were of a uniform size, an extensive collection of Picasso's bullfighting posters created for Ronda, the mountain top city's annual bullfighting festival. The artist's passion for bulls began during his childhood, and a quick study can find numerous references to bullfighting in his work. The contest between man and beast, the internal conflict of man-as-beast, appears frequently in his prints, sketches, paintings, sculptures and ceramics. Dapper Dan had ten posters, all signed. Being Picassos, they were stunning, memorable images of art.

"I never paid full price," he said, gloating.

The amalgamation of literary besting and Picasso boasting were signals I should not ignore. I ask him how it was he did not have to pay the full purchase price.

"Simple," he answered. "I ordered them from galleries, paid half-price as a deposit. When they arrived I challenged the gallery to sue for the other half. Sometimes I said they had been damaged in transit. No reputable gallery wants to be seen suing a client, not a *distinguished* client, a professor from a university." His vanity was as embarrassingly evident as a length of toilet roll caught in the back of one's trousers. He was admitting to theft and how he got off with the scam. I did what most people would do caught in that situation, I made a mock expression of shock, praised the posters, and after more trivialities and talk of how much he admired my wife's artwork, I paid my respects and left.

On the way home I had a realisation of the same type as my first meeting with J.K. Rowling, or J.K. Rowling-Innit, as I nick-named her. The encounter took place in an art gallery of sorts. Relatively unknown, I had asked her how much she received for her first children's book, published months earlier. She told me one pound sterling. I told her that was rip-off and she should get a good lawyer. On the way home I remembered the book had sold in millions. Her facial expressions rarely rise above a half-smile so I could not gauge if she was thinking I was an idiot to ask such a stupid question. The same thing happened on my way home from the professor's place. I remembered he had borrowed a small painting of my wife's to have as a template for a tapestry he wanted made for his sitting room wall. With Picasso's at knock-down prices, how safe was the painting? I did not have long to learn.

Months later, there was no sign of the painting's return. I wrote to him and got a terse email in reply. "The painting was *a gift*. Go away!" It was my turn to exclaim 'really?' – twelve thousand pounds of a gift? And so began our war of attrition. He responded, "How dare you imply I am a liar!" I thought about the baking of his madeleines.

At university I was fascinated by morality, what shapes it, nurture or religion, or peer example, maybe all of those things? *Absolute* morality is when universal standards of right or wrong apply to all people at all times irrespective of their culture or beliefs. I had the distinct feeling the professor was exercising *relative* morality, that truth and rightness is different for different people or cultures depending on the circumstances or the act in question. Did the professor of international repute think he had a right to out-smart people who trusted him?

I wrote back to remind him the loan of the painting was only until the tapestry weavers had had time to choose the colours of the woollen yarn to recreate the painting, the grades of colour, and the number of bobbins, before they got started on the loom's warp and weft.

For the next two weeks his letters got more and more frenetic, frantic and downright frightful, my pleas for the return of the artwork ignored. Something strange was happening, something had altered a corner of his mind. When a penultimate missive from him went above and beyond sanity I sent a carefully worded invitation to return the work, adding he ought to see a medical consultant because his comments were increasingly irrational, and I was genuinely worried about my old friend's health.

I put my conscientious observation to him in a series of carefully composed questions. Was he aware of his aggression? How did he feel about his compulsion to acquire aesthetically pleasing objects at low or no financial cost to himself, robbing their owner? Why was he so keen to kill off our friendship? The pupil and professor had swapped roles; I had become the professional psychiatrist to the pupil.

His final shot was a calculated insult. "I have never been interested in you or your work. I am only interested in the work of your gifted wife!" I could smell the smoke of smouldering plastic from his keyboard caused by the ferocity of his typing. Picasso's poster images came to the fore – the professor's affront was a red cloak to a snorting bull. The blade was out of its scabbard, steel glinting in the sunlight. I assumed my best matador stance ready to plunge the sword straight down the nape of the neck into the beating heart. I wrote him a final letter. "You have until the weekend to return the artwork or face a police summons for theft. Be advised, I always sue. And there is no mercy in my justice."

In previous years I had come up against a nasty neighbour. He sustained his attacks over many months drawing in others to his manufactured degradation. People do not do that unless they have tried in the past to intimidate others and succeeded. I learned to check a person's background before tackling adversaries. I checked the professor's background. The professor had form!

Years earlier he had been caught by a store security guard stealing women's underwear. The eminent psychiatrist, trained and ready to cleanse you of your compulsive habits, revelled in donning women's frilly knickers. Up before the Beak in London, the judge stared down at him and said, "Are you not the same academic who wrote the prescribed text *The Discipline of the Mind*?" The professor nodded his head enthusiastically half in expectation he was about to receive praise and leniency. "Yes, I am, Your Honour." "In which case," replied the judge, "is it possible that you might follow your own advice?" and fined him a wad of cash and a suspended sentence.

I suppose one should expect doctors of the mind to have experienced human frailty themselves if they are to cure the mentally sick. They have experienced mental instability.

I knew a manufacturer of women's underwear who lived next to me in Malibu. He wore, or should I say *tested*, his new designs personally, by wearing the bras and panties under a wet suit, and going for a swim around his bay. But he was not exorcising pain. I waved to him a few times as he snorkelled by and he waved back, unaware a swimmer in a hard rubber suit silk frilled edges showing looked decidedly foppish silhouetted against the sea's horizon.

With no sign of the artwork and no evidence it would arrive undamaged at its home, I called in the police to discuss the professor with a pronounced perversion. A tall young people officer arrived at my door accompanied by his much smaller female colleague. Over cups of coffee with a chocolate biscuit, no madeleines, I explained the situation, carefully, coolly, and asked that they retrieve the work. If handed over to them I would not press charges. The police officers looked at each other. "We are not sure about arresting a university professor, especially a guy in his seventies," said the tall one taking notes. "Do you have a photograph of the painting, and confirmation of its value?"

I was ready for their expression of reluctance to grapple with an old man of learning, a pillar of the community with status, a trait not unknown in a society beset with class consciousness. When the philosopher Bertrand Russell was giving a talk about staying out of conscription in the First World War he was set upon by some of the men in the audience, bullies ready and willing to fight the Hun. The policemen at the back of the hall did not move content to see a conscientious objector taught a lesson. His wife cried out. "Please help my husband!" They still did nothing. "But he is the son of a Lord, a politician, and an earl himself!" The policemen came to his aid immediately, escorting him out of the hall to safety.

The two officers munched on their chocolate biscuits. I told them he had criminal form and explained the episode, the grins on their faces getting wider as the story expanded. "Leave it to us," said the smaller of the two.

The next day they were back, still smiling. "He will return the painting" said the tall officer. "He admitted he had it." I was overjoyed for my wife, and relieved I was not about to confront the professor in the Court of Sessions. I asked them how they achieved what I failed to achieve. The female officer explained they had knocked on his front door a few times. They knew he was in because they had seen him keeking out a curtained window to see who it was. A few minutes later, they witnessed him climb out of a rear window and run off down the leafy street. I was astonished. I asked them what they did next.

"An old guy in his late seventies?" said the female officer, volunteering a quizzical smile. "We had a cigarette and waited until he ran oot o' puff, and then sauntered doon the road to hae a wee word wi him."

A day later, out of the blue, a close friend of the professor contacted me. I was right in my estimation that the muddled man was losing his wits for indeed he really was, a physical deterioration of the frontal lobe that governs notions of morality, the ventromedial prefrontal cortex. At least that was the excuse and the medical theory. He would talk to him and see to it that the painting was returned.

A few days later they both appeared at my door, the friend leaning on a walking stick, the professor clutching the painting. He pushed straight past me and walked up to my wife to kiss her on both cheeks and hand, no doubt, as if long parted lovers. My wife pulled her head away from the unwanted advance, the best therapy the old rogue could have got free of charge. He stuttered words of apology saying it was all a terrible misunderstanding. No one wanted to hear his excuses. His friend took him by the arm, pirouetted one hundred and eighty degrees on his walking stick, and ambled out the door to take him home.

The affair of Dapper Dan and the purloined painting was over but I was sorry it had ended that way. As I have had occasion to say before, a man can be an intelligent, bright scholar and still do criminal things. How that comes about I leave to Freudians and the Jungians.

17

THE OUTWARD URGE

Why do so many Scots leave their homeland? It cannot be because some winters are harsh. Sweden and Switzerland are just two countries that expect hard winters but we see few of their inhabitants desperate to lead a life elsewhere. Icelandic folk know how to handle extreme cold and dark days. The people of Greenland are not pleading to the United Nations to be rescued. Scots leave their homeland. Where do countries put all the Scots? There are hundreds of thousands down the centuries, emigrants by force and by choice. I was one. Like many another deprived Scot I managed to carve out a career by dint of getting a good, traditional elementary and higher education. Let no one claim Scottish education is remotely backward. It has transformed the lives of millions, including today's smug House Jocks. I sought work abroad only to sustain my vocation writing screenplays, and producing films. Scotland, a prosperous, vibrant nation, was still the emigration capital of the world haemorrhaging souls.

In the 1950s an aunt and uncle had taken the UK government's £15 grant to make a new life in Australia. They exchanged bleak winters and few job opportunities for noisy kookaburras and constant sunshine. What their sons and daughters think of the blistering heat, droughts, bush fires and flash floods caused by humankind's abuse of the planet is another question. For a time they must have thought they made the right decision. A recorded two million and more Scots left Scotland between the end of the first quarter of the eighteenth century and the start of the First World War in 1918, a hundred years of steadily decreasing population. The 1800s saw the Gaels lose over half their crofters and cottar families from the West Highlands. In their wake departed farm workers, ploughmen, shepherds, cattle breeders, blacksmiths, carpenters, weavers, stonemasons. Our two main cities Edinburgh and Glasgow grew to accommodate the homeless – filed one family on top of the other in badly built five-storey tenements with no lift (elevator), a hallmark of Scots nineteenth century architectural construction. Many, too many, decided abroad was the place to go.

No matter what the malignant Tory party says about keeping English jobs for English people, people of all nations have traversed the globe looking for work and trade ever since Marco Polo travelled to China, found his life's vocation, and returned with silk and tales of riches. Emigration is a right; the volume from Scotland is the concern, a homeland abandoned.

My research began in earnest when I was working on an original television script about the Highland Clearances. It was for the small screen not the big one. Like Tchaikovsky who knew the difference between a suite and a symphony, I like to think I know the difference between a cinema film and a television drama. Anyhow, I wanted the most people possible to see a significant aspect of Scotland's history and that meant a television broadcast.

Late in his eventful life, I was privileged in making friends with the Canadian historian and avid Scotiaphile John Prebble. He had a whole library of scholarship to impart. Through him I was surprised to learn almost all the colonial medical profession in North America in the late eighteenth and early nineteenth were Scots, or trained by Scots in Scotland. Kith and kin that screwed their courage to an envisaged ideal chose North America. Those looking for land to farm went to further north, to Canada, a lot to Nova Scotia, and just as many to Australia and New Zealand. A few decided South Africa a good destination.

Those Scots with skills, especially in leadership and diplomacy, were soon in government employment. Wherever they settled they made a deep and lasting impression on the development of the land and its life. Scots were quick to be assimilated by the local population compared to (say) Italians or Irish workers, newcomers ostracised by the locals who tended to keep to their own kind for a generation and strengthen ties. If you have never read a history book you know from watching movies such as *The Molly Maguires* (Irish) and *The Godfather* trilogy (Italian) the problems those races encountered. As for Scottish immigrants, we behaved ourselves – well, most of us.

Scots had experience of working under a reasonably efficient capitalist system. Many were descendants of people who had participated in the Scottish Enlightenment, inspired by new thinking and radicalism in economics, science, medicine, philosophy, and religion. Scots arrived with practical skills that could be put to good use. They had solutions not problems. They had vision too, and a valued authority of the personality. Hard work and hard conditions didn't bother them much. That gave them a distinct advantage over uneducated Italians and Irish, rather like Polish immigrants are valued today, good-natured hard workers. We may have lacked the advanced Italian aesthetic in design and architecture but we knew how to build a house! That took Italians to Hollywood to design movie scenery, to opera houses, or made them clothes and interior designers. Scots were the camera men, the sound engineers and the animal wranglers.

Historical records show as many as half of Scots emigrants were skilled or semi-skilled tradesmen. New emergent nations desperate for skills and experience welcomed them with offers of jobs, land and grants. Japan found a place for businessmen ready to export its goods, and handle its shipbuilding. The urge was outward.

The poor and the middle class sought a new life in the Americas and Canada. Written accounts of life aboard sailing ships record how some individuals did not last the voyage, the undernourished especially vulnerable, children too. Highland women refused to defecate on board ship without privacy among passengers. They were unused to a loss of dignity.

Most of us can name Andrew Carnegie, novelist Robert Louis Stevenson, and Allan Pinkerton, Scots who made their mark abroad. Others were just as successful in small business enterprise. Scots shopkeepers set up stores along America's western frontier running trading posts. Sheep farmers helped create and nurture vast flocks in Wyoming and Montana. I used to wonder why I kept hearing cowboys with Scots accents and actors with Scottish names in western movies until I did some homework. American history books tell us, for example, Donald Mackay and John Dickie practically invented shipbuilding in New York. American banks benefitted from the doctrine of Adam Smith, his theories of capitalism imported by Scots bankers, his actual unadulterated theories, that is, not the corrupted ones fabricated and followed by neo-liberals.

Scots were not always pleasant interlopers. There are instances in Australia's New South Wales where tough Highland Scots were brutal to the Aborigine tribes in an effort to appropriate the land the tribes lived off. Some kept young Aborigine women as mistresses while presenting them as servants. Those historical details are told in Don Watson's *Caledonia Australis*. One famous pioneering Scot, Angus MacMillan, who married a Gaelic speaker arrived by boat, practically opened up Gippsland in the south-east region. There is a statue to his memory.

Macmillan was an uncompromising Presbyterian with a bad temper. It was his undoing. He hunted down and wiped out a small tribe at Warrigal Creek. By a mixture of religious certitude and repressed sexuality, he was convinced the tribe had kidnapped a white woman. The massacre is legend. The kidnapped 'woman' turned out to be a ship's figurehead that had washed up on a beach. The Aborigines were worshipping it as an icon.

In Australia expat Scots were able to borrow from their banks back home and reinvest it in their personal enterprises. That fact took me by surprise. The generally held image of Scottish emigration is of the Victorian kind, and with some justification, harrowing images painted on large canvases of destitute Highland families sitting forlorn among meagre possessions at the dockside.

America and Canada absorbed a great many skilled Scots. They went there for higher wages than they could never secure in their homeland. Canadian officials keen to acquire new blood, recognised the influx from Scotland could open up new territories and establish new settlements. That in turn meant laying new railroads to distant places in the prairies. Canadian Pacific Railway softened the hardships of long journeys by building ready-made farms for the emigrants, with all the extras of barns and cattle fences thrown in. Seductive inducements offer a good life where there is hope.

Some Scots failed, of course, and came home again. Newspapers, ever looking for the negative story, were filled with examples of the weary and the failed. Some returned with money in their pockets. One such group was Aberdeen's granite masons. Coal miners did the same thing, took advantage of seasonal work in the US, returning home a few months in the year. The more tradesmen did this, the more they brought home tales of overseas opportunities. From this ebb and flow Scots took up the annoying habit of overlooking ability under their nose yet praising it when it returns from abroad.

At any rate, emigrants brought back news of vast lands and people who treated Scots and their language with respect. No wonder so many took advantage of places to settle, assisted passages, land parcels, grants, and superior living conditions. Others made their name in London such as J. M. Barrie author of *Peter Pan*, England seen as 'abroad', a different country. From London it was a two-day journey back to Scotland, with no ocean in between to drown in.

In the sixteenth and seventeenth century we put on our warm coats and gloves and set off in our tens of thousands for Poland, hence so many places in Poland with Scottish names. Poles came to Scotland to make a new life, finding weather and terrain similar. We exchanged small-time merchants and labourers. That friendship resulted in a steady influx of Polish from about the 1850's, an association with roots in Bonnie Prince Charlie's mother. She was Polish.

Elementary history books show us indisputable evidence that the most draconian emigration in the nineteenth century was *enforced*, steered by severe economic pressures – placed on the Highland and

Islands populace. England's power imposed a landlord culture as a means of taming Scots and grabbing land they left behind or were driven from, not an unknown situation in other countries where people living off the land for generations have no documents to prove they owned it.

England suffered emigration too, but not on the scale of the Scots haemorrhaging. You will not find vast tracts of land and villages left derelict over rural England. In days of the British Empire Scots tobacco lords drove Glasgow's rapid expansion; playing enthusiastic employee to England's territorial ambitions was very attractive, trading in slaves included, for some very lucrative, but no one can claim the wealth accrued did the poor any good. England created modern England with the help of its colonies. Scots, mindful they were essentially an English colony, offered their skills and energies at the service of England.

Today sees the population of Scotland rise over the 5 million mark for the first time in its history. Then again, a good many incomers are choosing Scotland as a place to live because English society has become less tolerable politically and socially. But Scots emigration has not reduced, not yet. I can't think what will change that other than nationhood reinstated.

Scotland ruled by England has been a three hundred year disaster of economic stagnation, lost opportunities, our resources plundered and our taxes squandered, our cultural hegemony diluted. Scotland's emigrants helped shape nations. Hence, we have all the skills and experience needed to rebuild our own nation for a new era. The unionist slogan 'Better Together' has to be one of the most ironic in human history.

18

THE LAST MAN IN EUROPE

Given a book as a gift with novelist and essayist George Orwell in the title was somewhat misleading; it turned out to be more a dissertation on gardening with scant mention of Orwell. However, it held a surprise. We know Orwell from his political, socially conscious novels, his exploits fighting Franco in the Spanish Civil War, and his Etonian education, very little about his private life. The author mentions Orwell was as domesticated as the rest of us. He liked gardening, mainly growing vegetables and roses. For Orwell, there was a sort of stability, grounding in the activity of digging and planting.

When spring appears my heartiness swells to see snowdrops defy the frost, less so to see banks of narcissi. Unlike the Victorian romantic wanderer William Wordsworth, a host of golden, really Indian yellow, daffodils does not quite lift my spirits, not as much as a carpet of bluebells in a Scottish wood of silver birch trees, although a bunch of daffodils stolen late at night from a front garden on the way to see a girlfriend did nicely in my poverty stricken teens.

In my earliest garden plots I made basic error after error; house plants always a disaster, practically dead on arrival. If the English have anything to boast about, it is their beautiful gardens, from exquisite cottage gardens with mixed vegetables and herbs sharing space with perennials, to an explosion of herbaceous plants and shrubs in a wide border, and on to topiary hedges and manicured lawns, design almost as tranquil as a Japanese Edo period landscape where shrubs are given their special place and not lost in profusion. The Scots have never quite found their own gardening style. We lived off the land, not redesigned it.

Orwell loved the English rose. It was brought from China in the 18th century. Roses had been cultivated in China for a thousand years and more. The four brought to England in 1792 were known as stud roses, for obvious reasons. Almost every English rose since comes from those four. I am not sure what Elton John could have chosen to sing at the funeral of Princess Diana if the English rose had not existed, beyond candles in the wind. Heavily scented roses can sway the senses, but they are hellish shrubs to look after. Roses are labour intensive. They get diseases easier than humans catch a cold. They are eaten by as many insects as bees pollinate them. The over-bred variety are weighed down by heads too crowded with petals, and the tighter the petal cluster the harder it is for bees to reach the protein rich pollen for their brood back in the hive, if at all. Wet days ruin blossoms. For some reason, the most alluring roses have monstrous thorns that tear the flesh, and the abundant multi-flowering types require constant pruning. In the same category, rambler roses are a nightmare to train. Modern roses display lurid shades fit only for the colour blind. I can think of a dozen shrubs, rhododendron, azaleas and climbing Wisteria among them that I appreciate as much as an old-fashioned rose.

My first moment fascinated by a host of flowers was coming upon a mature evergreen rhododendron in full wedding dress cascade of white panicles growing near the foreshore of Silverknowes in Edinburgh. I stood transfixed for minutes. 'Rodon' comes from the Greek meaning rose, and 'dendron' means tree – the rose tree. The second occasion was a white lilac growing by the railway line at the south side of the city, in Edinburgh's Morningside, the intoxicating perfume masking the pungent smoke of passing steam locomotives. And yet for all their drawbacks and deficiencies roses return terrific value for the immense effort put into growing them. The playing card soldiers in *Alice in Wonderland* thought nothing of sweat and tears painting the Queen's white rose bushes red, the colour she expected to see, their heads left intact, the soldier's heads, that is.

For a man better suited to the hard concrete pavements of the metropolis and the soup kitchens of the post-war era in London and Paris, Orwell's love of flowers calls for a little study. The works of Orwell were prescribed reading in my politically forming youth. I read everything he had written and published, novels, essays and letters. To my mind his novels are ponderous if educational, very matter-of-fact, heavy-handed and semi-autobiographical, such as *Burmese Day* relating his time as a colonial police officer in British colonial Burma. At the time it did not strike me as a vociferous condemnation of colonialism, more Orwell's interested in portraying the daily racism, the systemic abuses of imperialism, than capturing the social life of the region he worked in. Then again, I may have missed subtleties. What I did not overlook is Orwell's family are descendants of colonialists and the servants of the British Empire. His mother, Ida Mabel Limouzine Blair, grew up in Burma and her father was a teak merchant.

The exception to his attempts at pseudo novels English would call it rem is *Nineteen Eighty-Four* based on his experiences working for the BBC propaganda unit broadcasting to India, fiction relentlessly negative and bleak. His publisher did not take to the first title, *The Last Man in Europe*. One wonders what he would have gone on to publish if tuberculosis had not taken his life at age forty-seven, in 1950. *Nineteen Eight-Four* is society gone irreversibly bad. It was his last book. It has the distinction of being the preeminent warning of things to come among dystopian novels of his era, such as Aldous Huxley's *Brave New World*. Orwell is quoted hundreds of times a day, probably thousands, whole passages and phrases hurl around the ether, social site to social site, tweet to tweet, and they open opinionist newspaper columns. They linger in the mind. Who can forget his description of a fascist society, "If you want a vision of the future, imagine a boot stamping on a human face – forever"?

There is a lightness of touch in Huxley's predictions, a hedonistic playfulness, never grim, dark or malevolent like Orwell's pinched grey world and Big Brother's threatening giant screens. Huxley argued his view of the future was more accurate than Orwell's because Orwell relied on us believing the fiction of a government always in power one way or another, no revolutions, no rebellions, no overthrows of corrupt administrations, the human spirit conquered. Huxley did not reckon with the advent of neo-colonial economies, where wealth is sucked upwards distributed amongst the few leaving the masses struggling. Both saw a world dominated by America and weapons of mass destruction. Both foresaw a world obsessed with sex, as we see now, sexual pornography mainstream. Both talk of brutal populist leaders. Huxley talks of a drugged society, Orwell of continuous wars and repression. They begin their books with a sentence designed to signal a world which was familiar but unsettling: "A squat grey building of *only* thirty-four storeys," begins *Brave New World*. *Nineteen Eighty-Four* begins: "It was a bright cold day in April, and the clocks were striking thirteen." Thirteen?

There is one great difference between the two writers' end of days novels. Only Orwell's Winston Graham talks of flowers. He sees one caught in a glass paper-weight bought from a junk shop, a significant act of subversion. The beauty of the entombed flower fascinates him, a link to a distant past. Reading it again jogged my memory. I realised Orwell's work is full of references to flowers. The first that comes to mind is right there in Orwell's novel entitled *Keep the Aspidistra Flying*. He saw the aspidistra emblematic of England's buttoned-up, stuffy middle-class, keeping the sun intolerant plant flying like the Union Jack.

Revisiting his novels finds allusions to plants and trees. In Spain, in *Homage to Catalonia,* he talks of "crimson buds forming on cherry trees," a line of them in a deserted orchard, and "if you search the ditches you could find wild hyacinths, like a kind of poor specimen of a bluebell". Near abandoned machine gun nests he found bullet chipped cherry trees. "Wild rose with pink blooms the size of saucers struggled over the shell-holes round Torre Fabián." Behind the line he met peasants wearing roses over their ears. Those moments, the scent of nectar, must have made all the difference from the odour of rotting food, corpses and excrement.

After he left Eton, Orwell was forever short of cash. He was a book shop assistant for a while in London, his lodgings near the Portobello Road. The quiet moments gave him time to write essays, the works of literary giants on the shelves to read and study, and as it was a three days-a-week job, he could pad about London in the poor districts collecting material, and socialising in the evenings.

His first books brought him little or no revenue. He was not always fit to take on a consistent job, troubled by his recurring bouts of tuberculosis. This left him to mooch a room and bed for long periods from his parents or close friends. In time, in 1936, by meagre savings and loans, he managed a deposit to lease a small run-down cottage in the village of Wallington, in Hertfordshire. There was nothing there we take for granted, no electricity, gas or indoor toilet, and the roof was tin. What it did have was the rudiments of a garden space. The first thing he did was clear it of old vegetation and plant flowers but the climate was not conducive to roses or fruit trees.

The good socialist knew enough to understand growing one's own food is a pragmatic act. Cabbages, Brussel sprouts, potatoes, peas and leeks were summoned to his table. He kept a few goats for cheese, letting them graze on the village common. I cannot imagine the slender frail frame of Orwell, foot on a spade, turning over and breaking up heavy clumps of earth, but dig he did. His day journal records:

> "Cut down the phloxes, tied up the remaining chrysanthemums which had been blown over. Difficult to do much these afternoons now it is winter time. The chrysanths now in full flower, mostly dark reddy-brown and a few ugly purple and white which I shan't keep. Roses still attempting to flower, otherwise no flowers in the garden. Michaelmas daises are over and I have to cut some of them down."

By the time the roses were blooming he wrote, "In order that England may live in comparative comfort, a hundred million Indians must live on the verge of starvation, an evil state of affairs, but you acquiesce in it every time you eat plate of strawberries and cream." I am unsure about the relevance of the strawberries. The ones he ate came from his garden.

In 1948 Orwell surrendered the lease to a local school teacher, Esther Brookes, all the roses in bloom. In 1983 she reported to the local press that the Albertine rose he planted was "the glory of the garden," still in bloom. A few years later he wrote in his essay *The Lion and the Unicorn: Socialism and the English Genius* that "a minor English trait is a love of flowers. This is one of the first things that one notices when one reaches England from abroad." He goes on to wander a bit about aesthetics but by then it is clear he knows nothing of the technical side of art.

Stunned by the quick succession death of his widowed mother, his wife, Eileen of cancer in 1945 at the age of 39, and then his older sister, Orwell took a house on the island of Jura in the Outer Hebrides, to work on drafts of his seminal and final novel *Nineteen Eight-Four*. His fable *Animal Farm* published in 1945 was selling well and bringing him some much needed royalties. The house he rented was a large white-washed cottage called 'Barnhill'. He chose it after a short visit in 1944. He described Jura as "an extremely un-get-atable place". Southern English would call it remote, but then they call anything north of Dundee 'remote'. He was terminally sick, his TB much advanced. Barnhill was another temporary home. He shared it with his sister Avril, his housekeeper Susan, and his young son Richard.

The journey from the mainland to Jura involved two ferries, one from Kennacraig to Islay, and then another to Jura, a 20-mile drive and then a four-mile walk along a dirt track. Orwell did not like his work interrupted by hawkers, circulars, tinkers, or "please sign my copy of your book" celebrity seekers. I can find no record of how he integrated with the local community. There are English there now; wanting staff, the Jura Distillery won't be fussy about the origins of incomers or how they will disrupt the identity of the place in their efforts to 'save' it. The man from the metropolis did have one adventure. Corryvreckan made its presence felt when Orwell went out rowing with his son. The whirlpool at Corryvreckan hides in coastal waters three miles north-west of Barnhill. His boat got sucked into the spiral's deathly grip. They lost the boat and had to swim to a beach and cove. It was two hours before father and son were rescued by a passing lobster fisherman. Lashing about in cold water and hanging about in wet clothes would not have helped his health. Then again, he was a chain smoker.

It was there in 1946 that he worked on new drafts of his fictional masterpiece *Nineteen Eighty-Four*. (He died seven months after publication.) On his arrival he did the same thing as he did at his Wallington cottage, he tackled the creation of a productive vegetable garden with a few flowers. The soil was not the friendly spoil of Wallington, too peaty and stony, the effort consequently greater. He enriched it with seaweed fertilisers until the vegetables he planted took the hint and began to grow. His attempts at growing roses were not successful, cold sea winds blowing down the glen towards his house curled and withered delicate petals.

Orwell made little mention of Scotland in his travels and political essays. There is no evidence he admired Scotland but by some accounts he disliked Scots in his callow youth, displaying a trace of racism. His real name, Eric Blair, *Blair* is a Scottish name. Perhaps that is why he camouflaged his Scottish surname and chose to use the River Orwell as a substitute for his essays and books. Once on the Isle of Jura he must have had a change of heart. What he did mention in *My Country, Right or Wrong*, was terse and to the point. "The Scots talk a lot about their spiritual connection to their land being greater than the English to theirs, but in the end it's really about power." He was correct, an independent country suppressed.

He was aware of the existence of the Scottish National Party, and in considering their aims and policies, understood the protests of Scots ruled by London had merit and substance.

"Up to date the Scottish Nationalist movement seems to have gone almost unnoticed in England. To take the nearest example to hand, I don't remember having seen it mentioned in Tribune, except occasionally in book reviews. It is true that it is a small movement, but it could

grow, because there is a basis for it. In this country I don't think it is enough realised—I myself had no idea of it until a few years ago—that Scotland has a case against England. On economic grounds it may not be a very strong case. [He wrote that passage decades before the discovery, and England's appropriation of, Scotland's oil.] *In the past, certainly, we have plundered Scotland shamefully, but whether it is now true that England as a whole exploits Scotland as a whole, and that Scotland would be better off if fully autonomous, is another question. The point is that many Scottish people, often quite moderate in outlook, are beginning to think about autonomy and to feel that they are pushed into an inferior position. They have a good deal of reason. In some areas, at any rate, Scotland is almost an occupied country.*"

And another letter Orwell touches on the use of Gaelic.

"*No doubt Scotland's major ills will have to be cured along with those of England. But meanwhile there are things that could be done to ease the cultural situation. One small but not negligible point is the language. In the Gaelic-speaking areas, Gaelic is not taught in the schools. ..... At one time I would have said that it is absurd to keep alive an archaic language like Gaelic, spoken by only a few hundred thousand people. Now I am not so sure. To begin with, if people feel that they have a special culture which ought to be preserved, and that the language is part of it, difficulties should not be put in their way when they want their children to learn it properly. Secondly, it is probable that the effort of being bilingual is a valuable education in itself. The Scottish Gaelic-speaking peasants speak beautiful English, partly, I think, because English is an almost foreign language which they sometimes do not use for days together. Probably they benefit intellectually by having to be aware of dictionaries and grammatical rules, as their English opposite numbers would not be.*"

At the end of his thoughtful missive the colonial in him takes over again when in a patronising mood he suggests some additional Gaelic programming "once a day" would "buy a little good-will".

When Orwell returned from Catalonia, recovered from a bullet wound in his throat that almost killed him, it was of his garden he first wrote. "Too long neglected, I cleared it of weeds. Flowers now in bloom: polyanthus, aubrietia, scilla, grape hyacinth, oxalis, pears in full blossom." And as an aside, he added, "There are daffodils in the field, but they are strewn about as if dropped there by accident".

As a child, I discovered bright yellow flowers in the back green of a temporary home, picked a bunch, and brought them inside to my stepfather – flowers for free. "Those are weeds," he said, and carried on with whatever he was doing. I insisted they be placed in a cup of water, colour in a grey world. The scrawny delicate flowers were wild mustard, good for pollinators and a food plant for butterflies.

"Weed" is an imprecise term. In past time we used them medicinally and as herbs. The word derives from the Old English *weod* and means simply a plant, any old plant that's green and grows abundantly without you having to sow the seeds. When you are poor, and before the world of flowers and shrubs was cornered by growers, some 'weeds' were perfect to brighten a room, so long as they survived for a reasonable amount of time in a pitcher of water. Green alkanet, ground elder, creeping buttercup, cornflowers, and some orchids were welcome visitors in a vegetable patch. Every part of the bright yellow dandelion is edible. Scotland's humble yet proud thistle lasts ages alive or dried. Weeds are plants, often wildflowers – until they demand too much attention. They have been following us around since the Neolithic agricultural revolution, roughly 12,000 years ago. But like the English dislike too many foreign visitors, we learned to weed out weeds. Weeds made for an interesting study for a young boy with no hobbies and a curiosity about the natural world. Eventually I managed to earn a shilling in pocket money to buy the *Observer Pocket Book of Plants*. The weeds that Orwell so easily rejected in his garden as a nuisance were actually beautiful plants in themselves.

Flowers are important to all of us, one way or another. We talk of some people's complexion *blooming* and the *bloom* of youth. We use flowers to celebrate betrothal, weddings, funerals and decorating the coffin. St Valentine's Day sees millions of them given as tokens of our love and affection. We drape them in wreaths on our door at Christmas time, plant them in window boxes, and place them in a vase at the side of a hospital bed. We pay homage to them in all sorts of material, from ceramic to wallpaper. There are flower processions and flowers shows, London's Chelsea Flower Show regarded as the top of the tree for flower growers and garden designers, if I can put it that way. They are everywhere in paintings, jewellery, embroidered or printed on clothes. On the other hand, single roses, petals fallen around the vase they sit in signifies lost love and tears.

Orwell wrote of the scent of flowers masking the stench of death. His olfactory sense was as acute as his observations of adult hypocrisy. A landscape of poppies, surely the cliché of art, is beloved by amateur and professional painter. We use a poppy to symbolise the millions we send to war who never return. I doubt there are enough species of poppy the world over to represent every man, woman and child killed in wars since Orwell died in 1950 in University College Hospital, London, a vase of flowers by his bedside from Sonia Orwell.

19

THE STUBBIE

We have seen them in countless films, the sturdy fire hydrant, and probably parked close to one on a visit to a city in the States. They sit on the sidewalk, humble to look at though its duty is great, a silent sentinel. Universally recognisable, their existence is the difference between life and death. They stand square shouldered to the sky, proud in the city's bright livery or flaking paint and rust. They are indispensable. They are America's fire hydrant.

Extinguishing fires swiftly was a challenge ever since neighbourhoods were built. Back when the USA was still indigenous native land, and buildings, especially homes, were essentially built of wood and stucco, hydrants did not exist. A fire could spread quickly, to douse the flames neighbours lining up to pass buckets of water from a horse trough, or the nearest water pump usually kept close to the blacksmith and the stables. When that failed there was nothing for it but to stand back and watch a home burn to the ground. The Great Fire of San Francisco in 1906 burned for three days and wiped over five hundred blocks of two and three storey buildings, most homes. An earthquake ignited buildings, and fire broke out in half-a-dozen places leaving shocked and disorientated citizens little chance to stop the conflagration spreading. Today, if a car catches fire the hydrant is there to alter a smouldering engine into an insurance claim with soggy carpets and ruined electrics.

ESSAYS 2

The Chinese, always a thousand years ahead of the West, installed large cauldrons on their street corners. That was the same method used during America's colonial days until cisterns were invented. In the early 1800's the hydrant was a simple standpipe enclosed in a wooden case. It's generally accepted by hydrant historians – yes, they do exist – that the first was installed in Philadelphia in 1865. The inventor of modern fire hydrant is recorded as the then Chief Engineer on the Philadelphia Water Works named Mr. Frederick Graff, Snr. Around 1801, Mr. Graff invented the first post or pillar type of fire hydrants. What he invented was considered a "wet-barrel" design chiefly because the part of the hydrant above the ground had a valve on top of it, containing plenty of water.

In 1909 a better design was registered, short and made of cast iron. It was nicknamed The Stubbie, and the name stuck. In time the shape was made taller, easier to reach and handle by firemen in a hurry. Some were fluted, made to look a little like a Doric column. By the 1930's the new standard was everywhere. The arms outstretched as if in crucifixion, that classic design is recognisable anywhere. There are millions throughout America. Slim, squat, fluted, smooth, chunky, they come in a variety of styles and livery, colour the choice of the local fire department. In California they are predominately yellow or mustard. As with icebergs, the greatest part lies under the surface. Some have their top caps in a contrasting hue to tell at a glance their exact water capacity.

We are familiar with their function, thanks to the movies, where if there's one in the plot it is guaranteed to get hit by a car and gush water up to sixty feet in the air. In sweltering hot days in the city children uncouple the stay and play in the domestic spray.

If there's no hydrant near a house fire the fire department has the right to take water from your swimming pool without notice. I have a vision of a sleepy resident handling a hangover throwing off his nightgown for a morning dip and landing slap-splat in the bottom of an empty pool.

People paint Stubbies to make them look like little people. I saw one dressed up like Super Mario, another as Arnie Schwarzenegger

THE STUBBIE

but it did not last long, something of a contradiction from the movie star who began his career pumping iron on Muscle Beach. One famous hydrant in New York stands proud adorned in the Stars and Stripes. It's on 104th Street and Broadway, Manhattan. It's the most photographed of all fire hydrants, a national treasure.

Hydrants might look as if unsophisticated lumps of cast iron but they have exacting specifications to ensure hydraulic efficiency. They are fabricated strong and sturdy so they are easy to replicate. The correct internal bore of the pipes is critical to ensure constant pressure, and the operating nut is manufactured with short threads so a hose can be connected with only a few turns, preferably no more than three – hence, on hot days the nut is easy for kids to undo on hot days without a spanner. (The race is on to invent an easy off, child proof cap.) The pressure they hold back for their emergency use is an average of 60psi, flowing about 1295 gpm (global precipitation measurement) the water forced through a 2.5 inch nozzle. In Los Angeles they are place 200 feet apart and no more than 500 feet from the building they are designated to protect. The USA has so far retained feet and inches, but mystified by 'stones' as a measurement of weight.

Built to withstand extreme high temperatures – San Diego can rise to 120 in the shade – the traditional hydrant is under threat in far northern cities such as Chicago where the ground can freeze hard and deep. There they are gradually being replaced by flush, underground appliances that won't ice-up in Arctic conditions.

They are collector's items, the older, scarcer much prized. Prices of the earliest design are high at auctions. Some people have a collection of them in their garden, while others photograph as many as they come across. "Myrtle! Look! A Series 2500 Ductile! I gotta take a picture." Obsessive pedants and firemen too, send letters to movie studios chiding producers for placing the wrong period hydrant in a scene.

Obviously the fire truck does not carry all the water a burning building might need to put out the flames. Therefore, you must *never* park in front of a hydrant. Locals know the rule. That gap in the line of parked cars you are delighted to spot, and aim for before another driver grabs it, is left free because the fire engine parks there. Ignore the red line and you'll get your car towed away to the Pound *plus* a humungous fine. As street furniture the American hydrant, also known as 'fire plugs' is more important than the lamppost or the traffic light. Their dignity remains intact in all weathers, rock solid, a friend in need, in all situations. They're stoic, never fazed when drenched in canine urine, H20 on the inside, K9P on the outside.

When used in films, a hydrant geyser is dramatic, adding energy to the image and the scene. The hydrant is as familiar as yellow cabs, steaming vents, and corner diners. Fire hydrant showers were a pleasure denied to us Scots street waifs on the rare flaming hot summer days. We witnessed the gushers in films and television dramas made in America There was that scene in *The Godfather* when impetuous Sonny, played by James Caan, is lured to beat up his brother-in-law – in reality the two actors detested each other, the punches real – and returns to his death at the tollbooths on the drive home. In the fight scene there is a fire hydrant spewing water over his victim. Sonny would have been better using the hydrant to cool his temper.

The Stubbie stands as a document page in the history of the white man's expansion across America, his cultural stamp, as familiar as hotdogs and hubcaps. And how can we forget, that is some instances a fire hydrant is used to quell the anger of legitimate protestors. And that's another story altogether.

20

GIVE THE BEAR A HUG

As I write, Russia is trying to open a corridor for over a million refugees fleeing the invasion of Ukraine to reach safety. By the obduracy of the West, refusing to agree a compromise with Russia, the bear fed up watching NATO installations getting ever nearer its border, Europe will have to accommodate millions of new immigrants after resisting the request of Ukraine to join the EU. The cost to the West and the damage to our economies, in addition to the heartbreak of uprooted families, never occur to the warmongers.

Meanwhile, the first minister of Scotland, too weak a character to seize Scotland's liberty, forgetting England took Scotland out of the EU against the will of the people, happy British censorship has closed down Russian Television (RT), so we do not hear the other side of the argument, acts as if we sit in the United Nations. I liken the stance to the weakling who hangs out with the bully repeating what the bully says, pretending to be just as tough.

I lived through Perestroika, the radical reformation of the Soviet communist party, a turning point in world affairs betrayed by the West's greed, its need for domination and its intransigence derived from having the greatest number of death weapons. What I know of the genesis of the Ukrainian tragedy is universal; truth is a major casualty of the actions on both sides.

Russia is a truly vast country, so big that when a huge meteorite crashed into it, gouging a two mile canyon through a pine forest, hardly anybody noticed. Russia has eleven time zones. It is easily the largest country in the world by area. The last census in 2020 arrived at close to 145 million people; some are Christians, some Orthodox Russian Church, many are non-believers.

There is no doubt in my mind, that of all the great men and women of the twentieth century Mikhail Gorbachev is arguably the most eminent of heroes of that troubled era. He put an end to the Cold War. He received the Nobel Prize for Peace, and then everybody in the West forgot about him. The last he was seen was as the key character in a television pizza commercial.

On becoming General Secretary of the Communist Party of the Soviet Union (from 1985 until 1991), Mikhail Gorbachev, understood the majority of Russian people wanted radical change from the stumbling progress of pseudo-communist failed economic strategies. By mass meetings, discussions and agreement in villages, towns, factories and cities, the people agreed a part-socialist, part-capitalist system was the answer, opening Russia to trade with the West, best of all.

Gorbachev arranged a summit meeting with that old hammy actor himself, President Ronald Reagan. He told him, Russia was introducing a Western-style democratic system of governance, headed by a President of Russia, the Soviet Union dead and buried. He wanted the support of America. It would be truer to say he needed the unwavering support of the USA if he was to succeed. Neither nation could afford escalating costs of piling up greater and greater weapons of mass destruction, and paying for army units deployed around the world, cost to govern the same reason that saw England give up India. Gorbachev explained his plans to Reagan, but crucially, for the Russian people to remain safe, to feel safe and thus give him their backing, he wanted NATO to remove their rocket installations from their strategic placements around Russia. The *quid pro quo* was, "Germany would NOT move one inch to the East". To show his sincerity, his side of the bargain, Gorbachev would instruct the Berlin Wall be removed allowing the unification of Germany, and that by dissolving the Soviet Union, he would create free states still allied to an open for business Russia.

Knocking down the Berlin Wall, obliterating East Germany and its Stasi secret police, was a risky but incredibly generous step. It profoundly lessened East-West tensions in a stroke. On hearing the news people moved into the streets to express their joy. When Reagan stood on the other side of the wall on a high podium and spoke his well-rehearsed declaration now on film, "Mr Gorbachev, tear down this wall!" the old faker already knew it would happen.

President G.W. Bush (Senior, not Junior) pretty much lived up to these commitments. So did President Bill Clinton at first, until 1999, the 50th anniversary of NATO. With an eye on the Polish vote in the upcoming election, some political analysts have speculated, Clinton admitted Poland, Hungary and the Czech Republic to NATO removing them from Russian influence. Russia grumbled but did not object.

Later, discussing matters with Reagan's successor, President Clinton, the USA gave President Yeltsin the same promise given to Gorbachev years earlier, that the West would instruct NATO to move its forces back . There was no role for NATO on the ending of the Cold War.

Years earlier Gorbachev made the terrible error of trusting the word of the USA and not getting a signed and sealed deal. Once Germany was unified, the USA took the opportunity to move more forces *into* East Germany. When Russian authorities protested the agreement was broken they were told it was "only a verbal promise". NATO, a puppet of US foreign policy, moved in on the premise Russia was weak and would not retaliate. They were right. The West did nothing to help Gorbachev when his Politburo colleagues saw him as an ace sucker of a grand order. He was deposed. The man most likely to integrate Russia with western free trade and keep the peace East with West was consigned to the history books. A new Russia emerged just the same, but with old-time faces. The West was introduced to hardline alcoholic Boris Yeltsin installed as Russia's first President. Immediately he set about using strong-arm tactics to beat back voter protest and regain public control, at one point shelling his own parliament building by army tank to rid it of

Gorbachev's sympathisers. Yeltsin wanted the new Russia his way, reflecting his view of what it should be.

Russia was in disarray. Seeing a business opportunity, and working on the basis of the brutal neo-liberal doctrine that a nation in shock can be raided and altered swiftly, American bankers met Yeltsin to make him offers from the West. He listened to the contingent of high-powered US financiers, keen to buy everything on the cheap, Russian banks, factories, gas lines and land. But Yeltsin had guile. He was a shrewd politician of the old school. He said he would think about it, but instead dispersed those state resources to oligarchs in a single month, causing the leader of the American delegation to exclaim, "The Russians are untrustworthy bastards!" I guess it takes one to recognise one. The USA's attempt to plunder Russia after the fall of the Soviet Union and the UK's endorsement of the foolhardy action was a policy blunder of epic proportions.

That policy was exemplified in the brutal ne-con economics of Milton Friedman, now in the history books when he proposed the USA should "wipe our Russia". It is still US policy. President Truman's same basic attitude, "let them kill as many as possible" referring to Nazi's invading Russia, also informed the post-war doctrine that bears his name, along with the establishment of NATO and the C.I.A., both of which he is credited with founding. When he died he was praised as courageous and decisive.

A large part of the conflict goes back to George W. Bush in 2008, reaffirmed by Obama, to invite Ukraine to join NATO. No Russian leader will ever accept that, to invite NATO to park its nukes on its doorstep. Ukraine is far too significant for Russia strategically, historically and culturally to allow an enemy sit on its doorstep. Pretending it is one man's evil, President Vladimir Putin, is just lying and delusional. As far as Russia is concerned incorporating Ukraine into NATO is welcoming a hostile military alliance into its backyard.

President Vladimir Putin's command to invade the Ukraine and reinstate a Russian parliament from the one ousted by USA intervention in 2014 is a serious error of judgement. Ted Galen

Carpenter, senior fellow for defence and foreign policy studies at the Cato Institute, wrote:

> 'The Obama administration's shockingly arrogant meddling in Ukraine's internal political affairs in 2013 and 2014 to help demonstrators overthrow Ukraine's elected, pro-Russia president was the single most brazen provocation, and it caused tensions to spike. Moscow immediately responded by seizing and annexing Crimea and a new cold war was underway with a vengeance...'

The Russians are not the problem. The problem is NATO. The North Atlantic Treaty Organisation has always been the problem. Those inculcated these last years to believe President Putin is the devil incarnate will reject everything written here. The West has done a good job engineering consensus, but until February 2022, Putin was available to discuss a compromise. No matter what Russia asked, or argued at the UN, it was rejected. He will be replaced by a new president of Russia. Do we begin the demonization cycle all over again?

Russia is surrounded by US offensive weapons. At one point, US forces were taking part in military manoeuvres in Estonia, a couple of hundred *yards* from the Russian border. No Russian leader, no matter who it is, will tolerate Ukraine joining a hostile military alliance. We should hug the bear not keep poking it in the face.

For the West to maintain decades of a cold war is madness beyond insanity. Almost as soon as we think we have elected rational leaders and their feet are under the head office desk, their demeanour alters, and they start acting the tough guy. Seeking peace marks out a politician as a really tough politician, Mahatma Gandhi proved that. The other kind chases orthodox thinking, and easy decisions almost certainly owned by the powerful weapons industry. I am sure if we reduced military spending to a small standing army in each country the money saved we could feed the poor.

Why does the West insist on trying to convince us Russia is a monolithic, omnipotent evil empire with commies hiding under every bed in the West ready to strike? We listen to the music of

Russian composers, we read Russian novels, we go to see plays written by Anton Chekov, and yet our leaders think we are brainless fools. On the basis of this delusion our politicians initiate an increase in taxes to create more weapons of war, and boost their war machine.

The reality, Russia is a second-level country fast falling behind Germany, watching China beat the West at its own game. The American republic is falling apart at the seams trying to maintain the vast cost of being a world power. Our answer is moronic and dangerous – extremists demanding we blow up Russia.

There is a simple way to deal with this endless inflammatory sabre rattling. **Do *not* deploy weapons of mass destruction.** Ukraine should remain a neutral country, just as the Russians asked. In Scotland, in a free Scotland, get rid of Trident missile submarines berthed on the Clyde, free Scotland from England's death grip. The red button on Trident warheads is controlled by America, not England.

The time has come for the West to make common cause with Russia. We almost had it in our grasp were it not for the warmongers needling President Putin. The benefits that accrue from peaceful co-operation are massive in comparison to wealth hovered up by global companies patching up a bombed country. President Joe Biden, and whosoever is prime minister of the United Kingdom, the prime minister of the Ukraine, plus President Putin, assuming he too is still in office at the ending of this proxy war by the West, the Four Horsemen of the Apocalypse who see war as the answer to fix tribal differences; we know it has the propensity to wipe out humankind. As it is, Ukraine takes the world's attention off the global crisis upon us now, cataclysmic floods and fires, droughts and high sea levels from climate change. The two great powers of the Northern Hemisphere owe it to their own people to work together, for if they choose war, human civilisation is at an end. Peace is the objective, nothing less.

21

THE ARCTIC FOX

Dr John Rae was known as the 'Arctic Fox' for his remarkable ability to trek vast distances in deep snow. Rae was an outstanding explorer who discovered the link to the Northwest Passage, an Edinburgh trained surgeon, cartographer, and recorder of the the lives of Esquimaux people, a renaissance man in the true meaning of the expression. A study of Rae elicits some interesting facts about the way the British State dispenses with people who dare to present a narrative that opposes the one it wishes the populace to accept. It does not always need the involvement of the British press to ruin a reputation, though it helps.

The British Establishment is embodied in a handful of public figures; they can alter historical fact, dent achievement, and destroy careers and reputations before you can say 'that isn't true!". It took only a rehearsed aside from Queen Elizabeth on her way to the chapel on a Sunday to cause many Scots to switch from voting 'Yes' to nationhood and mark their ballot paper 'No'. (Remarkable how easily Her Majesty can slide from one religion to another, from Church of England to Scots Presbyterian.) In Dr John Rae's case it took a concerted attack on his character by Lady Jane Franklin endorsed by none other than the novelist Charles Dickens. There is a reason Rae died in a garret almost forgotten – Lady Franklin and Charles Dickens saw to it.

John Rae was born in Orkney in 1813. Tutored privately paid by his relatively well-off parents, his childhood seems to have been healthy, his personality growth well-adjusted. In his youth he had an aptitude for sports, running, hill walking, climbing the slopes of Scarsdale in the southern area of Orkney, and assisting his father with farming his vegetables and sheep. Orkney folk's reliance on the land for their sustenance and existence, the hard toil and the weather, put him in good stead for his future work in the wilds of Canada. John Rae was a huntin', fishin' and shootin' kinda guy, almost anything that moved that was edible, to put no finer a point on it.

Orkney historian Bryce Wilson relates, "When he was six, Rae's father "took him to Stromness to see the Hudson Bay Agency" and their ship whenever in harbour. "Their hospitality and tales of the 'Nor'wast'" must have been thrilling for a young man to hear. In his autobiography, Rae wrote:

> "My chief and almost sole amusement during vacation or play hours were boating, fishing and riding of which my brothers and I had ample opportunities of practicing. The two excellent boats were provided by our kind father, the one small, light and handy for fishing and a sort of tender to the other which was about 18-feet long and admirably fitted for a crew of boys."

Despite his enjoyment of team work rowing boats with six pairs of hands in swelling seas, Rae was a solitary individual, preferring to hunt grouse, wild ducks, and rabbit on his own in wild marshland. Again, this would have been excellent experience for his weeks in the Arctic tundra. He record in the outlet of Stenness Loch, sometimes he caught as many as a dozen sea trout, food for a week. In the neighbouring island of Hoy he learned how to hunt for bird's eggs on the sheer cliffs. "Usually two or three men went in company, passing ledge to ledge, or lowering one down by rope from the cliff top".

Orkney was the perfect terrain to toughen up a boy in preparation for the vicissitudes of Arctic exploration and survival as a man of adventure, yet he maintained his modesty. "We of the Hudson

Bay Company thought very little of our Hudson Bay work. For my own part at least, I thought no more of it than any ordinary journey."

Orcadians were much valued as employees of the Hudson Bay Company. In his book *Transactions of Manitoba – Historical and Scientific Society, 1883–1884,* Professor George Bryce could have been describing Rae himself:

> *"There can be no doubt the people from the Orkneys, who are of Norse ancestry, and are quite distinct from the Celtic Highlanders by their patience and perseverance, quiet disposition and industrious habits, and their power of endurance, were spectacularly suited for the hardships of such a wilderness life for dealing with the Indian tribes in that 'canny' way which begats confidence in other men."*

Two of Rae's elder brothers joined the Company, John's turn pretty certain, but first his calling as a medical man took him to Edinburgh. He trained as a surgeon at the Royal College of Surgeons, but once on a ship with other young Orcadians, he landed at Moose Factory, the company's post in James Bay, an inlet of Hudson Bay. His journal records:

> *"Perhaps there is nothing that strikes a person more forcibly than the first sight of icebergs and floe ice. The beauty and purity, vastness and variety of the former are so attractive that you feel at first as if you could never weary of seeing and admiring them, yet to lie for weeks along side of almost the same floe began to pall, and we all wished a change of some kind."*

Once in the north of Canada, given supervision of village locations along the length of the Bay, Rae was soon greatly respected as a medical specialist and an explorer of tremendous fortitude, mapping the coastline, writing about the terrain, and researching the natural history and anthropology of its people. He tested himself against weather and terrain, doing it with a degree of understatement.

"I had to plunge waist deep into a river of ice to retrieve a canoe, there was handy way to change my clothes, I was not quite comfortable."

The Governor-in-Chief of the Hudson's Bay Company, Sir George Simpson, identified Rae as the best person to map out the remaining miles of the coastline, "to complete the geography of the northern coastline." In carrying out his commission he met a racism not confronted in his Orkney homeland. His reliance on native methods to guide his mapping was viewed as dealing with uncivilised locals. He could little notice of the colonialism, but he was to come into contact with the same condescension later in his career.

The sorrow is how he died, almost penniless in London in 1893. In between times he helped alter the world map as far as northern Canada and the islands beyond are concerned, called 'Northern America in his day,' and contribute immensely to our understanding of the Esquimaux tribes. That was too much for those who presumed celebrity belonged to them, and by God's law, were English.

At that time, manly men who did manly things in Orkney were certain to attract the attention of the Hudson's Bay Company. Orkney was a chief recruiting post for men of strong disposition used to the rugged life. Orkney lies further north than Fort Churchill, outpost of the then fur trade on the shores of Canada's Hudson Bay. Stromness Harbour was the place to stock up with provisions and water, await a fair wind, and make for Hudson's Bay. It was only natural a man of Rae's self-sufficient temperament and thirst for adventure would become an eager employee. Rae's father noticed his son was restless and suggested he take a year out of starting a medical practice in Kirkwall and work for the Hudson's Bay Company, which is exactly what he did, only it lasting more than a year, and the 'temporary' job as a surgeon made his name internationally.

Rae proved to be an exceptional explorer often taking on mapping duties exploring miles of snow-covered coastline on his own. And he learned the Esquimaux ways, their language and customs, how to make snowshoes, how to build an igloo, how to catch fish and game and cook it. His skills were second-to-none. He dressed as Inuit, and strong as an ox, could walk 100 miles in a few days, taking precautions to protect himself from the night's freezing cold, light a fire and building a shelter. But his biggest achievement was discovering the Northwest Passage, the last route through the myriad of islands that litter the ocean in that inhospitable part of the world. This was what was stolen from him by his English peers.

The search for the Northwest Passage, a quest to avoid the arduous journey around the Horn of Africa, was almost a continuous search for many centuries. In 1778 Captain James Cook got as far as Icy Cape in Alaska. The quest, however, continued to engage the Victorian mind, finding a way east to west or west to east. An expedition led by Sir John Ross was thought lost the crew perished, but they returned explaining the hardships they encountered, though with the goal unachieved. William Edward Parry had tried three times on official expeditions, and latterly reached Lancaster Sound, but got no further. It was he who recommended to the Admiralty to try one more time, and faith was placed in the rotund figure of English Royal Navy Officer, Captain Sir John Franklin. Initially, Franklin he was up against the opinion of some esteemed captains of whalers who felt there was no necessity, indeed, "no service" in finding a way to reach the Pacific Ocean. In 1817, the president of the Royal Society Sir Joseph Banks, supported by the Second Secretary of the Admiralty John Barrow, felt it was time to renew the initiative and find a way through.

Behind every successful man there is a woman, goes the saying. In Captain John Franklin's case behind every unsuccessful man there is an over-ambitious, pushy wife. Lady Jane Franklin was well-known for interfering in her husband's administration work, censoring his incoming letters, and giving him lessons in statecraft. They lived in Tasmania, back in the day called Van Diemen's Land, a penal colony over which Sir John was lieutenant-governor. In 1843, Sir John, derided as a victim of petticoat domination, was censored for incompetence, and ordered to return to England. His wife, Lady Jane, was not prepared for her husband to end his career in disgrace.

On returning Lady Jane learned that the Lords of the Admiralty were looking for someone to find a route around Greenland, see if Baffin Island actually existed, and plough on through ice floes to the western end from the Atlantic to the Pacific. She thought the challenge the perfect task to cap her husband's faltering career; he would be lauded as a great hero in the most glorious expedition of England's seafaring history, the opening up of the Arctic. Her husband was almost sixty years old and grossly overweight. She ignored reality and physics, the pounding a man's constitution would take on such a hazardous journey. In her imagination her husband would become a national hero, she the consort respected forever.

Sir John was at the bottom of the list of candidates for the job, but Lady Jane got him to the top, mostly by rubbishing the achievements of the other candidates and boosting his two previous polar expeditions as near-discoveries rather than the abject failures that they were.

In 1845, Franklin set sail in two ships, HMS *Erebus* and HMS *Terror*, aiming for a place in the history books, but not as Lady Jane hoped. Two years later, when it was plain he was not going to reappear trailing tales of glory, and a map of the Northwest route, Lady Jane added £3,000 to the reward money offered by the Admiralty for anybody who could locate and bring home her husband and crew. She clung to the delusion he was still alive, living in his ship, though the rations they took would not survive a full crew's appetites for two years in hellish winters ships stuck in ice.

Things turned bad when Franklin's *Erebus* and *Terror* disappeared entirely, a fate that had happened to other ships for longer periods. People were not unduly worried; the crew of 'missing' ships had a habit of turning up sooner or later some after been missing for years. Lady Jane Franklin remained concerned and lobbied the government, the Prime Minister, Lord Palmerston, and the Admiralty, even the Tsar of Russia, to send ships to find them. In 1848, Sir James Clark Ross's ship, with Rae aboard making use of his ten years of Arctic travel experience, found nothing – *Erebus* and *Terror* almost certainly under the ice by then. A reward of £10,000 was set up for anybody who could find news, a sum including £3,000 of Lady Franklin's own funds.

The man identified to stay on the case, so to speak, a choice endorsed by Lady Franklin, was John Rae. Rae's first problem was his employers. The Hudson's Bay Company refused to pay him anything extra for the additional task over-and-above his normal work. Against better judgement, Rae set out on a second journey in 1850. He was briefed to ask indigenous tribes to look out for white men travelling in from the north. This he did. He could speak local Inuit languages, and travel far on snowshoes. On his first walkabout and unbeknownst to him he got quite close to where Franklin's ships met their end.

From then on Rae made it his task to find trace of the crew. He tried three times, doing what others failed to do, asking local Esquimaux to bring him any knowledge they had of Anglo travellers lost. On the third try he found evidence things might not have gone well for Franklin's men. There were the remains of a storehouse and tents.

It was Rae's forth journey that provided conclusive evidence of Franklin's fate. He had all the advantages an explorer needed to reach a destination, the most critical; he learned the language of the Cree Indians and the Inuit. If you want to penetrate new territory and understand profoundly a society, you must know how to speak and write their language. If you are fluent in someone else's native language, their people will readily accept you and you can better understand the cultural aspects and nuances of that society. Rae acquired those skills, and he learned the ways of surviving in the wild. It was the Indian and the Inuit who guided Rae to the places Franklin's men perished. They trusted him.

Rae, and men he had taken with him, met Inuit in Pelly Bay who told tales of about thirty Kabloonans (white men) they knew had starved to death near a river to the north. Rae did not accept that as *prima facie* evidence but he bought a gold cap band from them he knew to be Admiralty stock, the first trace of the tragedy.

At Repulse Bay, Rae talked to other tribe's people who related how the crews had perished in the freezing wilds, some of the group splitting and going a separate way from others. More relics were handed to Rae. He followed their directions and found mummified bodies in tents and sheltering under a boat. Rae collected as many artefacts as he could safely carry including a silver plate with Franklin's name etched in it. Worse was to come. He found irrefutable evidence they had resorted to cannibalism to survive a few fearful days that life was to give them. Rae put all this in his journal, transcribed in a full report to the Royal Society of London, together with an inventory of all the items he had been given by Inuit he met, and talked to his Report in person when he returned to London in August of that year.

"I have the honour to mention, for the information of my Lords Commissioners of the Admiralty, that during my journey over the ice and snows this spring, with the view of completing the survey of the west shore of Bothia, I met with Esquimaux in Pelly Bay, from one of whom I learnt that a party of 'white men' had perished for want of food some distance to the westward, and not far beyond a large river containing many falls and rapids. Subsequently, further particulars were received and a number of articles purchased, which places the fate of a portion, if not of all, of the then survivors of the Sir John Franklin's long-lost party beyond a doubt – a fate as terrible as the imagination can conceive.

The substance of the information obtained at various times and from various sources was as follows:-

In the spring, four winters past, [spring 1850] a party of "white men," amounting to about 40, were seen by some Esquimaux, travelling southward over the ice dragging a boat with them, the Esquimaux killing seals near the north shore of King William Land, which is a large island. None of the party could speak the Esquimaux language intelligibly, but by signs the natives were made to understand that their ship, or ships, had been crushed by ice, and they were now going to where they could find deer to shoot. From the appearance of the men, all of whom except one officer looked thin, they were then supposed to be getting short of provisions, and they purchased a small seal from the natives. At a later date in the same season, but previously to the breaking up of the ice, the bodies of some 30 persons were discovered on the continent, and five on an island near it, about a long day's journey to the north west of a large stream, which can be no other than Back's Great Fish River [named by the Esquimaux Ooy-ko-hi-ca-lik] as it's description and that of the low shores in the neighbourhood of Point Ogle and Montreal island agree exactly with that of Sir George Back. Some of the bodies had been buried, probably those of the first victims of the famine); some were in a tent or tents, others under the boat which had been turned over to form a shelter, and several lay scattered about in different directions. Of those found on the island one was an officer, as he had a telescope strapped over his shoulders and his double-barrelled gun lay underneath him.

From the mutilated state of many of the corpses and the contents of the kettles, it is evident that our wretched countrymen had been driven to the last resource – cannibalism – as a means of prolonging existence.

There appeared to be an abundant stock of ammunition, as the powder was emptied in a heap on the ground by the natives out of the kegs or cases containing it; and a quantity of ball and shot was found below high water mark, having been left on the ice close to the beach. There must have been a number of watches, compasses, telescopes, guns, all of which appear to have been broken up, as I saw pieces of those with the Esquimaux, and, together with some silver spoons and forks, purchased as many as I could. A list of the most important of those I enclose, with a rough sketch of the crests and initials on the forks and spoons. The articles themselves shall be handed over to the Secretary of the Hon. Hudson's Bay Company on my arrival in London.

None of the Esquimaux with whom I have conversed had seen the "whites," nor had they ever been on the place where the bodies were found, but had their information from those who had been there and who had seen the party when travelling.

I offer no apology for taking the liberty of addressing you, as I do from a belief that their Lordships would be desirous of being put in possession at as early a date as possible of any tidings, however meagre or unexpectedly obtained, regarding this painfully interesting subject.

I may add that, by means of our guns and nets, we obtained an ample supply of provisions last autumn, and my small party passed the winter in snow houses in comparative comfort, the skins of the deer shot affording abundant warm clothing and bedding. My spring journey was a failure in consequence of an accumulation of obstacles, several of which my former experience in Arctic travelling had not taught me to expect.

JOHN RAE MD., CF., Commanding Hudson Bay Company's Arctic Expedition.

Those last words of Rae gave the British State, more used to elevating England's heroic failures to sainthood than told they ate their dead to live, the opportunity to denounce his findings and suggest reliance on the word of local natives was unwise, to put it mildly. In so doing they discounted hard evidence that would have stood up in any court in the land, with or without a body.

The Admiralty accepted the Report in full. Members of the press, who had never endured the deathly winds of the Arctic, were mixed in their opinions; they had the sensibilities of their readers to consider. Some journalists opined he had delivered a report to secure the reward, but Rae pointed out he had not known a reward was offered. There was public debate that he should go back for one more fact-finding expedition but he refused.

Robert Burn's famous line from his poem '*Tae a Mouse*', 'the best laid schemes o' mice and men gang aft a-gley,' ought to include 'women', or perhaps Lady Macbeth is more apt. Lady Franklin was instrumental in the downfall of her husband. If he had perished she was determined to raise his reputation to the skies. Once more, the English way of elevating their failures to heroic stature took hold in the national psyche.

John Rae was commissioned to look for Franklin. Though he did not find Franklin's body, he found irrefutable evidence Franklin and all his crew had died. What Rae had not perceived was Lady Jane assuming the role of professional widow, her husband's death confirmed on seeing 'the melancholy proofs of my husband's demise, a broken chronometer, a small silver plate, his name engraved upon it, and several spoons that bore his crest." As for cannibalism, how dare that nasty upstart of an Orkney man, a mere fur trader, suggest cannibalism and taint the good name of her husband. A wonder she did not call Rae a 'lightweight'. Lady Franklin was intent on revenge!

Recovering from her trauma, Lady Jane set about destroying Rae's character, his (generally) accepted discovery of the Northwest Passage and the Rae Straits named after him, straits that led to the route. Her campaign was going to leave no prisoners. She denigrated and defiled Rae to her elite friends, earls, landed gentry, knights, lords and leading politicians. She encountered some pockets of disbelief; after all, Rae was not without his admirers, and a long illustrious history of scientific exploration. Lady Jane was not without *her* admirers, so she enlisted the help of the day's most elevated literary celebrity, a great writer, immensely popular and influential, a lady's man on the quiet, Charles Dickens.

Born a year before Rae, Dickens already had some of his best work published: *Oliver Twist*, the hardy perennial *A Christmas Carol* and *David Copperfield*. The poor loved him, not only for his stories and characters based on people he had met, but because he was an ardent social reformer. Lady Jane knew people from all classes would listen to Dickens. And they did. Like many of his contemporaries enjoying imperialist times, Dickens was prone to racism. Of a dark-skinned London-born citizen he said, "He is not a foreign-grown savage, he is the ordinary home-made article, dirty, ugly, disagreeable to all the senses, in body a common creature of the common streets." To some degree Dickens' intolerance helped give him confidence to denigrate 'lesser mortals', prejudices handy when blasting the reliability of the Esquimaux who brought evidence to Rae.

Scotland was a not a place that much interested Dickens, in fact, it is difficult to find a Scots character in any of his novels. (In a visit to Edinburgh's Canongate Kirkyard in 1841, Dickens took note of a headstone epitaph 'Ebenezer Lennox Scroggie – a meal man' (corn merchant) using the name for Ebenezer Scrooge in his perennial *A Christmas Carol*.) Nevertheless, he was given the freedom of Edinburgh and wrote admiringly of the city on his one and only visit. He was very careful, of course, not to be seen criticising Rae, a Scots hero and much admired by his fellow Orcadians, when so many of Dickens' books sold to Edinburgh's Anglophones.

Once under the spell of Lady Jane, Dickens succumbed to her intimidating charm. She was furious 'ghastly' cannibalism was ever mentioned. Dickens agreed. He was not as stupid as to be completely manipulated, to embark on a wholesale condemnation of Rae. He knew to praise a man with a strong reputation and of a resolute character, admired by his peers in the Royal Society. Dickens acknowledged Rae had a duty to report what he had learned and seen. Instead, in a lengthy leading article in the *Household Word*, he chooses to damn the Admiralty for publishing unedited extracts from Rae's report to the Royal Society. Dickens dismissed the allegations without denigrating Rae but was ultra-careful not to condemn Rae's conclusions.

> "There is no reason to believe that any of its members [the Franklin expedition] *prolonged their existence by the dreadful expedient of eating the bodies of their dead companions. Quite apart from the very loose and unreliable nature of the Esquimaux representations, we shall how …that it is in the highest degree improbable that such men and the officers and crew of the two lost ships, would, or could, in the extremity of hunger, alleviate the pains of starvation by these horrible means.*"

Dickens exonerates Rae as if guilty of some accusation or other, a literary sleight of hand. "*We can release Dr Rae from this inquiry, proud of him as an **Englishman**, and happy in his safe return home for a well-earned rest.*" [My emphasis.]

Dickens' semantics completed, he challenged almost all the evidence in Rae's report, stating it worthless because of its "third-hand nature, given through an interpreter." Dickens studiously omits mention of Rae's ability to speak the local language. Esquimaux are depicted as heathen, ready to say anything for the trade of a fur pelt, trinket, or bottle of whisky. "We believe every savage to be in their heart covetous, treacherous, and cruel, and have yet to learn of any tenderness in their nature" added Dickens, mixing fiction with bigotry, as if he knew the tribes intimately.

Dickens goes on to suggest the Inuit murdered Franklin and his crew and concocted a story of cannibalism to hide their guilt. He did so despite the Hudson Bay Company backing Rae's findings to the hilt. In the tradition of many an English heroic failure, Franklin's journey was commemorated by several geographic names, including two islands in Antarctica and Greenland: Franklin Sound north of Tasmania and Franklin Strait in Arctic Canada. His wife was given name to Lady Franklinfjord in Svalbard.

Rae never stopped fighting to correct his reputation. He is buried in his homeland, Orkney, a statue erected to his memory off the main street's edge in Stromness. In 1986, corpses of Franklins men were found well preserved in permafrost, mutilated, showed all the signs of cannibalism. Dickens was wrong. Forensic science proved it. Rae's findings were vindicated.

John Rae's professionalism and his integrity did not stop English politicians claiming the man who discovered the Northwest Passage was John Franklin. Rae was demoted to a naïve traveller, awarded a little over half the reward, and left to anonymity in his final years. He died almost impoverished and forgotten. In time, of course, everything Rae had detailed on the last months of Franklin and his crew proved to be absolutely correct.

It was not until 2012 that some brave politicians took this miscarriage of history to Westminster demanding Rae be given his rightful place in history, that he be given proper recognition as the true 'Discoverer of the Northwest Passage,' and that that title be removed from Franklin's tomb.

On a visit to London, Tagak Curley, the Inuit rights champion, was photographed scoffing at the statue of Franklin marked 'Discoverer of the Northwest Passage'. "He never reached it," Curley averred. "The people liked John Rae. He learned their ways. He was not arrogant like the English explorers and traders."

The denigration of Dr John Rae is an example of how the British establishment takes care of its own, how in doing so it contrives to find scapegoats, will deal in sophistry, betraying the inherent racism of the colonial mind, its prejudices, and its delusional self-image as civilisers of the natives.

As testament to the kind of man John Rae was, here is his view of the Inuit.

> *"I have had some opportunities of studying the Esquimaux character; and from what I have seen, I consider them superior to all the tribes of the red men in America. In their domestic relationship they show a bright example to the most civilised of people. They are dutiful sons and daughters, kind brothers and sisters, and most affectionate parents."*

At Rae's death, the Norwegian explorer Roald Amundsen sent Catherine, Rae's wife, a letter saying Rae had been his inspiration. Amundsen had succeeded in being the first non-Esquimax to sail the Northwest Passage by navigating the exact channel in his schooner the Gjoa, that Rae had indicated during a mapping expedition, observed from the western shore of the Boothia Peninsula in 1854.

In a television documentary, the narrator discussed the 2014 discovery of Franklin's sunken flagship, *Erebus*, trapped at the eastern end of the Passage and not at the exit. Rae's part in it all was not mentioned once. HMS *Terror* was discovered in September, 2016, and again no report mentioned Rae. By coincidence news of the discovery of some bodies of Franklin's crew appeared in UK newspapers a day after an attenuated version of this essay was published, cannibalism confirmed. There is some way to go to rehabilitate one of Scotland's finest explorers and scientists.

22

BIGFOOT

Bigfoot was an Abyssinian cat. And Bigfoot was big, *really* big. His paw size could fill a tea cup. He was big even as a kitten when I went to see him in his cattery, and shown his father. The father was huge. I had not ever seen a domestic cat that size, not even a Main Coon.

In appearance Bigfoot resembled a lynx, short-haired but with a full-length tail. His coat was an orange-brown. The history of the cat remarks upon how the Abyssinian is thought to be the forerunner of all the Victorian moggies we know and cuddle. That heritage may well have gone further than Egypt and the pharaoh's tombs, back as far as South East Asia, the Indian Ocean. You can see the lineage in the colour of each banded hair, soft white at the base running to brown with a red tinged tip in the right light. His ears were tall and straight, not folded or floppy. His eyes were almond-shaped, a piercing dark green. The stand was regal, imperial as a Sultan of Ethiopia, long lean, statuesque. Bigfoot was all muscle and sinew. And athlete, educated in the best cattery.

As he grew to half size I watched it catch a bluebottle lurking above the window close to the ceiling. It never moved its gaze from the fat doomed insect. Staying absolutely granite still, the cat used a stool that lay before it and then the side of a table to make a geometric straight line to the insect and zap it dead in one swift move, moving from floor to ceiling's edge so seamlessly and swiftly

I had to replay it in my head in slow motion to assimilate the act. This was one impressive beast.

It was a cat of independent mind. It disliked being caressed or stroked. This was no lap-cat. Physical contact was only ever on Bigfoot's terms. Lift him up to embrace him got you a hard paw smack in the cheek, held there pushing until you backed off and put the cat back on the ground. When it wanted affection it came to you and sat on your lap, otherwise it went where it pleased. There was no jumping on your chest when asleep to purr and paw you awake and let it outside. You fed it and were expected to be content it remained a silent companion, honoured it chose to share a space with you.

It loved to play games, always winning, much smarter than the average human. If I lay flat on my tummy, Bigfoot behind the sofa, and I crept around to take him by surprise, I rarely managed to negotiate the bend of the couch before a paw would lash out and strike me first, and then with the other three feet, disappear into the kitchen out of my reach. He took to indoor battles when he needed exercise.

If not beating me at chess, it would sit on the window sill staring at squirrels in the trees, or glare at a feral pigeon strolling by, while being photographed by passing pedestrians astonished to encounter such a magnificent specimen of the feline species. He rarely acknowledged the presence of passing admirers, although he was stoic enough to remain stock-still while they took his photograph. Yes, Bigfoot was a born aristocrat. Nothing phased his demeanour.

My earliest pet was one shared by thousands of other children, and a few cats, no doubt, a hamster. Having a hamster was a mistake. They are nocturnal. They come out at night with a vengeance. We wake them up during the day to play with them. At night we lock them in the metal cage which they rattle with their teeth to escape. I tried a dog for a short stay but that did not work, my lifestyle did not coincide with a dog's routine. I did notice dogs snore but Bigfoot *snurred*, heavy breathing, usually silent. Since then, although I respond well to characterful animals, I prefer we Homo sapiens showered children with affection not pets, and certainly not toy dogs, animated powder puffs kept in a Gucci handbag, combed and groomed three times a week and fed the best fish and meat. I would never dream of washing Bigfoot. That way lay a struggle to the death; safer if I used my tongue.

In the film business and in the world of television commercials there are cat wranglers. By whatever means, they manage to teach cats to do a few basic things, but only what comes naturally to them, no undignified tricks, no human-like antics such as walking on their hind legs or balancing a ball on the end of their nose, they won't fetch and deliver shot game, or jump through fiery hoops. Which reminds me, teaching a cat to stay, sit or roll over is about as easy as teaching them Latin. Bigfoot did what Bigfoot wanted to do and that was that.

There is an anecdote demonstrating the difference between a cat and a dog. Watching you erect a shelf on a wall, a dog will think you are the most assured, skilled carpenter it is his good fortune to know. A cat will watch you with scorn, knowing you are using a Number 3 screw and Rawl plug instead of a Number 7. They let you know how stupid you are by simply staring at you for minutes on end. What cats cannot do is show pleasure or happiness on the face. They only show rage or fear.

At the time Bigfoot was a house mate I lived in a small mews house, too small for a creature of Bigfoot's wild habits, his territorial imperatives bottled up, nowhere to roam. Fully grown, he was immensely powerful. In the end, I made a decision to give him to an elderly couple who lived outside the city in a big house with a back door that led out onto a long park and glen. There Bigfoot could chase squirrels to his heart's content, get as much exercise as he wished, which he did, only stopping momentarily for people to take the occasional portrait photography, or call the police to say they had definitely seen "an escaped lynx" in the Braidburn Park grassland, a puma on the prairie.

Bigfoot was a beautiful creature, but like most cats, a lot less loveable after dropping a lifeless bird at your feet and look up at you for praise. Cats do not respect the sanctity of life.

For his part he had a good life. He lived to a ripe old cat age, 18 years, I am told. His owners were so distraught at his passing they placed a notice in their local newspaper. A wonder they did not add 'no flowers – send tins of best tuna'. I took it for granted the Abyssinian known as Bigfoot would be buried with his play things and best tuna in a pyramid shaped tomb. I admired his independence of mind, his no need of human company until meal times, knowing he could open a drawer and use a tin opener if I was not around.

23

THE RISE AND FALL OF THE NATIONAL PARTY

I knew in my bones Scotland would *lose* the first independence referendum in its history, toss away the gift on a plate, so certain that I placed a £100 bet in William Hill at 7 to 1, to *win* the vote. I did the patriotic thing, I made the futile sacrifice. And why not, as comedian Arnold Brown was want to say. Now we have three parties, each wedded to Scotland's rights, but two less eager to accommodate the agenda of the British State. There is the ALBA party and the ISP (Independence for Scotland Party), founded by a group of women disillusioned by the SNP's unwillingness to prepare for a new Scotland.

Colonised over 300 years, what were the chances of the ill and the sick getting up off their mattresses to vote the colonial invaders home again? We had hardly more than a year of a nationwide debate to turn *Britishness* into *nationhood*. No amount of frantic idealism was going to reverse overnight centuries of imposed English values and the disease of an ingrained subservience. And so it came to pass that a fool and his money are soon parted, in my case, to a bank in Gibraltar where William Hill has registered his betting company.

As I left Davy Byrnes' pub in Dublin days, a haunt of James Joyce and many another Irish independent voice, a republican shouted "Do you think Scotland can do it?" I paused moments and then shook my head. "Too many colonised minds to show courage," I answered. Had enough folk seen the light, a third of the UK land mass would have ceased to be British territory.

The tragedy lay in the figures. A majority of Scotland *had* voted to govern their country. The electorate of Glasgow with the biggest population and of Dundee witnessed the working class understand they had nothing to lose and everything to gain. My home city of Edinburgh, proud capital of Scotland, with its citadels of privileged private schools where all roads lead, voted against freedom. But when Edinburgh University researched the figures it was discovered 37% of those who voted 'No' wanted greater powers for Scotland, and a great many of them switched from 'Yes' to 'No' in the last days, hoodwinked by an illegal and fraudulent 'Vow' offering more self-governance, a panic response from Westminster hustled on stage by Scotland's House Jocks. No sooner had a commission of politicians been chosen to work out which powers we should be given – not taken, *given* – the unionist parties voted down the reforms proposed. Life as a nationalist accommodating English-orientated parties was going to be little different from life without a parliament.

Until the advent of nationalists in positions of power, Scotland suffered a false democracy; all our political parties were paid off-shoots of the colonial usurper. No matter which one you voted for you got more English power. To understand why the Union is not worth resuscitating you have to stand well back, back to the late Sixties and early Seventies. When I was in short trousers the Union could not have been more secure. Britain was still a world power, waning but still influential. In the Sixties, London dominated everything, or took over everything if the source made money. In that category fell popular music, classical music, television programming, fashion, photography, fine art, magazine production, newspapers, novels and writer's agents. If you were anything wanting to be something you gravitated to London.

I was one of many who gave it a try. I subsisted in London penniless, seeking fame and fortune, living off Rumbaba sponges the cheapest food I could buy, secretly sleeping in a camper van access to drive out blocked at the back of a public garage. I left each morning before the staff arrived. London was an education, the magnet for everything. That process had been a fact for two hundred years, enough to worry English intellectuals who saw the land denuded of farm and craft workers, they abandoning the place of their forefathers for the lure of the metropolis and better paid work. The SNP at the time was a blot on the misty moors of the Highlands, an irrelevant and oft derided eccentric sect that attracted more ridicule than serious interest. One of its founding members, Hugh MacDiarmid, was forever getting thrown out of the SNP and invited back in again. He was news; the others considered comics in kilts.

Scotland's mainstream parties were Labour and Tory. Scotland was that contradictory thing: proud of its Red Clydeside yet rejecting any thought of independence. In fact, the Great Paradox saw revolutionary socialist John Maclean at his oratory height and Scotland voting Tory. Only in times of adversity did dissent ferment in the tenement villages of Glasgow. When a Labour government ruled Scotland we grew contented again despite being robbed blind of our wealth by Labour as much as by Tory administrations. We assumed Labour meant protection from Westminster colonialism. We were wrong.

In the middle of the 20th century, throwing off war austerity, we felt part of something else that wasn't wet, driech Scotland. A bright new future sold to us as Carnaby Street fashions. Deaths of our service men and women in the First and the Second World Wars had encouraged Britishness. The collective sacrifice was reiterated to us in all sorts of ways by English-centred television channels, *as it is now*, every day, in press articles, television documentaries, films, and endless ceremonies to the dead, manufactured by England's propaganda machines. I cannot think of another nation so obsessed with death, generations of youth sent to die in unnecessary wars and then commemorating their obliteration, while never atoning for the deaths of foreign innocents they have murdered.

To add to that imperial attitude, the establishment of the Welfare State made us feel Britain is a good place to be. We did not, after all, have any other source of income. The British Treasury took all our wealth, including funds from the US Marshall Plan – a post WWII massive bribe to see things the US way – hardly a penny spent in Scotland.

By the Sixties, pride in a British empire seemed insensitive, and we began to reject its values. We still had the Commonwealth countries to comfort us – *common* and *wealth* being the most cynical title for countries we thought had nothing in common with England, and from which we stole wealth. We were blind to the hypocrisy. Seeing Queen Elizabeth accepting flowers from an indigenous child in British Guiana, for example, helped to cement the image of a great Union still a powerful force in the world. Britain ended the war bankrupt but we Brits felt we were only down to our last bag of rubies.

For over 300 years Scotland has been governed by London for the benefit of England. Scots are often upbraided by English for forgetting to say thank you because we helped build the British Empire, as if we had a choice. After India, Scotland was Britain's biggest cash cow, and now that England has departed from the world stage, we are most certainly its main subsidiser. We paid for our own oppression.

How can you build a nation with no Parliament and no democratic system of looking after the populace? How do you take pride in people of talent running Scotland's civil service and our great institutions when the jobs do not exist or are not offered to Scots? You watch people leaving for careers overseas. In fact, the infamous 'Cringe' that afflicts Scots, where we devalue those around us with the expression 'he cannae be tha' good cos Ah kent his faither,' that appeared a lot earlier than we think. We took greater pride in those who left our shores and became a success in some far flung place than the few who stayed and made a name for themselves. It took from 1946 until 2022 for a Scot, Nicola Benedetti, to become director of the Edinburgh International Arts Festival, and only a few years before that, Scotland given the sop of one indigenous production included in the official festivities. That generous step kept down reimbursement of travelling costs, of course; no international plane fares or hotels bills to pay.

Moreover, the nationalisation of British industries by Labour administrations strengthened Scotland's false perception of living in a partnership of equals. If we put Labour in power in London, Scotland would get a better deal. We did exactly that with Tony Blair, and he stole Scotland's oil and took us into an illegal war with Iraq. England's interests are rarely Scotland's interests. When Scotland's Secretary of State was banging the lectern about Scotland not accepting Tory policies he was actually toting for England. His Labour policies were not Scotland specific; they were first and foremost 'British,' and which nation was the largest in population and therefore the prime country to benefit – why, it was England. But things were about to change and the brutal guinea pig policies of Margaret Thatcher's reign, demolishing Scotland's steel industry and our shipyards, once the envy of the world, took the rose-tinted spectacles off our nose.

By then, uncontrollable events inside and outside Britain undermined the age-old stability of the Union. One of the first to burst the banks was joining the Common Market in 1973. Remember, the 1707 Treaty was essentially *a trading agreement*, not only a way of rendering Scotland compliant. Signing up to the Common Market reinstating Scotland's old trading routes to Europe. The Seventies changed Scots. England's markets ceased to be Scotland's only outlet. Now we had multiple trading partners, the very thing that England blocked in order to impoverish Scotland and bring it to the negotiating table in 1707! With Britain joining what was to become the European Union, Scotland did not have to rely solely on trade with England. There was freedom in trade.

Joining our European friends had other benefits. A primary factor floating Union stability was the perception of a collective existential threat from a foreign foe: France and Spain in the 18th century, Russia, Vietnam and then China in the 20th century.

Meeting Europeans who were meeting their Soviet and Chinese counterparts brought forth better knowledge of countries we were told were evil places. With the rise of the Soviet Union's Mikhail Gorbachev with a master plan to dismantle it and create instead a federation of Russian states, we saw the end of the Cold War removing the fear of nuclear attack, or at least lessening it. NATO was an irrelevancy. Small countries like Scotland could look after their own affairs. Within five decades over one hundred new independent nations appeared, many out of them former British colonies.

In Scotland, old tribal enmities and shibboleths remained to be overturned. The Catholic Church was spectacularly antagonistic towards anything associated with the SNP. Not for nothing does our ecumenical music man, Sir James Macmillan, compose for the pleasure and applause of cardinals, and does it while portraying supporters of self-governance as philistines, third-rate and godless. Catholics saw a Presbyterian stronghold; some of the fiery Calvinist rhetoric that issued from its best orators added to the distrust. The Ulster Orange Order saw Catholicism as the enemy, and tried hard to bring fire and brimstone into Scottish politics. But as church congregations faded away so did adherence to the Pope's edicts, and resistance to the SNP as a political force.

The Sixties and Seventies liberalisation of sexual laws, and the freedom from sexual taboos, plus the Pill for women, were all resisted by the Catholic Church. The wave of new free thinkers and a refreshing scientific attitude to the mysteries of life and the universe freed the intellect. The times saw the Catholic Church lose well over half of its followers in a decade. The SNP saw its membership rise, a party that welcomed all sorts, from all sorts of backgrounds, from poor to working class to middle class and the posh Jock too. As we moved into the age of secularism, Scotland began taking note of its own history and traditions. We re-evaluated our past and lifted it to the status of modern studies. By the Nineties the Church of Scotland was toiling to get parishioners into their chapels. The 'Wee Frees' of the Highlands and Islands found their influence reduced to pomposity.

The Protestant culture symbolised by the village Kirk, once the bedrock of Scotland's daily life, together with pseudo military youth organisations, the Boys' Brigade, the Boy Scouts, and to some extend the Girl Guides, began to atrophy. Zealous fans of the Union, such as members of the Rangers Football Club, spoke openly about their desire for an autonomous Scotland. Until the rot began, working class adherence to the two main political parties most committed to the Union, Conservative and Labour, left no space for the growth of nationalism. Now there was space for the SNP to breathe, to speak with a unified voice, and to convince. Winnie Ewing's shock 1967 victory for the SNP at the Hamilton by-election had been a portent of things to come.

First, the SNP had to pull together policies fit for the 21st century. Internally, the SNP had a rethink – curiously the slogan '*It's our Oil*' was jettisoned – and slowly but surely the result attracted new membership from all walks of life, and all political parties, from communists to Conservatives, from Buddhists to atheists. That sectarian electoral pattern in existence so long, especially in the west of Scotland, faded away. It had reached a crisis between the wars, when the Church of Scotland leadership made the gargantuan error of petitioning the UK government to prohibit Irish Catholic immigration. The animosity left deep scars. At last people began to revolt against discrimination for jobs selected by sectarian category. By the late Nineties the old ways had withered, sectarian voting patterns dissolved. The habit of Protestants supporting the Conservatives and Catholics giving automatic allegiance to Labour was no longer the rule. As those beliefs, those certainties fell away, the populace began to question why Scotland danced to England's piper, and why Scotland had to beg for, and justify, an annual budget when the money awarded by the UK Treasury was nothing more than a paltry portion of taxes *taken from* Scotland. In time people realised Scotland's progress was at the mercy of English nationalism and English priorities.

Curiously, the destroyer of communities,, Margaret Thatcher, was the same Tory who stated an SNP landslide was a legitimate democratic cue to restore independence. Her successful assault on the miner's union, implemented with cunning and police violence and a lot of help from the right-wing press, was repulsed in Scotland as much as Wales until resistance could hold out no more. Coalmine after coalmine closed down, the communities around them turned into bleak, depressing towns sporting a 'visitor's mining museum'. Her imposition of the hated Poll Tax on Scotland as a guinea pig was more evidence of England's abuse of its neighbour. The social dislocation made people understand they were not in charge of their own destinies. People who did not live in Scotland decided who worked and who did not. Decisions that affected Scotland were taken by people elsewhere, people who did not care about Scotland's needs or interests beyond hunting, fishing and shooting, or who owning a track of pine forestation as an investment. The reaction was strong and decisive. Scotland became a Tory-free zone in electoral terms. Another pillar of the Union crumbled and collapsed. Power fell away from the Labour Party seen to side with their mortal enemy the Tories against Scotland giving rise to the myth that Scotland is traditionally a left-wing country in political outlook.

Not for the first time Scots began to count the colonial English among them, the ones that influenced their lives, who saw Scotland as a stepping stone to 'better things' in London. On the street, a Scottish banknote refused in English shops as legal tender was mocked by Scots growing in confidence. We invented bank notes and printed our own, why did the English racist think that silly? We compared our faux democracy with the real thing practised in other countries, Ireland, Sweden and Norway, key examples of states with similar population sizes, five million. English appointments to high office in various institutions ran into a wall of criticism. Were there no equally qualified people living and working in Scotland? BBC Scotland, purveyors of safe tartanalia, found itself the target of protest for ignoring the glaring rupture in Union loyalty and the benefits of Scotland as a nation state. We questioned why we were not told the level of taxation taken by the UK Treasury and that which was admitted was so much more than handed to Scotland as an annual budget under the Barnett Formula.

Lord Jonathan Sumption, justice of the UK Supreme Court, argued in a 2013 lecture, that these levels of public expenditure "inevitably had profound effects on attitudes to the state in Scotland, which differ significantly from the rather more equivocal view of the state taken by most Englishmen". How marvellous – an English judge, not a Scots judge, spotted profound changes in attitude on both sides of the border and spoken openly about it, a divergence in political cultures cleaving the Union like a shelf of Arctic ice.

The foundation of the Scottish parliament in 1999 saw Labour take charge, with the SNP in second place, and the Tories trailing behind. Devolution moving towards independence was by then unstoppable, although some tried, Scots MPs among them proving a colonial mentality takes a generation to shake off. The task of rubber stamping a debating assembly, and then termed 'executive' was given to prime minster, Tony Blair. (Alex Salmond switched it to its proper function, a parliament.)

As Blair feared, reinstating Scotland's debating chamber energised people who wanted a better country, and, fulfilling his worst nightmare, saw them demand real powers to govern Scotland without pleading for more gruel. Blair was to add that agreeing to devolution was one of his major errors. Under Blair old Labour had become New Labour, but to Scotland it was business as usual Labour. When the SNP gained its first shaky minority administration, proven to govern with a competent, steady hand, the die was cast. Scotland's parliament became the spur for Scots to examine every aspect of the lives, their history, their culture, their economy and their future. This, then, became the basis of the historic SNP victory in 2011.

In 2020, the SNP reached a crossroads. Having ignored three mandates and as many opportunities to use them, given to them by the electorate to process a second referendum on autonomy, discontent has created a clamour for the constitutional change the SNP so often promised. The SNP is tired and bereft of imagination. It has no vision or imagination. It looks to champion ineffectual or minority policies, the easy targets, and sweats over the small stuff.

Studies of colonial power record the process of disaffection with national parties holding off the main event, parties who allow opponents to penetrate their organisations and values. First, the national party delays the Big Day. It gives lots of reasons for not fulfilling the core policy of its manifesto – restoring independence. The time is not right, unexpected crises mean energies must be spent fixing things. They then invite their cronies to government and some who were past opponents, advisers who feel caution is their watchword, courage reckless. Delay becomes a formal policy. Dissent is squashed or outlawed. They embrace the agenda of the colonial power.

This brief study of the rise of the SNP tells us that until Alex Salmond led the party, it depended a lot on how people discerned its worth, *not* by its intellectual arguments, but by how badly Westminster ran the United Kingdom and how badly it treated Scots. Under his leadership the SNP triumphed in almost everything it tackled, implementing radical, progressive new rights, sweeping aside accepted constraints on everyday life, such as tolls on our bridges, and commissioning a new road bridge over the Firth of Forth which was completed on time and under budget. He managed to have the prime minister of the day, David Cameron, agree to a referendum on independence by signing the Edinburgh Agreement which set the precedent for others if needed, and in its signing, underlined Scotland is a separate sovereign nation. Salmond was honourable. He resigned on losing the Referendum. If he had stayed in his post, pushing onward, we could have seen independence won by a plebiscite vote held during a national election for almost as soon as he resigned the electorate gave the SNP a landslide victory, and the polls registered 58% in favour. By his final act while in office he miscalculated badly. He put the national party in the hands of Nicola Sturgeon, his second-in-command and protégé, an emotional stunted, buttoned-up politician of very limited political ability, though hard working. That is not a compliment. A national party is elected to secure the safety of the nation's sovereignty. She has neither the statecraft nor the courage to do it.

THE RISE AND FALL OF THE NATIONAL PARTY

Once again the SNP is faced by the old enemy, an implacable, far-right Tory Party in power at Westminster determined to treat Scotland as a province, giving Scotland less respect than Northern Ireland, indeed, less respect than Gibraltar. England's nationalist upsurge has a goal to regain its own parliament and embrace delusions of empire with inflated occasions of pomp and circumstance. Simultaneously, when it ought to have been at its most politically vigorous, the SNP is mired in badly thought through policies, cases of sleaze and conspiracy it could have avoided, and dragged out of the European Union against its will by the British State. The SNP is out of step with the concerns and anxieties of the people who put it in power. Dissent is everywhere. Self-determination is superseded by self-flagellation.

The flaw in the creation of the UK is there for all to see, one nation holds 85% of the population and the vast majority of seats in the assembly of nations, thus controlling the destiny, the good health of all the others. Historians studying the Union are agreed its days are numbered. An amalgamation of Celtic people controlled by unreconstructed imperial elite is wholly unfit for the 21st century.

The risk-averse SNP, hell-bent on chasing mundane, trivial social matters, appears unable or unwilling to do what it was elected to do, give Scotland back to its people. We are back to a time when Scotland's decolonisation depended on how the electorate can stomach Westminster's tyranny.

Under a brutal Tory party dug into Westminster with a huge majority, put there by many working class English submitting themselves to the English class system – a charlatan educated at Eton is better as a leader than a grammar school boy who is man of the people – Scotland is experiencing a calculated withdrawal of its political powers, a full-frontal attack on its status as a sovereign state.

All this was predicted when Scotland was cheated out of its future by a colonial mindset in September 2014. Purgatory is a desperately bad place to be, waiting in the hope someone will come and rescue us. England has never left an invaded territory better than it found it. England's enlightened despotism is not even enlightened any more. The House Jock sees the Union Jack and feels part of an imperial history. The independent-minded Scot sees the Skull and Crossbones and wishes he was free.

24

A CULTURAL DIFFERENCE

How pleasant to unearth new facts about early Scotland and do it without use of a metal detector. Anything that is liable to reinforce intuition, sensitivity based on empirical evidence, catches my attention. Not so long ago, I asked an architect friend whose advice I value, what he thought best identified the Scottish vernacular that made it different from English rustic, the classic Tudor wattling and daub. If our cattle are different from those tended by the Anglo-Saxons, our breeds of dogs, our language and our terrain, surely our houses are different too. What marks out Scottish domestic architecture as unmistakeably Scottish?

While Professor Ian Ritchie thought about the question I used the moment to think of the answer he might give: castles, or something along the lines created by the master builder Charles Rennie Mackintosh, or a fusion of house styles from Nordic nations, perhaps, with the Spanish roof tiles thrown in for good measure.

His reply was not what I expected. "Harling" he said emphatically. Yes, plain white hard dash harling, lime renders or cement. Our harsh winters demand more than moisture absorbing brick, so common for house building in England. Even modern engineering brick, a brick with a harder surface, looks odd in a Scottish setting although it is now common used for new 'affordable' homes. The observation holds true wherever you look in towns and villages, but it is a surface examination.

His remark agitated me. There had to be more to it than plain old cement or lime rendering. How about a window shape, a turret, a use of stone of which there are a myriad of ways to construct a building with stone, a material the uses of which Scottish stonemasons are supremely skilled. How about good old stone, surely one of the great crafts of Scotland? He agreed the design of turrets in our castle architecture is indigenous, but for the wealthy only. It was Robert the Bruce who ordered castles burned so that marauding English divisions would be unable to use them, the power elite of his day, robbed of their posh homes.

Was there more to Scots and English domestic architecture than meets the eye? New research proved that there was indeed a cultural difference.

To get an exact identification we have to go back further in time, to the Romans and before. Archaeological research reveals the domestic architecture between the peoples of Scotland and England were already *culturally divergent* long before the Romans arrived in Britain, long before they pitched a thousand troops in Cramond, outside Edinburgh, and began marching north to see what pickings lay there.

In a new study of Iron Age settlements such as Brochs, duns, crannogs and souterrains, researchers identified that they are found widely scattered across Scotland, *but are not evident in northern England or further south.*

What significance has this revelation? In lowland Scotland we were speaking in the Brythonic tongue, a tongue relating to the southern group of Celtic languages. Those consisted of Welsh, Cornish, and Breton. They were spoken in Britain before and during the Roman occupation, surviving as Welsh and Cornish after the Anglo-Saxon invasions, and taken to Brittany by emigrants.

These distinctive differences in our archaeological record are significant because the construction of crannogs and souterrains during the 4th-2nd centuries BC demonstrate this divergence occurred long before the Roman frontier zone may have severed societies, that is, when they built Hadrian's Wall, running across

Northumberland, or Antonine's Wall, running between the Firth of Forth and the Firth of Clyde. Antonine's Wall was known to the Romans as *Vallum Antonini*, a turf fortification on stone foundations, built at the order of Roman Emperor Antoninus Pius. Not much remains of the wall but the need to build it is a sign the world's greatest army of its day was defeated in attempts to tame Scotland. A well-preserved section of the ditch of the Antonine Wall and a short section of the stone base of the rampart can be found in Roman Park, on the west side of Bearsden, Glasgow.

This may have played a crucial part in explaining why the Romans failed to absorb Scotland into their empire, despite three major military campaigns that appear, at least in Roman accounts, to have been reasonably successful, that got as far north as Aberdeenshire, before rain, cold, midges, hit-and-run raids by Scot and Pictish tribes, and ill health got the better of warm blooded Mediterranean soldiers.

This failure is often attributed to the changing political and military priorities of Rome. New thinking suggests it may owe more to the nature of Iron Age society in Scotland, which archaeologists are beginning to recognise was anarchic in nature – not chaotic, but composed of autonomous households and communities lacking institutionalised leadership.

Like the driver who is lost yet refuses to use his sat-nav (satellite navigation system) because his pride is stronger than his knowledge, our ancient tribes were quick to stick to what they knew and absorb ideas when needed, but not accept new ways unsolicited. Nae furringer wae new fangled ideas wud dare tell us things wha cud be dun better.

Unlike southern kingdoms, the Romans encountered to the south, Scots were near impossible to absorb into the Roman Empire's way of doing things. Our basic anarchic sense and dislike of imposed authority was well and truly ingrained.

There's clear evidence that the adoption of Roman culture does *not* occur in Scotland until the 5th century AD, after the Romans had abandoned Britain. This is when secular as well as ecclesiastical Latin inscribed stones, bearing Latinised names of indigenous inhabitants, and Christian terminology and symbols, were erected across southern Scotland.

Freelance archaeologist Dr Ronan Toolis is the man behind the analysis I extrapolate. "This only occurred when Iron Age society in Scotland had become hierarchical," writes Dr Toolis. "The evidence implies that far from being passive participants in acculturation, it was only with their active participation and likely at their own instigation and on their own terms, that communities in Scotland truly adopted aspects of Roman culture."

Moreover – and this is the part that helps explain why there has always been an enmity north with south – expressions of power and prestige distinctive to early medieval Scotland suggest profound cultural divergence continued in the centuries that followed the demise of Roman Society. Pictish symbols, whether carved on stone or inscribed upon artefacts, like massive silver chains and silver ornaments, are only found in Scotland. While these are overwhelmingly concentrated north of the Forth, they are also encountered within non-Pictish contexts to the south and west in the Lothians, Lanarkshire, Galloway and Argyll. They are wholly Scottish in origin. The same is not found in Anglo-Saxon England.

The direction of influence was not one-way, English culture to Scotland. Putting two-and-two together, in ancient artefacts, massive silver chains, which are also unique to Scotland, are concentrated in the south-east of the country, reflecting their cultural origin here, the result of the appropriation of Roman silver as a way of expressing status and power. When it came to the trappings of authority we knew what to copy and what to discard. That silver chains are also found north of the Forth but not south of the Tweed and Solway demonstrates again mutual cultural values in the expression of power and prestige among the Britons of southern Scotland and the Picts of northern Scotland, but not apparent among the Britons, Angles and Saxons of England and Wales.

Nucleated forts – a type of early medieval hill fort unique to Scotland – are also absent south of the border. These often occur in discrete clusters of elite settlements – in Galloway, Argyll, the

Scottish Borders, Fife, Tayside and Aberdeenshire. Excavations reveal several of these forts to be royal strongholds showing evidence of international trade, the manufacturing of gold and silver jewellery and royal inauguration rites. Similar sized clusters of prominent households occupying brochs across lowland Scotland during the first two centuries AD may represent an Iron Age precursor to the pre-eminent households that emerged in the 5th–7th centuries AD. To quote Dr Toolis:

> *"It may be clusters of early medieval elite settlements reflect how society in Scotland was replicating a process of households accruing power and status that had been arrested in development, either because of Roman aggression or internal social upheaval, in the early centuries AD. While there existed cultural affinity in some aspects north and south of the border and regional variation is apparent within Scotland itself, these do not negate the cultural divergence apparent north and south of the border and the aspects of cultural affinity that the regions of Scotland uniquely share."*

What Dr Toolis is pointing out is how accurately we can discern national trends as easily as local habits from Iron Age culture onwards in Scotland, and we can see differences between national trends. However, culture should not be conflated with identity. The peoples of early medieval Scotland may have identified as Picts or Scots but they nevertheless shared cultural traits unique to Scotland – the way they built their dwelling places.

The main analysis of this research is not easy to perceive immediately: archaeological evidence suggests that Hadrian's Wall was *not* a cause but instead *an effect* of existing cultural differences between the peoples of what later became Scotland and England, and this cultural divergence continued beyond into the medieval period. Separate cultural trajectories led to the separate formations of the two kingdoms, entirely independent of Hadrian's Wall. To put it in crude terms, Hadrian's Wall was likely built because a centurion on horseback surveying the land said, "We've tamed that lot in the south. This lot to the north are bastards. Build a wall here to keep them out of our territory!"

So there you have it. We like our way of doing things and that includes building our homes, it suits our needs, and it gives us a cultural identity. We've been fighting to keep it that way for hundreds of years and are still in the struggle.

25

HIGH HEMLINES

A chance discovery of an old black and white photograph led me to a book on a pioneering climbing club for women. The grainy image was of a woman hanging from a sheer cliff edge, holding on to the rock face with one hand and one foot, leaning out as if waving to the person behind the camera, but what was strikingly odd were the clothes she was wearing, a short jacket over a high necked blouse, a full length waist-to-heels heavy woollen knitted skirt, basic leather ankle shoes, and for a hat, what looked like a large chapatti sitting atop a cow pat. This was Edwardian woman as sports pioneer.

The temptation to chuckle at the sight of large pile of army bedclothes draped over women is smothered soon as one thinks of mountaineering, one of the few sports where spectators are few and even fewer laugh at the participants. We watch in awe.

My first sight of a woman climber was a *free* climber, the kind who has no safety harness, swinging precariously by her fingernails from under a Nevada overhang a hundred feet in the air, not a rope to be seen. Catherine Destivelle wore skimpy clothes, hands in fingerless gloves, one hand at her back in a leather pouch off magnesium oxide, chalk powder to counter sweaty palms, the bag attached to her belt, the other wedged into a sliver of gap in the rock. That vision was the equivalent of hitting a tooth with ice where the nerve is exposed. A sense of terror was my first reaction, and it lingered throughout her climb. What if she falls? Was there not an easier way to commit suicide? She moved about, swinging left and right and up like a gibbon with grace and agility, one leg catching a step of stone higher than her head, all of it spectacularly impressive – and heart-stopping. I hope she took the loose change out of her pocket before she started her climb.

We Scots must be second only to China for all the inventions and pioneering work we have to our credit, a great many carefully listed and discussed in *The Scots Who Invented the Modern World* by Professor Arthur Herman, a book no self-respecting Scot should be without. There is nothing in the book about women as mountaineers or indeed inventions for mountaineering; I know Hamish MacInnes invented the light-weight folding aluminium stretcher suitable for mountain rescue teams to carry but there my knowledge ends. He also published his own autobiography and lost the use of a room at his home packed with boxes of his book that would not sell.

Who were the women who decided life at the top meant a hazardous climb? The women accredited with the formation of what had been a man's sport are Jane Inglis Clark, her daughter Mabel, and friend Lucy Smith, were all from Edinburgh. They decided on a club of female enthusiasts and named it the *Ladies Scottish Climbing Club* while sitting on a large boulder near Lix Toll, Perthshire in 1908, and their men folk off in front on a climb. It was a case, if you can't beat them, organise your own team.

The title alone, *ladies* rather than *women*, and *Scottish* as secondary prefix, signal an activity open to well-heeled, middle class women with the time and energy to cope with a day or a week away from home ministering to their husband's routine and supervising domestic chores. To be a woman and be a climber you had to have money. Climbing is a costly hobby, pick axe, crampons, special ropes and metal ties are not cheap, and there is still the price of getting to the location to begin an ascent. Expenses are sky high, to use a pun, when travelling abroad to climb peaks in the Alps or the Andes. Those goals were all down in the club's books as challenges to conquer. On top of that there is the problem of telling the misogynist husband you are away on a climb for the weekend, and he shall just have to survive without you.

When the three founders had their light bulb moment the Scottish Mountaineering Club already existed and Jane's husband, William, was the secretary. Climbing was not unknown to them, they had accompanied husbands, or guided by men on relatively safe climbs at one time or another. The three women craved more adventurous climbs without men choosing the way or leaving them midway because the remaining journey was "men only" stuff. Straws drawn, Jane became president of the club, Lucy treasurer, young Mabel assumed the role of secretary, and a fourth found, Ruth Raeburn, became the librarian responsible for maps and journals a good choice for her knowledge of the Scottish hills and mountains was second-to-none. They invited the Marchioness of Breadalbain to become their Honorary President and she agreed. They held a committee meeting and decided on the club's constitution and purpose: "to bring together Ladies who are lovers of mountain-climbing, and to encourage mountaineering in Scotland, in winter as well as in summer." In short measure they attracted ten members. Within a few years they had 70 members, women from all over Scotland, enough for several groups to be organised on chain climbs, and more than enough to share costs.

Training took place on the volcanic strata of the Salisbury Crags on Edinburgh's Arthur Seat. They must have been a singular sight ascending the rock face while people below exercised their dogs and watched giggling or in awe, and people above shouting down to ask if they were in trouble and needed a helping hand. To qualify as full member the founders set the criteria, and did not make it a doddle of a task. These were women who felt they could be as good if not better than their male counterparts. Members had to ascend four peaks of at least 3,000 feet with two snow climbs and two rock climbs. From there came the real challenges, climbs of mountains such as the Beuckle (Buachaille Etive Mòr) and Suilven (Sùilebheinn) in the west of Sutherland. If those climbs felt daunting they did not quench the ambition to climb a peak in the Himalayas.

In the beginning it was one step at a time. And those steps always had an experienced male mountaineer as guide. In years to come, men were local guides, not husbands. In fact, one of the earliest things the women questioned was 'leaders'. Why should a man lead if there are women of similar or better experience? They decided crocodile climbs, that is, a long straggling group, should have several leaders and if they get lost in a sudden mist or cloud and the line break up, each is assigned a guide.

Pouring over photographs of all-women parties of climbers outside their mountain huts, long-handled picks in hand like wives of navvies laying railway tracks, I was amazed at the clothing they had to wear. There was the first woman I had seen in that old photograph wearing an ankle length skirt. Beside her, another in the same attire but wearing a long heavy coat over the woollen garments. Their blouses were woollen. One wore a necktie. Some wore a Shetland jersey and muffler. Brogue shoes were the norm, some with Edwardian gaiters over the top to keep out moisture from soggy grass and marsh ground.

What an effort it must have been to seize the day while carrying a ton of bad weather clothes plus ropes, bedroll, tent gear and food. The more devil-may-care among them took to wearing heavy duty knickerbockers under their skirt, or men's breeches, and once on the mountain side, leaving skirts and city togs folded behind a rock. On record is an incident when, on a group's return to fetch their clothes, an angry looking Wee Free shepherd was waiting to give them a lesson in female godliness! It was not until after the Second World War that cheaper, lighter and warmer clothing became readily available as manufacturers began to cater for the increasingly popular sports of hill walking and mountaineering.

The club published a journal. In it, and taking a feminist attitude to her chosen hobby, and without knowing it breaking a glass ceiling, founder member Inglis Clark wrote:

> *"Mountaineering for women is the very best of sports, for here there is no rivalry, no seeking applause, and no possibility of heart-sickening*

sense of defeat. We leave our differences behind, and when climbing there is time to feel, to think, to be one's self. Mountaineering for women seems to have come as part of their emancipation, especially from the old conventional restraints. Indeed it is almost impossible for the girl of today to realise the great difficulties and prejudices that had to be overcome to those early days of climbing for women."

The obvious wisdom in Inglis Clark's thought may well have been an antidote to the prevailing orthodoxy of male climbers. The English mountaineer C.B. Benson in his book *British Mountaineering*, written about the same time, goes out of his way to be gratuitously patronising to women who follow in the wake of an ascent.

"We men must ever keep a watchful eye on the ladies, and see to it that they are never in danger or being hurried or over-tired, for the woman who has once over-walked herself seems doomed to be more or less an invalid for life. Doctors in this age of feminine athletics are constantly having girls on their hands who [sic] *have once overdone it and never be quite the same again."*

Golly, gosh. There was a similar antipathy to women riding that new-fangled contraption, the bicycle, sitting astride a narrow leather saddle; they were most definitely ruining their reproductive organs. What would Benson have to say today about ludicrous men who self-ID as women, too physically and mentally weak to win sports in all-men teams, but able to stand on the top podium in women's sports? We inhabit a crazy world where if a male athlete loses he has the choice of becoming a female athlete and beating women by his additional strength. How many chop off their tackle to pass as women? If they chicken out of going the whole hog, where do they tuck their tackle?

Behind Benson's matriarchal concern for "ladies" physical well-being is the supposition they climb differently from men. One thinks of those days as old-school religion, women, get thee behind me, but chauvinism prevails. In 1989 one famous Scots mountaineer wrote in an article in the Scotsman newspaper: "*Glencoe is quite a technical area for rescuers and not very amenable to women climbers.*"

It must have taken some time to recover from the booing and jeering. Women can be just as derisory about other women as men are of men, but the club is one of the few where competition is not encouraged. Team work is the be-and-end all of group endeavour. Lack of competitiveness prompts me to mention my early attempts at playing golf were put off by two events. The first was meeting highly competitive males on the golf course. They began the day making fun of the cheap second-hand clubs I was using, and then, red faced with the exertion, veins standing out on their neck to bursting point; invite me for a game where "we are all equals on the course". Back in the club house for that customary drink, I was told women were not allowed to be members. I learned to dislike golf at an early age.

In truth, I admire anybody who is proficient at a sport. I enjoy watching the greats play tennis, but have no aptitude for any sport that involves balls, the only two good ones I have managed to hit was when I stood on a rake. I would not dare take up climbing as much as a run of carpeted house stairs. My first and only visit to see Isambard Kingdom Brunel's Clifton Suspension Bridge lasted all of three minutes. I looked over and down into the ravine and drew back alarmed, swaying unsteadily, overcome by nausea. My thyroid hated heights.

The *Ladies Scottish Climbing Club* suffered no such anxieties. They went on to create their own records and achievements. One early member, Annie Hirst, was the first woman to climb all the Munros – the 282 Scottish peaks higher than 3,000 feet, and without a man in sight. By 1955 the women completed an all-female expedition to Himalaya.

The stigma of women on mountain climbs saw it lose its patriarchal taboo in 1964 two of its members; Betty Stark and Evelyn McNicol were invited to join an international Scottish Peruvian Expedition. In 1987, Cynthia Grindley and Angela Soper were the first women to conquer the Old Man of Hoy. By then, women has lost the insulting Hollywood image of pith helmeted, back pack carrier, scream at anything with more than two legs, neurotic females who followed the men and had to be rescued by the leading male, obliged to marry him. In 2008, the club's centenary year, the membership enjoyed a Bolivian meet, and a Stravaig mass ascent of Buachaille Etive Mòr. Respect. I think in that year I had refused to follow visiting relations to the top of the Scott Monument in Edinburgh.

In 2008, the club's centenary was celebrated with a party in period costume on top of the Beuckle. President Helen Steven recalled the youngest founder, "I knew Mabel and remember her as very warm, rosy-cheeked and welcoming – she came into a room like a burst of sunshine. But she was hard as old nails. They were all characters…" The history of the club is contained in a detailed survey of its achievements entitled *Rising to the Challenge* by Helen Steven.

Honestly speaking, I have never seen a movie about mountaineering I liked, muscle-bound men hanging impossibly from shoogly rope ladders, or hauling their dozy girlfriend up from the cliff edge one-handed. We know they are shot against a green screen or two feet from the ground, the actual death defying moments done by stuntmen. As for the Ladies Scottish Climbing Club, how pleasant to know when women feel adventurous they climb a mountain. They do not invade another country.

One other thing; data covering a seven-year period up to shows that women accounted for only 10 of 114 fatalities. Men it seems use a mobile phone app for navigation from warm glens up to cold mountain areas, misread weather indications, and get lost. Women prefer an ice axe and crampons, maps and a compass. Smart – eh?

26

THE DECLARATION OF ARBROATH

"For as long as a hundred of us remain alive, never will we, on any conditions, be subjected to the lordships of the English. It is in truth not for glory, nor riches, nor honours that we are fighting, but for freedom alone, which no honest man gives up but with life itself."

Two things are missing from that soul-stirring passage from Scotland's *Declaration of Arbroath*. The first is any mention of women; back in the day they didn't hold power unless a monarch or a monarch's wife, an omission corrected now there are so many women in positions of governance. Men hope they govern well, or at least, not as badly as men. The second omission is the lack of foresight. The authors of the Declaration did not foresee that a long period of adapting to a co-existence with 'them next door' might convince trusting Scots to forget their nation is sovereign, a fact exploited by every English politician with a swagger stick and a colonial mentality. England's relationship with Scotland has always been one of forcible alliance. The English elite never tire of the struggle.

Incurious of how we are governed by London is one reason Scots convert over 300 years of London rule to proof life in a provincial system is acceptable. They judge by the here and now. Two clear conclusions arise; they have little knowledge of how cruelly a colonial arrangement undermines progress, and also it generates an attitude of, 'I'm alright, Jack'. This is a psychology where facts, figures and empirical experience are ignored. What history they know of they consider of little value. They do not see Scotland as anything more than they space they inhabit. They have a certainty without being able to say what they are certain of. Being British and in a Union is comfortable; to examine it only unearths a can of worms. In that atmosphere it is difficult to convince people of coherence in the argument – a free Scotland can be a better place than a Scotland subservient to England's interests.

Mentioning the Declaration of Arbroath in polite society and one can guarantee a Longshanks-lite will claim the Declaration has no meaning in the modern age. The Declaration – and not forgetting the Claim of Right of 1689 – stands as the defining statements of Scotland as a nation state. The prevaricator will argue the Declaration was a bog standard letter written solely to receive the Pope's blessing, but as it never received as much as an autographed photo of *Priest of the Month* in reply, it survives only as a worthless piece of parchment. This response is patently absurd.

No written reply exists from the Pope, but he did as the document asked, he wrote to Edward I and asked him to desist from land grabbing, plundering, and generally being a bastard, which is as good as an endorsement. Tell a patriotic Englishman Magna Carta is a soiled rag of no significance to English law and he is liable to shrug his shoulders, its meaning lost over centuries. On the other hand, an English constitutional lawyer will explain the tenets of Magna Carta are woven into the very fabric of England's common law.

By the same criterion the Declaration is a bond between elite entrusted with the future of their country and the populace, draped with the seals of Scotland's powerful earls and barons – eight earls and probably forty barons – written in Latin, sent to Pope John XXII in April or May 1320. It was most likely drafted in the scriptorium of Arbroath Abbey by Abbot Bernard on behalf of our nobles and barons, one of the few moments in Scotland's history when a strong, democratically-minded war leader, Robert the Bruce, managed to convince our bickering clans and septs to unite as one for a bigger prize, Scotland liberty in *perpetuity*.

Scotland is a nation. It is registered with the United Nations as a nation. Scotland is one of Europe's oldest nations. Following the integration of the Parliament of England and Wales and the Parliament of Scotland in 1707, Scotland *remained* a nation within the new Union state. Scotland has never relinquished that inviolable position. The Declaration was written during the struggle for our rights – the same rights so many treat so casually today – rights embodied in the war of independence begun in 1296 with England and Edward I's attempt to rule Scotland. The Declaration and the Claim of Right are key documents that help fix Scotland as a separate nation. The Claim of Right is an Act passed by the Convention of the Three Estates, a sister body to the Scottish Parliament in April 1689. It is one of the key documents of United Kingdom constitutional law and Scottish constitutional law.

> *"I rise to remind the House that the Claim of Right for Scotland is a principle that recognises that the people of Scotland have the sovereign right to determine the form of government best suited to their needs. This right is well established; it was first set out in the Declaration of Arbroath in 1320 and was most recently endorsed by Parliament in the Commons in a debate in July 2018—a debate in which I was privileged and proud to speak. In Scotland, this House* [House of Commons] *is not recognised as sovereign. The people of Scotland are sovereign, and they are angry that this House, this Government, are over-reaching themselves by trampling all over Scotland's devolution settlement..."* Patricia Gibson MP, North Ayrshire and Anna, Hansard, 27 January 2020.

With the death of Alexander III and his granddaughter Margaret, Maid of Norway, Scotland was left without a head of state. In 1306, Robert the Bruce grasped the thistle to secure Scotland's liberty. As now, England was not Bruce's only *bete noir*. There were Scottish naysayers, plotters, fair weather friends, and turncoats to worry about. Lined up on a battlefield, the world's best trained army, an English regiment, could be seen and assessed, their foot soldiers, superb archers, and horsemen a fearsome sight. The loyalty of vacillating Scots was more difficult to discipline. Bruce wanted no repetition of Sir William Wallace's downfall when coalition men left the field at Falkirk at a critical moment in the battle. A duplicitous confederate can do greater harm to a cause than a recognised enemy.

No pope likes their theologian property and wealth the casualty of warring skirmishes. Pope John wanted peace in both kingdoms. Like any other small country harassed by a larger neighbour, Scotland grew tired of interference in its affairs. On the other hand, England was not bothered by a man hundreds of miles away, dressed in religious garb transported around on a shoulder-high chair. At that time Scotland's relationship with the Catholic Church was at an all-time low. Displeased at Scotland's rejection of a papal edict demanding a truce with England, Bruce and his supporters felt it good psychology to offer renewed respect to Pope John by asking him to validate the Declaration, a sly counter-diplomatic offensive, if you like. The Pope on your side removes his sympathy for the other side.

I would like to think most Scots know of the Declaration's existence but fair to say many will know little of its contents beyond the paragraph quoted at the start of the essay. It ought to be standard curriculum in Scottish schools. For now, study of only one central paragraph is sufficient. The authors of the document were careful to show respect to England as a separate nation. The wording shows deference to England's place and skilfully takes care to emphasise the Declaration is about people, *not* possessions.

The Most Holy Fathers,

Your predecessors gave careful heed to these things and strengthened the same kingdom and people with favours and numerous privileges, as being the special charge of the Blessed Peter's brother. Thus our people under the protection did indeed live in freedom and peace up to the time when that mighty Prince, the king of English, Edward, the father of one who reigns today, when our kingdom had no head and our people harboured no malice or treachery, and were then unused to wars or invasions, came in the guise of a friend and ally top harass them as an enemy. The deeds of cruelty, massacre, violence, pillage, arson, imprisoning prelates, burning down monasteries, robbing and killing monks and nuns, and yet other outrages without number, which he committed against our people, sparing neither age nor sex, religion nor rank, no-one could describe nor fully imagine unless he had seen them with his own eye.

"Exhort the king of England to be satisfied with what belongs to him", says the letter, which just as easily could be said about Westminster's vindictive policy of removing powers from Scotland. As mentioned earlier, records indicate the letter was delivered to the Pope in Avignon, and he did write to England's new Monarch, the less able than his predecessor, Edward II, urging him to cease hostilities.

Signatories to the Declaration, some autographs omitted but known by their seals, read like a Who's Who of the day. The bulky document with its seals and tassels must have been awkward to store, the majority of seals are missing now, the Declaration, stored so badly since a portion of it rotted away. In alphabetical order they are:

Sir David Brechin: Used his wife's seal. Untrustworthy supporter of Bruce, hanged.

Arthur Campbell: Campbells of Strachur, supporter, Constable Dunstaffnage Castle.

Reginald le Cheyne: Lord of Duffus and Inverugle, land in West Lothian, supporter.

Patrick Dunbar: Eighth Earl of Dunbar, supporter after Bannockburn 'convinced' him.

John Duraunt: Unknown, probably a landowner in south-west.

Sir Gilbert Hay of Erroll: Supporter, granted heritable office of Constable of Scotland.

Sir Alexander Fraser: Married Bruce's sister, Mary, became king's chamberlain.

David Graham: Supporter, received from Bruce land of Old Montrose in Angus.

John de Inchmartin: Sheriff of Perth, later knighted.

Sir Edward Keith: Supporter, subsequently Marischal of Scotland.

Alexander de Lamberton: Landowner in Angus, former supporter of Edward Balliol.

Malcolm Lennox: Fifth Earl of Lennox, received sheriffdom of Dumbarton.

Thomas de Menzies: Lands in Perthshire and Dumfriesshire, strong supporter.

Thomas de Morham: Stirlingshire and East Lothian landowner, last of his lineage.

Sir Roger de Moubray: English supporter, turncoat, involved in 1320 conspiracy.

Sir William Oliphant: Lord of Dupplin and Aberdalgie, awarded land grants.

Sir Alexander Seton: Made king's household steward, owner of land in East Lothian.

Malise Strathearn: Earl of Strathearn, strong adherent of the cause, his mother was not.

Sir Ingram de Umfraville: Fought for English, made peace with Bruce, went home.

If that list does not give the reader a strong flavour of Scotland in the 14th century, its divided loyalties, the argumentative and the vacillator, they will not understand why some Scots argue for Westminster rule forever though the Union has been a fraudulent, one-sided institution for most of its length, and is now wholly unfit for the twenty-first century.

27

SMART CARS AND SMART VISIONARIES

My first car was a tiny pre-owned orange Austin Mini. Back then I thought no one needed a vehicle bigger. Why be ostentatious? I used it to tour Scotland over a week, beetling around the coastline and then into the interior stopping at Loch Ness late at night, sleeping in its cramped space back-rest flat, binoculars ready to see the monster at dawn. A passing motorist told me I was at Loch Maree, not Loch Ness. My geography was as bad as my geometry.

A marvel of engineering packaging, the Mini was really a micro car, in the tradition of the post-war austerity micro cars such as the Bubble Car, but with four wheels and excellent stability. It did not seem microscopic in size in its day, just small. Outside a Rolls-Royce or a Bentley, cars were not the canal barges we see on roads now, and SUV's not yet invented.

The BMW MINI of today towers over an Austin Mini of old. Cars have grown in size in all directions since the cheapskate British car industry left engine refinement and driving development to the car owner. You can see how big cars have become when parked on a British regulation parking bay. Bay and vehicle dimensions do not fit. You are liable to hit the car next to you when opening your door. Normal saloons and estate cars were not as fast as our contemporary cars. Brake and tyre technology was relatively basic in the Seventies; hence safety issues were low down on the list of design priorities. Cars did not need massive bulk to absorb crash speeds. As engines became more powerful, engineers began looking at a car's body strength and braking ability.

Before returning to the efficacy of small, compact cars, especially for city use, it is interesting to look at Aston Martin, the company that made its DB5 the most famous car in the world thanks to James Bond films. Forced to reduce their emissions levels, the CEO hit on the sneaky solution of bringing in a small car of low emissions to take the edge off their unacceptable emissions output and so save money. Car manufacturers, ever among the top ten lobbyists of government policy, had managed to get tough legislation watered down from single car emissions to the *collective* level of a company's entire range of models. Aston Martin bought a couple of hundred Toyota 1.3 iQs, Toyota's answer to the Mercedes Smart-for-Two micro car. (Smart versus iQ – geddit?) Funds low, Aston left the engine as it came out of Toyota's factory, but gave the face and rear a handsome Aston Martin design, and leathered the interior, charging four-times the price of the same model in a Toyota dealership. They are so rare today their values have shot up, or rather, second-hand car dealers are chancing their luck.

When the car critics of the automotive industry saw Aston's iQ, now awkwardly called the Aston Martin Cygnet, they had a good laugh, and jibes about ugly ducklings and a terrible error of judgment filled their magazine columns. The vehicle got a drubbing and jeered out of the car park. It failed to sell in any number. In reality, the car was a good idea, though less so for cheating emission controls. If you are wealthy and can afford to run a big expensive car, keep it in the garage and show your environmental credentials buy using the marque's smallest model to run around town shopping or collecting children from school. Why crowd out city streets with giant vehicles transporting one driver and five empty seats? Use a small car for city errands and keep petrol costs down. In cities and towns, utility and function should come before status and extra-helping size.

After I sold my much loved wee Austin Mini, and after buying two more British made cars I could not get rid of quickly enough so badly were the put together, I bought a Volvo Estate. It was family time. In the Eighties there was still room on roads to park, but they were beginning to become crowded. My ownership came before Ford bought Volvo when it was teetering on the edge of bankruptcy. Once upon a time Scotland was Volvo's biggest market after Sweden. They were a kind of forerunner of today's SUV, big, crafted from a brick, and highly reliable, safe in snow, floods, crashes, and could hold a family of five plus a dog, and lots of luggage. A Volvo started first time in the coldest of weather. The car might still be running today, so well put together and durable was the slab-sided people and stuff carrier. A 1966 Volvo P1800S holds the *Guinness World Record* for a car with the highest mileage on a single engine, over 3,000,000 miles. When 4 x 4 SUVs became popular, the category invented by Toyota, the Volvo lost its status and sales fell away.

Taking advantage of unregulated capitalism in the Nineties, Ford, keen to raise the quality of its brand image, went on an imperialist rampage, a frenzy of brand shopping, scooping up companies as if animal trophies for the boardroom wall. Ford bought Jaguar, Land Rover, Aston Martin, and companies in South Korea and Thailand, before it realised ruination of running an empire issues from the vast amounts of investment needed to keep everything afloat and a ton of middle-management. Ford soon found itself as hard-up as the companies it had hovered up.

After ten years of struggle, Jaguar-Land-Rover was sold to the Indian steel conglomerate Tata, and the Swedish government bought back Volvo before selling it to the Chinese giant, Geely. (Sweden decided not to save Saab; it was too far in debt.) Ford may be credited with saving those companies but their engineering and bean counter accountancy attitude to car making soon devalued the brands. Few drivers wanted a Jaguar with a Ford chassis, Ford engine parts and Ford switch gear. Geely bought Volvo for £1.8 billion.

Around the same time a clever Swiss entrepreneur was thinking about moving from cheap watch making to cheap car manufacturing, a city car. But he knew enough to understand cheap should exude classiness and be classless in order to justify the car's position in the ranking of vehicles to covet. In a word, a small car had to have street credibility, it had to be *cool*.

Nicolas Hayek was the genius behind the conception of the two-seat Smart car. He was the force behind the renaissance of the Swiss watch industry. He invented the Swatch watch. They sold in millions and became as must-have fashion accessory, cheap to own and good design. Born in Beirut, Hayek was a larger than life character, confident, a born pioneer and a matchless self-publicist. How a French speaking Lebanese arrived at the negotiating table to face the world's biggest car makers via a Parisian university is no more implausible than Sean Connery becoming the world's top movie star from his days as milkman in Edinburgh and never changing his Scottish accent. Hayek had convinced Swiss producers to diversify, to move away from their traditional highly-skilled labour intensive assembly methods of watch making, to simplify watch movement by sharing a quartz movement that could work in any watch. Once he turned the ailing Swiss watch industry around, he turned his thoughts to cars and car makers. Surely he could shake them up with an innovative way to build and assemble a car?

Taking his cue from humble Swatch designs, Hayek created a micro car on paper that had plastic body panels easy to remove, easy to replace like a Swatch watch. Plastic does not rust. Replacing a deformed panel is cheap. The safety of passengers was enhanced by encasing it in a steel cage. Advertising showed the car hitting a concrete wall with minimal front end damaged and only a smashed windscreen. The interior was designed to take two full sized passengers in comfort, and a fridge sideways in the rear hatch. Two Smarts could sit end-to-end on a standard parking bay, or park between cars, nose-to-the-kerb. Petrol consumption was an average of 50mpg.

Selling the concept was a mountain to climb. The omens are never favourable for new thinking, new forms of mobility up against a conservative buying public and ultra-cautious car makers – hence Tesla cars are all yesterday's fashion in appearance. As with so many inventions that challenge the conventional, Hayek's micro car received scant attention from the big is better car industry. Small cars were assumed to be slow, characterless and not suited to long inter-city journeys. In the nineties the car business was booming, new companies churning out the same designs as everyone else the world over. To my mind, the Smart car was the most innovative vehicle actually produced in any number right up until 2010 and the advent of the all-electric vehicle. Only the recreation of the little Fiat 500 got close to the Smart. No wonder European streets are full of Smarts and Fiats.

Hayek asked Volkswagen to assess his concept. Volkswagen surveyed the idea, their engineers enthusiastic, their procedure to create the car slow and painful until the boss of Volkswagen resigned and then Ferdinand Karl Piëch took over, an aloof autocrat of the Austrian old school, and grandson of the gifted engineer, Ferdinand Porsche. He rejecting the car with a pompous "No one will want this elephant's foot", and promptly pinched the clever packaging for Volkswagen's new vehicle, the city Up model, but with four seats. His went on to concentrate staff on creating his vanity project, the two-tonne, 250mph faux Bugatti Veyron, a monster with a fireguard for a radiator, and a financial loss on every one though sold at a million pounds each. The car, an automotive equivalent of proving one's manhood, he failed to notice the cheating his company was doing over exhaust emissions.

Hayek persevered. He was a fine salesman as well as persistent. Mercedes Benz bought his designs and immediately set about making it a more executive-friendly concept while keeping its wonderful dimensions. They dispensed with the multi-coloured body panels swapped like a Swatch watch, and upped the price. In the journey they lost the fun element that Hayek wanted incorporated, cheap transportation for the masses.

On its inception English automotive journalists unanimously derided the Smart as they had done to the Aston Martin Cygnet. They trashed it and carried on selling their magazines with expensive unattainable supercars on the front cover, such as the big, fat Bugatti

Veyron. The Smart4Two, as it was christened, was a vehicle quite clearly fit for modern cities with busy narrow streets, where your sat-nav took you to your destination and you parked on a postage stamp.

I bought one, pre-owned as is my habit; letting someone else take the VAT and depreciation hit. Each time I get inside the cabin it brings a smile to my face. It brings a scowl to the face of BMW drivers when I shoot past them on the motorway. The transparent Perspex roof makes the cabin light and airy. I like the way the car locks the doors automatically as you drive off from a standing start, and the way the rear window wiper gives a single wipe when the car is put into reverse. You sit high for good visibility. Access and egress are superb, a basic craft lost on modern-day car designers. The paddle shift gears on the steering wheel are a joy to use, one pull up or down changes gear in a nano-second. The speakers offer excellent sound quality. Parking is a doddle, the smallest space is fine. Above all, I like how it does not crush my wallet when filling the tank.

And I can attest to how strong is its safety cage. I parked it on a slope but forgot to put the handbrake on tight, and bending down to the passenger floor to pick up files was suddenly overcome by nausea. I looked up just in time to see the car running downhill the last few feet smack into the back of a van. The thwack reverberated between the houses. I got out the car to assess the damage – nothing! Not a dent or a scratch. Calling the Smart dealer received the reply, "It can take a 25mph hit without deforming the bumpers, sir," he said. The few drawbacks it has are down to poor road surfaces that pitch and toss the small wheelbase around, and potholes that rattle teeth. City councils encourage us to drive small engine or electric cars yet force us to buy jeep type buggies with big tyres to cope with washboard surfaces.

There are too many SUVs cars chasing too few buyers, and too many manufacturers catering for people of wealth. The poor are asked to take to bicycles and in all weathers, or buy a bus pass and use public transport. How the elderly and the non-ambulant are expected to use bicycles or motorbikes is a question zealous cyclists won't answer.

Before Ford took over Volvo, the Swedish company built cars the human way, no conveyor belts, just ten cars sitting on the factory floor and a team allotted to each car, taking pride in fitting the parts one by one until the car was ready to roll out onto the test track. They fixed faults as they appeared. Moreover, Volvo sold their brand on the basis of safety and durability, how their cars looked was secondary. The Smart car emulated Volvo. The auto press did not care.

A modern car should be built to last decades and built of sustainable materials, light weight, not propelled by petrol or diesel, and compact. That brief is liable to be met by car makers in Asia, from China or Japan, two nations with a history of innovation and low economy transportation concepts. Manufacturers slow to change, who cannot adapt quickly enough, will not survive. Not for nothing did Clara Ford, Henry Ford's wife, refuse to drive his backfiring, oily, starter handle Model A car. She drove an electric car of her day, a 1914 Detroit Electric. It returned over 80 miles on a single charge from a dozen old-world batteries, and did not frighten the horses. Twenty miles an hour was fast enough, exactly what we see painted on inner city roads now.

Ferdinand Porsche had fitted electric motors to the wheel hubs of a carriage almost thirteen years earlier. But he was not the first, that accolade belongs to a Scotsman. Historically, the electric car was a Scottish invention, our engineers being among the most innovative in the world. You can see a surviving example in the Grampian Transport Museum. The *Electric* was the invention of Robert Davidson, a chemist, engineer and inventor, born in Aberdeen in 1804. Davidson is credited with creating the world's first electric vehicle. Davidson used a very simple battery, essentially a wooden box that held a liquid-acid electrolyte and a series of zinc plates. This was connected to an electromagnetic motor of Davidson's own design, a replica of which is on display alongside a mock-up of his battery. Alas, no car company existed in Scotland to take up his invention. Davidson was a visionary ahead of his time. He went on to create the world's first electric railway locomotive in 1842; it ran for the first time on the Edinburgh to Glasgow line, a breath-taking 4mph.

Hayek was also a visionary. He had a dream. He felt car makers were ignoring a whole sector of buyers, people who wanted a small, stylish, environmentally friendly vehicle. Car makers are still aiming for the well-heeled.

When Honda patented a devise to fit on engines that did away with expensive catalytic converters the American car giants ganged up on the company and had the device banned. They had invested in catalytic makers. The oil giants, car maker muscle, and chasing big profits stopped diverse forms of automotive progress for almost a hundred years. Car makers are the victims of their own lethargy and conservatism. The rise of Elon Musk's Tesla took them by surprise. The time to innovate, to be revolutionary was yesterday. It may be too late for the slowest.

28

SMACKEROONIES

The Bank of England issues £1 million notes (Giants) and £100 million notes (Titans) held permanently somewhere in its Threadneedle Street premises. They issue the mega-notes to give confidence in the value of their normal currency. Scotland invented paper money. We issue our own banknotes, a twenty-year out of date portrait of the English Monarch nowhere to be seen on them.

The three Scottish pound issuers are, simultaneously, authorised to print Scottish pounds of the same face value. The British State has been doing all it can to find ways of stopping Scotland issuing its own currency for they understand the significance of an independent country having its own currency, and they know it is a constitutional matter, any move to stop production liable to anger other nations.

In the man-to-man to-the-death debating match televised between combative Alex Salmond and soporific Alistair Darling, Salmond refused to rise to Darling's vexatious question, "What currency will you use?" a reference to the day after independence. This was Darling clearing the way for his colleagues in the other unionist parties to claim they would stop Scotland using the pound sterling, something they cannot do, but a threat is as good as the reality.

Laying aside the triteness of arguing over a Plan B when all that matters is withdrawing from a corrupted union, Salmond actually said he had *three* plans. Like a general mounted on his warhorse meeting his opposite number mid-battlefield before the conflict starts, the face-to-face exchanging a pardon on surrender or a riposte and a scowl, Salmond was not going to disclose his auxiliary plans to the invader.

Darling's remark and the subsequent tyrannical announcement of the then chancellor and thug George Osborne stating "Walk away from the Union and you walk away from the pound," caused alarm among the ill-informed in Scotia, and the easily scared. Salmond's silence, it transpired, was reported as a tactical error. I do not believe it was. The exploitation of the currency issue by press commentators and media was the problem. Wobbly supporters echo the colonial line, namely, the electorate will not trust an independent Scotland if we do not know what currency folks will use, as if no country has ever dared take its independence using their own currency.

We will use the pound sterling for a short time, as Ireland did on becoming a republic, and move swiftly to our own currency, when enough is printed to circulate among the populace. There are those who feel Scotland should use its own currency immediately to avoid the Bank of England dictating interest rates, but that assumes Scotland has a nationalist government that demonstrates alacrity in preparing for independence.

Money is that strange thing, a faith, a *belief* that the piece of paper or coin you hand over will secure goods in exchange. Eons ago we got by with shells and beads and bartering a blacksmith's service for a rabbit or a goat, the same belief in their agreed worth.

'*Scotland Be Brave*' ran the legend on the Referendum poster, and duly inspired … we fell prey to the lie Scotland is a poor nation. To accept responsibility assumes boldness in decision making. First know the truth. We are a wealthy nation. Second, name our currency in advance. The stand-up comedian Kevin Bridges likes to call our future pound notes Smackeroonies, others suggest the Groat. I think we should use what we called it, The Pund Scottis.

Pund Scottis was the unit of currency in the Kingdom of Scotland before the kingdom agreed to share a single parliament with the Kingdom of England in 1707 but it was hundreds of years older than that. It was introduced by David I, in the 12th century, on the model of English and French money, divided into 20 shillings, each of 12 pence. Why petition for a continuation of our subservient role in an asymmetrical sterling union when we have our own currency?

English Euro-sceptics have an argument of sorts against the Eurozone only for all the wrong reasons. Contrary to the ludicrous straight banana lies of Brexiteers, the EU is a place of democratic practice, but some of its decision making ought to be made more public. The one institution screaming out for radical reform is the EU Central Bank. It is a repository for the most brutal theories of the Chicago School of Economics, almost all discredited since the death of its hallowed messiah, Milton Freidman.

Populated by Chicago School luminaries who hold tight to extreme-capitalist ideology, the EU Central Bank is unable to throw off its ideological straight jacket, its governing maxim, loan to a nation's banks, never invest in the nation. The nation is expected to accept artificial austerity so that the banks recover, able to pay the EU Central Bank interest at high rates. The money goes from bank to bank, and back again gathering interest, never landing in *our* account.

The answer is a radical reorganisation of the EU Central Bank and probably following it, the Bundesbank. In them lie the ideology of the Chicago School of Brutal Economics and the economic diktats of EU states national policies. The difference between the Bank of England and the EU Central Bank is not always obvious: the EU Central Bank is not allowed to print or borrow money. It survives by investment and interest charges on loans. The Greek government knows how painful that can be. The Bank of England is duty bound by instinct and old pals to follow Westminster instruction. Confronted by an autonomous Scotland, it might feel obliged to turn antagonistic for one reason or another to Scottish economic reforms Westminster does not like. No one should forget England has always imposed its rule by force. It follows that it has to be safer to dump the Pound Sterling and not use the Euro if and when Scotland rejoins Europe. It is not obligatory to use the Euro if an EU member; a member is asked to consider it when eligibility fits the criteria. In alphabetical order, Bulgaria, Croatia, Czech Republic, Denmark, Hungary, Poland, Romania, and Sweden have declined the Euro and stuck with their own currency. Ireland uses the Euro but seems to have suffered no ill effects.

According to the view of English patriots the Euro's great weakness is there is no single nation state to back the Euro in times of trouble (correct) and no European institutions can or should play that role (wrong). Let's take this logic a step further. England's governing isolationists claim no single currency can serve the interests of a multi-national state. But wait! The United Kingdom *is* a multi-national entity. That being so, indisputably so, then Scotland should issue its own currency forthwith, or forever relinquish being a *bona fide* nation. If England's Brexiteers are right about the Eurozone, then we have a moral duty to make Scotland independent of London. The only reply a Brexiteer has to that is the one full of cellulite: Scotland needs England. We are better informed now; we know the reality is the polar opposite, England needs Scotland.

There are formidable economic arguments in favour of a nation having its own currency. Scotland invented and printed the first paper notes, their existence now hugely beneficial for an independent state. Presently, our three Scottish banks issue Scottish pounds under an agreement with the Bank of England which limits the quantity of printed money. Upon independence, and to keep everybody happy, we can avoid major financial upheavals, the Scottish government can commit to maintaining (say, for two years) the same rules of quantity supply. The most experienced advice available is united: "*control of the three banks' note issues should be transferred to a Scottish Central Bank which commits to maintaining a currency board that allows for a seamless transition to a free-floating Scottish pound within a couple of years*". (Call it our Central Bank.)

I place that last paragraph in italics because that is the view of at least three eminent economists who have studied Scotland's situation: Yanis Varoufakis, David McWilliams, and Professor of Accounting Practice and Political Economist Richard Murphy, a Greek, an Irishman and an Englishman! The outpourings from those who would have Scotland impoverished to prove we cannot exist without English rule are shown to be ludicrous. Those who warn of imminent catastrophe, people throwing themselves off the top of financial institutions, skyscrapers, railway bridges, or castle ramparts, it being Scotland, are playing silly buggers. The experts are agreed: we won't see mass suicides; Scottish notes are already in circulation, "*no ATM disruption, no re-writing of short and medium term contracts and no fear of bank runs*". Don't take my word. When experts are agreed the opposite point of view cannot be held to be true.

Turning to the issue of public debt: Scotland does not have a public debt. Part of the Union deal bars Scotland from running up debt. Debts can only be approved by Westminster and are the responsibility of the bank of England. The UK shoulders debt and it alone will keep all debt in the event of independence. This is an underlining reason for a self-isolating England to keep hold of Scotland. Some think we should accept some of the UK's debt as a negotiating ploy. Why? For a country to begin a new with no debt is almost unheard of, a huge plus. Then again, we could rent Trident's Rosyth Docks for (say) £5 billion a year for five years tops, as Greenland has done with that country's remaining US air force base, and we can ask for a few million more for the clean up once Trident has gone south.

By suggesting we keep the Pound Sterling, albeit for a limited time, we are dealing the best hand to London as a bargaining chip for securing the continuation of a lopsided currency union. Our own currency minimises the amount of UK debt we care to accept.

Any thought of the bank of England remaining as Scotland's bank of last resort, a kind of legal guardian, is highly dangerous. A belligerent neighbour for over 400 years, England is guaranteed to implement draconian, abrupt lifestyle changes on indigenous Scots, as Thatcher did with so many of her imposed policies, and all Westminster governments since. The usurper invades to plunder not to assist locals to prosper.

Mark Carney the former governor of the Bank of England, a Canadian by birth, spoke honestly when he confirmed sharing sterling can happen, but manipulated and bullied by a tyrannical Westminster, how much wiser it is to use our own currency. That aside, it matters not a jot what the governor thinks. The Bank of England will always stay tuned to the needs of southern England and the City of London; the City operates as a perpetual drag on Scotland's economic growth, it poses a permanent threat to the solvency of the Scottish government. A quick glance at any small country doing well, even one that does not share Scotland's natural resources tells us Scotland is currently scammed to the high heavens.

Scotland can never secure sovereignty within the sterling zone because a shared central bank will *always* force Edinburgh to dance to the tunes of the City and England's agenda. Let us dump the hideous Barnett Formula in which mafia thugs take most of our earnings and leave us just enough to keep the shop open so we pay up again next month. Staying in the EU does not mean forced to use the Euro, *ergo*, using our own currency is the solution. Best of all, the EU does **not** control interest rates.

As that dotty warlord Margaret Thatcher said: "Those who control interest rates control the political!" Scotland is not a basket case. It never was, and it never need be. It has no humanitarian crisis. We are not suffering famine or long-term drought. By exiting the sterling zone, Scotland stands to gain nationhood without suffering any of the catastrophic economic costs. We can reject malicious unionist prejudices. We can do it because we have never been subsumed into England fully, neither culturally, economically, geographically or spiritually, though England has tried its hardest to have us become North England. Tied to an annual English 'allowance', we cannot reform the Bank of England, nor can we eradicate colonial manipulation while in an unequal union, but we *can* reform Scotland.

Eminent economist Yanis Varoufakis offers common sense free of charge: "An independent Scotland, with its own currency guaranteeing autonomy from Euro-sceptic England, can help an emerging alliance of peripheral European countries establish a new Eurozone architecture; perhaps one that Edinburgh may want to join...." to which I add, first we must dump England and its bank.

Using our own currency is as natural as using our own toothbrush, only we keep money in banks and pockets, not next to a toilet bowl.

29

THE POLISH STONEMASONS

Describing the creation of a garden is a waste of time for the reader when restricted to prose in an essay without illustrations. What I want to describe, however, is a small element of a garden's construction, my own and most certainly my last. Indeed colossal and towering – turning a rubble strewn precipitous slope into a stable flat area fit for planting anything. The achievement does not belong to me. I pay homage to the people who helped me create what is most likely to be my last effort at rearranging a rustic landscape to suit my vision. They are special people, Polish people.

By sheer chance, after two years of a search for a cottage and a series of increasingly disappointing failures, I came across one on the edge of Edinburgh in a semi-rural district. It lay only a mile where I had spent my childhood near the foreshores of Silverknowes, in a disused Victorian pile that had one outstanding feature, a crenulated turret from where you could shoot imaginary arrows down at school friends playing English invading soldiers, or the Sheriff of Nottingham's men demanding payment of taxes. For the few scorching hot days the turret was a place to sunbathe naked.

The building sat in seven acres of what had been an estate that included a blacksmith's bothy, orchards of fruit trees, cultivated shrubs, and giant oak trees that sheltered red squirrels. There was free food for the taking if one had a mind to forage for it. I harvested what I could when the fruit was in season, gathered mushrooms I knew where safe to eat, wild garlic, wild strawberries, and in the estuary nearby I sought crabs under glutinous sea anemone, mussel-bound boulders to cook in a pot, rich supplement for a meagre choice of nutrition when supermarkets did non-existent. Free food and free education, some of the best watching entranced sweat-laden Jimmy the gnarly, coal and grease stained blacksmith and farrier fire up his forge to white hot heat – I can still smell the fire – and shoe a Clydesdale horse, the giant beast docile as a dormouse, and as a kind of release from the drama and a change of mood, I chased rabbits with Meikle his Jack Russell, exhilarated, until one was cornered and knew fate had arrived. Until that point, I had never met a person who was not Scottish.

It was about as idyllic a time span a lonesome kid could wish for, the house tenancy part salary from the city council, a 'tied' house, the term given to property owned by the town council once useful, now too big to utilise for any single purpose. It was given to my stepfather, an ex-soldier of no great character, then a jobbing gardener. The family was restricted to three rooms in one corner of the third floor. His stewardship ensured the building was not vandalised. The council would do that. Ultimately, they decided to bulldoze the lot and create a golf course for working folk, the other five in Edinburgh not being enough, and some only expensive clubs for posh folks. Finding a modest cottage not too far away from those misty remembered adventures was returning to one's roots.

Unlike the imposing stone pile with the turret built early in the nineteenth century, the cottage was built in 1900, the land bought from the local shepherd by a building company owner for a home. It too was built of stone, but ugly random rubble coated with harling against Scotland's harsh winters, and painted white. The property was in a bad state; the elderly couple keen to downsize and live elsewhere without the cost of renovating the cottage to a modern standard. The repairs to be done were bad enough, the garden worse. I had returned to the cottage five times to check detail, things one misses on a single inspection, drawn back because it had privacy on all sides from other houses. On that fifth time the sun was shining warm on my face. I realised the place was a suntrap. Here was a chance to recreate my childhood lived down the road so many years ago, but with a house worth living in. I could create a kind of heaven on earth. The immense amount of repair work to be done would eat up modest savings, and what could not be seen, the stuff that hides behind walls and under floorboards, dry rot and no damp course, was potentially lethal to a man relying on the sale of his writing for an income. I had renovated property in the past, and large scale projects were not a frightening prospect, only the money in one's pocket makes the difference between confidence and walking away.

The garden was a brae slope running from a long wall, down ninety-odd feet to a short, flat area, and then another drop of ten feet into the backyard of a house below. Halfway down the grassy slope there was a thin retaining wall built by the first owner that looked and proved to be ready to collapse. The property was hardly mind months when, after ten days of incessant rain the brae shifted, collapsed in the middle with a dull rumble during the storm. Tonnes of soil began to move toward the private house below. This was an emergency.

On every house build budget there is a contingency sum, or ought to be, a cover for the extra-costs not calculated bound to occur, but a soil slide was never envisaged in my worst imaginings. I had already paid a few thousand pounds to have seventy-feet alien Norwegian spruce cut down and removed, replaced by indigenous multi-stemmed silver birch trees. A landslip was unexpected.

Consulting a friend who was an engineer provided the answer, gabion baskets. Those are wire baskets filled with inter-locking rocks. Once a row is completed, each basket is tied to the next along top and bottom with steel wire. Stability is the prime target. Gabions were the invention of the Egyptians but constructed of pleated papyrus reeds. They used the baskets to hold back channels of sand when creating water channels from the Nile to their plant beds. The Romans perfected the idea and used metal baskets. I chose a brand covered in plastic so the gabions had over a hundred years of life, outliving me and the next house owner easily, and withstanding rust and rainwater that still found its way under the slope. In fact, Edinburgh's Roman encampment had reached the property wall, a legion of 1,000 soldiers and horses, the harbour where a large carved stone lion was discovered in the mud of the estuary. The history of the place was attractive to the Sicilian side of my heritage.

The first cost that arrived was a killer, a five-figure sum the size of a mortgage deposit. The horrendous quotation was on top of engineering drawings and submission to the city's planning department. Would I have to sell the house, and having not lived in it, who would buy it with a huge bill to pay for shoring up a crumbling embankment? The second quotation from a medium-sized company was no less of a shock, although half the amount of the first estimate.

What made the cost so high was the inaccessibility of the site. There was nowhere to bring in a JCB or a Japanese mini-digger and not as much as a rough track for delivery trucks. Everything, every ounce of material, would have to be dumped at the house gate and carried by hand or barrow to the slope and shuttered down a chute to the levels worked, like a coal mine but in reverse. I was caught between a rock and a hard place, or rather, two-hundred and twenty tonnes of rocks to fill two-hundred gabion baskets. There was no choice, no reselling a house with a moving brae. But where to find a crew who would do the job for what could be afforded?

In desperation I turned to the Polish stonemason team who were in the process of taking down a poorly built brick shed to rebuild the disintegrating boundary wall exposed by the shed. Could they help? They could and at a fraction of the cost, formally contracted. Knowing how onerous the task was going to be and no one could slacken, we agreed I'd supply meals and refreshments on the job – some days a Polish fry-up – and of course, I paid for the materials. I was overjoyed to make the acquaintance of good people with a predilection for hard graft at economical rates. To make new, lasting friends was a dividend.

The stonemason squad had come to Scotland in 2005 when wages were higher here than anything they could earn in Poland. They followed in the honourable footsteps of thousands of Polish people who had emigrated to Scotland and thousands more who fought Hitler's armies as they ploughed into Poland and set up their concentration camps.

Andrzej, Piotr and Mariusz are all brothers – The Brothers Szarko. Polish people had been friends to Scotland for generations. In the sixteenth and seventeenth century we put on our warm coats and gloves and set off in our tens of thousands for Poland – hence so many places in Poland have Scottish names. Poles came to Scotland to make a new life. We exchanged small-time merchants and labourers. That friendship resulted in a steady influx of Polish from about the 1850's, an association with roots in Bonnie Prince Charlie's mother. She was Polish.

The stonemasons who volunteered to build my gabion embankment were a fine bunch of the male species. Piotr was the eldest, the brother who endorsed group decisions; Andrzej had the best English, at ease communicating with clients, conversant with a good few Scots dialect words and phrases, and Jacek Ogórek was their co-worker who just kept smiling and working no matter what he was asked to do, from barrowing rocks or empting earth, to fetching ladders and spades, picks and shovels. They had a stonemason, Grzegorz (Gregory) Jaworski, to help with the heavy lifting on specific days. I would do as much as I could. They were in their thirties; I was double their age, puffing and panting, sweating and aching.

Quick, efficient learners, they got experience in Scottish ways of building working for a renowned Edinburgh firm before having the confidence to establish their own company, replete with muscular pick-up truck, their company name proudly emblazoned on the side. Having never built a gabion embankment, the team agreed to work under the supervision of a professional gabion engineer, but as the embankment took shape, he realised the Poles were so proficient, regular inspection visits were unnecessary.

THE POLISH STONEMASONS

To describe the task ahead of us as exceptional – building an embankment seven gabion baskets high, three more rows dug deep underground, twenty-one baskets long without mechanical digger or crane to lift in loads of rocks – is an understatement. It was almost impossible. But I had no choice. Each day saw the slope move a few more feet downhill. A Herculean effort lay before us, the maximum commitment required. The brothers put their backs into it, presumable sleeping all the hours of the night.

By now I had begun to call my plot of land Little Poland, the squad were Polish, the delivery drivers were Polish, and even the relief postman was Polish.

Days of toil were carried out in good natured mood aided by bright sunny hours, but back-breaking. Fill a barrow with heavy rocks, push the barrow to the top of the brae, wheel squeaking with the weight on the axle, tip the load down the chute, two of us at the bottom sorting out the rock sizes and handing them one at a time to the man standing in a gabion, locking the rocks together, biggest in the base, smallest on top as the rock pile filled the gabion space.

Each gabion is six-feet long, three-feet high, and three-feet deep. They arrive flat-packed, a bit like IKEA furniture but without the screws and wood plugs needed to reassemble them, or a few key elements missing. Some prescribed had six-feet long tails of mesh on which had to be piled Type-1 crushed stone and then soil on top of the crushed base, compacted material to weigh down the rear of the gabion. It had the physical reality of building an Aztec pyramid, and when finished, with its ledges for walkways, looked exactly like one.

The very bottom row under the earth was three baskets deep, front to back, the same for the next two rows, and two baskets deep thereafter until the very last at the top, which was one basket in dressed stone to serve as the top safety barrier wall. We gave ourselves six weeks, six days a week working like Egyptian slaves. It took seven. Luck was with us, it was seven weeks of sunshine from May through to July with only a few days of rain.

The crew kept working during heavy rain, and this was not masonry work they were used to. A Scots crew were liable to shelter in the cabin of their trucks drinking tea or reading a tabloid newspaper if rain was heavy. You paid them working or lousing. The Polish squad made a shelter and beavered on. They divided themselves into diggers of earth, fetchers of barrow loads of rocks, and fillers of baskets. I managed to fill some baskets before age and a painful back took me out for the day.

I was impressed by their camaraderie. It was uplifting. A Scots crew would exhibit similar banter and jokes, but there was something bonding in the team before me, much deeper than guys from different households doing a day's hard labour and then going home again.

Polish people like to chatter away to each other about almost everything under the sun, especially politics. They laughed, joked and reminisced about things seen televised on the news, or from their homeland, pushing each other to complete a full set of baskets before the day was out. They played the Polish pop music on a portable radio. Andrzej, Piotr and Mariusz, Jacek, and Grzegorz worked like the proverbial Trojans from 8am to 4pm with a 7am rise. If they made an error, which was not often, they fixed it on the spot, jeering in mock judgement at the perpetrator or their group stupidity.

There is one remarkable example worth the telling of how motivated Polish workers are to see a task to fruition. When the first twelve feet of soil was dug out from the base of the slope to take the first row of gabions, there was nowhere to put the spoil. Twelve feet down and six feet back for each gabion is a lot of earth. We discussed the problem for a time, and, noticing it was nearing lunch hour, I offered to go to the local store, buy food, and continue looking for a solution on my return. When I returned I was met by an amazing sight. They had not stopped work to await my return with lunch. They had solved the problem of where to put earth when trapped in a tight space.

The squad had improvised three landing areas an equal distance apart up the slope. The guy in the pit shovelled earth up six feet over his head to the platform above. The man on the first platform shovelled earth from there up to the one above, and so on, and so forth until the earth landed in the only place it could be kept temporarily – the very top of the slope. As the gabion baskets began to rise out the ground, one row upon another, a layer of earth would be shovelled from the top down the slope to fill the area behind the new-filled gabions. The gabions were stacked at a slight incline, leaning backwards into the brae, a double safety measure to hold back the entire slope if it every thought about moving downhill again.

On the seventh week, the job was done. From the front, the 25-foot gabion wall of massed quarry rock was an impressive edifice, a considerable barrier against nature's apocalypse. The top was now dead flat, a plateau, almost a turret overlooking the glen and woods below like the Victorian mansion I had frolicked in as a child. I could create a garden on the new flat area, an Italian one, what else, on strict Roman lines.

Piotr, Andrzej and Mariusz were born in the little town of Barwice in North West Poland. Their mother is the atypical Polish housewife, looking after home and family, their father working as a road services driver. They kept chickens and used their garden ground to grow vegetables. They gathered mushrooms from the woods and knew how to tap the sap from silver birch trees to make a satisfying beverage. When they arrived in Scotland they had no idea how to get work but knew they could be useful in the building trade, a good way to survive. As Andrej says modestly "We got offered the kind of work we do now and we wanted to be as good as we can. We had plans to go home again, but liked Scotland too much to leave."

On the day when most of the major work was over, Andrzej said, "You will miss us when we have gone." I thought he was referring to the band of brothers not available to do repairs as they arose, but he said instead, "I'm the son you never had." I allowed myself a wry smile and he knew I approved of his remark spoken half in jest.

To the Brothers Szarko, *Zawsze będę wdzięczny* – I shall be forever grateful.

30

THE BASTARDISATION OF THE BBC

'Bastardisation' is my creation. It conveys exactly a process that took place over a number of years affecting BBC Scotland's ability to reflect a whirlwind change in Scotland's politics. Suppression of facts, history and news items including the BBC's own Scottish staff. What has happened in the years just prior to the Scottish independence referendum of 2014, and the years since, justifies my view that BBC Scotland is wholly irrelevant to any economic or cultural progress for Scotland. I shall do my best to explain how this came about without quoting George Orwell on his time working for the BBC propaganda unit in London.

The BBC was once seen as the apogee of a career built in journalism or arts administration. It appeared to present Scottish culture in an enthusiastic way but it was only surface, The *White Heather Club* was a kilt and traditional Scots songs affair churned out from the Entertainment department, and spruced up for special events, Hogmanay or Easter. There was a weekly arts programme of thirty minutes duration, usually personality focussed, a studio interview with a few minutes of film on location. There was televised news, or regional, as Aunty BBC liked to call it, presented from what seemed a broom cupboard somewhere in the Glasgow headquarters, and from smaller local radio units dotted around Scotland from the Highlands to the Borders. BBC Radio Scotland had a better track-record, occasional discussions on the Scots language, some discussions on Scots history, and children's programmes. What made them stand out from other radio programmes was participants talking in a Scots accent of one sort of another.

Every so often BBC Scotland would cover itself in glory. The corporation did not make soap opera series. Those it left to the vulgar STV – Scottish Television. BBC could get classy when it put its mind and money to the task. Dramatisation of Lewis Grassic Gibbon's trilogy of elegiac novels *Sunset Song* brought acclaim and pride. A Scots novel filmed on location was an event. Trumpets blared, kettle drums rattled and cymbals crashed. Newspaper articles appeared interviewing director and stars, and the author's books sold more copies. No one noticed that the London press made little fuss over Scottish productions. And no one noticed that two thirds of the licence fee out of Scotland stayed in London, one third sent back to Scotland split between staff and programmes. We were being robbed not blind but while working for television or watching television.

On the technical side, studio operators gravitated to a productive, salaried life working for the BBC, cloistered among banks of fader equipment in windowless rooms. Make-up artists, costume designers, personnel staff, video editors, camera men and sound engineers were interesting people to talk to, they had lots of stories to tell about famous people they had worked with, and experiences; an eventful life. Women got jobs as news readers. BBC Scotland had its own orchestra. University students were given a year's training, the employment thereafter dependent on how smart and industrious senior supervisors found them to be. As you entered the building reception staff greeted you like an old friend, security staff saluted. Working for the BBC you were somebody. Nothing you did there was banal. "What do you do," was the first line to open a conversation at a social gathering. The second was "What car do you drive?" To answer you worked at the BBC and drove a VW Golf GTi told people you had reached the ranks of the well-heeled middle-class.

I could get startled by the unexpected: a respected news reader journalist moonlighting for MI5 so blatantly I had to ask him to tone down his arrogance. Short-listing staff for interviews for promotion one department to another, I opened their progress file only to find they had been marked down for rejection, or delayed promotion, because of their Scottish independence affiliations. I often had to rebut accusation of so-and-so staffer being left-wing or right-wing, a claim rarely flung at frontline staff working for commercial television companies. In my experience, those at the top, middle and upper managerial levels tended to be right-wing, general employees tended to be left-wing, especially studio or location directors who were schooled in the craft of asking awkward questions.

One can be fooled easily. The distinguished journalist Brian Redhead, renowned for sporting a scruffy beard and hounding politicians with incessant questions, presented the UK's morning news programme, entitled *Today*, from Portland Place in London. Redhead was a working class lad from Newcastle-on Tyne. He had been the Northern Editor of the *Guardian* newspaper before joining the BBC. His place of birth and his former job at the *Guardian* automatically labelled him 'socialist'. Tory politicians made it known they saw him as a media 'red under the bed'. On one occasion, the Tory chairman Norman Tebbit, a thoroughly unlikeable character even before he opened his mouth to speak, harangued Redhead about his socialist affiliations. Redhead refuted the accusation with barely hidden disgust, demanding the politician answer the question the public wanted asked. Tebbit kept flinging the insult in Redhead's face. It is debateable whether Redhead survived that particular tongue lashing or not. His star waned after it became front page news. When he died, it was discovered Redhead had been a long-serving Tory member of his local English village. Did Tory politicians know that, and if they did, were they indulging in the double bluff? It takes only a phone call to the cabinet office from Redhead's constituency for a colleague to say "He's one of us". Or was Tebbit as ignorant as he was ruthless?

The slump in respect for BBC Scotland is thought to have been recent, propelled by the ascendency of the national party to power and monopoly of the Holyrood Parliament. In truth, it began long before that, in the last part of last century. It happened quickly and without any help from the literary dwarfs paid by press baron Rupert

Murdoch, an empire builder intent on gathering communications systems to promote his political outlook and wiping out the BBC's influence as fast as his agencies could organise it. Behind the scenes, BBC pay was poor compared to commercial television companies. People were expected to work to tough deadlines, unions demanded better working conditions.

The galloping gangrene afflicting a once venerable outpost of the BBC was an inside job. The rot began with a diminution of Scottish programme output; the reduction of programme budgets; BBC London siphoning off hundreds of millions of the licence fee from Scottish households, and all-UK transmission becoming a London-only decision. While staff tightened their belts, executives widened theirs a few notches. Executive salaries ballooned – "society has to pay for the best talent" – the same self-serving fatuous elitism uttered by fat, fraudulent bankers. The golden age of the BBC was transmogrifying into the age of the high-salaried executive and the lowering of programme quality to the lowest common denominator.

There are more self-lacerations: the withdrawal of decision-making to London; the squandering of license money on cancelled projects often in many millions of pounds; sacking talented staff and replacing them by competitive submissions from freelancers and independent production companies UK-wide; full-time posts discarded for short-term contracts; loss of public trust issuing from the theft of ideas submitted by independent producers; loss of trust from heavily biased anti-Scottish independence programmes and their commentators; all that on top of a flourishing ethos of mediocrity. BBC Scotland was treated as an outpost – the betrayal of a nation it purported to serve.

Holding up a mirror to a big institution is almost impossible when an employee. Dare to do it and you are apt to see a green ogre staring back at you, or your personal desk belongings in a cardboard box awaiting your collection before you leave the building. I knew one middle-manager who was made redundant on a Thursday. On Friday he arrived for work but could not find his car parking space. Overnight his name had been erased. A month after I left the BBC, I called to check if I was eligible for a secondary pension. Administration could not find my name or records. A newspaper gossip columnist, frantically trying to lower my past BBC status for daring to criticise BBC Scotland's lamentable coverage of the arts in Scotland – 'forgetting' she got regular work from the Janice Forsyth Show – *did* know where I worked, informed by a BBC insider happy to pass confidential material to a hack. Leaving the BBC is like leaving the Communist party, you are never forgiven.

The director of BBC Northern Ireland was a kindly man, but I got the impression he was putty in the hands of his large, intimidating head of programmes, an Ulster man who sounded like the Reverend Ian Paisley when he got angry. If he was not MI5 he should have been. When it was time to leave, the director paid me a compliment for my pioneering programme series. The director of programmes made a negative comment. BBC was an unpleasant place to work, Northern Ireland especially so. On my first day as Head of Youth Programmes I was collected from the airport and taken to the BBC studios. The elderly secretary doing the driving switched on her car radio to tell me the programme playing was one of the best news shows from the province. Later, I learned she told the same badass director of programmes how annoyed she was that I asked questions and did not listen to the radio show in complete silence. Instant value judgement is a BBC hallmark.

Unable to make any headway into Ulster communities, bereft of inspiring facilities or source material, I asked to be moved from Northern Ireland and given a job in BBC Glasgow. To their credit, the BBC agreed. I was put in radio until a role found in television drama department. Boredom and humdrum routine set in very quickly. Churning out one, two and three-hour long programmes all day was demoralising. There was purpose in working on a film or television drama for a year or more, see it produced and premiered, and watch it praised and toured. For the life of me I could not see the purpose in pumping out immediately forgettable dough ball shows day after day, endless dollops of banal chat, people talking about themselves book-ended with pop music. With the BBC's classic patronising swirl, the content was designed for "the housewife alone at home".

The role of hamburger seller or cigarette salesman was not one my skills. I was given four trainees to help with the day's research. Two were always slow learners, one was eager to please, and the fourth certain to be arrogantly ambitious way beyond their ability.

The BBC prided itself on the quality of its training yet forgot to train me in how to supervise a studio broadcast. I was thrown in the proverbial deep end one day, and made the fatal error of popping my head out of the studio door to ask the actor and raconteur Peter Ustinov if he could go to the microphone as we were on air in four minutes. By chance the English-born director of programmes was visiting and witnessed my fifteen second discussion with Ustinov from down the corridor. On my annual report it said, 'left his post during a broadcast'. I mention 'English-born' because many senior staff in Scotland were incomers, or on a two-rear stint in the 'region', as BBC liked to call a sovereign nation. What they brought to a different culture they knew little or nothing of is a mystery, other than eradicating Scots accents on the radio and favouring London celebrities visiting Scotland for interview. Like carpetbaggers everywhere, a post in Scotland was seen as a stepping-stone to a better job in London.

The corporation had its share of sleaze, ever since Lord Reith discovered his secretary *in flagrante* across his desk with an engineer on Reith's unexpected return early one evening. This established the precedent one finds in large organisations, a sexual undercurrent to daily chores, and the inevitable attraction of office intimacy. A senior colleague asked me to go to lunch with an agent who called in once a year to sell BBC his latest talented clients, a singer, a musician, a journalist. The dinner turned out to be an occasion to pimp one of the women he brought with him and then sell his latest talented client for a stint as a presenter.

For a long time anybody who was homosexual was shunned. (I regret the loss of 'gay' as a description of happiness, there are so few adjectives to describe elation.) A much loved member of panel shows, Gilbert Harding, was outed as homosexual after his death. This shocked Puritan radio listeners who had loved him like a wise father. Homosexuality was still illegal in the tolerant state of merry England. On the same subject, I recall an argument with an intelligent editor who thought Tennessee Williams slept with men (true) and thus he hated women (untrue). He thought William's gayness reduced his female characters to witches and malicious *femme fatales*. Any actress will testify that Williams wrote wonderful roles for women. Perhaps that insight is why so many women feel appreciated and safe in the company of gay men. When the law changed in England, and homosexuality was no longer a crime, the BBC discovered gay celebrities everywhere and began promoting the campest of them to front game shows. Suddenly, everything had a sexual connotation. Behind the scenes, sleazy heterosexuals were stalking young girls.

At the other end of the BBC, London, straight guys, disc jockeys and celebrities were having a good time with fans. The infamous paedophile Jimmy Savile and the Australian entertainer Rolf Harris, two of the most notable, were grooming young girls while BBC employees looked the other way. Savile was rumour, a persistent one that would not lie down. At his death, someone high heid yin in the corporation was smart enough not to broadcast Savile's funeral ceremony yet had stopped a broadcast of a documentary outing his evil reputation, an exposé produced by two BBC producers, Merrion Jones and Liz MacKean. It had been a monumental battle for Jones and MacKean to gather the information and induce people to speak up. But BBC bosses kept delaying the broadcast, shilly-shallying over its content. Savile was a 'national treasure', someone beyond reproach, knighted by the Queen. So too was Harris.

Jones and MacKean were ostracized by the BBC for daring to tell truth to the nation. They left the BBC in disgust. Their documentary was broadcast by ITV. By then, Savile was dead and buried, safe from the law, justice, jail and victim retribution. The polished black marble headstone above his grave read: "It was good while it lasted," the seedy *double entendre* probably referring to the orgasms he enjoyed.

The BBC's capacity to capitulate to political pressure while rejecting honest complaints from the public, reminded me of BBC Scotland's attitude to Special Branch and MI6. BBC Scotland broadcast a documentary on the Zircon Satellite, a spy satellite Prime Minister Margaret Thatcher said did not exist – she misled the UK Parliament but was not sanctioned for the falsehood. The forces of the British State descended on BBC's headquarters in Glasgow after a demand to hand over the recording tapes was refused.

Events began in November 1985 when the Scottish investigative journalist Duncan Campbell was commissioned by BBC Scotland to research a six part, half-hour documentary series called *Secret Society*, produced by Brian Barr. The UK's Government Communications Headquarters known as GCHQ became aware a BBC crew were sniffing around RAF Menwith Hill. The cat was out the bag when Campbell interviewed Ronald Mason, the former Chief Scientific Adviser to the ministry of Defence. Mason had let slip mention of the Zircon Project designated 'Highly Secret', secret in that the British Government was preparing to spy on its own citizens. Campbell had planned to use an episode of *Secret Society* to reveal the existence of Zircon, but he discovered the head of the Public Accounts Committee knew absolutely nothing of the project. The committee is appointed by the House of Commons responsible for checking government expenditure. There was tacit agreement expensive military projects should be subject to scrutiny by the committee.

Campbell felt ignorance of the Zircon project was a violation of this agreement, skulduggery by another name. Not a bad scam when one understands the project had cost the taxpayer over £1.5 billion in 2020 values. Alarmed at questions from Campbell, Tory politicians withdrew from interview, embarrassed at the alleged ignorance of the spy satellite's existence. The point of recounting this shameful episode in BBC Scotland's troubled history, was the then director handed over the tapes as soon as Special Branch arrived at the BBC's door in Glasgow having previous announced he would guard them as he would his life. What the Scottish press stayed silent about was Special Branch operating in Scotland is a violation of the Treaty. Then again, it never occurs to the invader that sending in men to root out troublemakers is anything less than their right. As soon as the Treaty of Union was signed, over one hundred military outposts were established across Scotland to keep the natives subdued.

Understandably, Campbell felt abandoned by his colleagues and soon departed from the BBC. "The Government's actions are oppressive, as has been shown by their treatment of broadcasting. We saw the spectacle of police being sent to raid the BBC headquarters in Glasgow in the middle of the night. We saw the Zircon tapes seized as an elaborate blind."

Living in Edinburgh and losing three hours of each day driving to Glasgow and home in the evening keeps one away from after-hours temptation, boozy trips to the BBC club pub, office trysts and extra-marital affairs. My days as a BBC employee were prosaic and worse, I did not possess my own life. In theatre, I had been used to working with people enthusiastic for the project. In the BBC colleagues were after the promotion. One negative word, one envious backchat comment from a junior colleague was enough to cause paranoia.

The rot starts at the head. The BBC's own respected *Newsnight* journalist, Paul Mason, felt so moved about the collapse of standards from his end of things in London that he went public about the reason for his resignation, his disgust at the way the BBC has turned itself into a purveyor of half-truths and deceptions. He tweeted: "Not since Iraq have I seen the BBC working at propaganda strength like this. So glad to be out of there." Nowhere was Mason's alarm expressed more forcefully than his view the BBC has forfeited its claim to impartiality. The BBC I knew, and have witnessed since, was a stalwart of Westminster ideology, a mouthpiece for the anti-democracy lobby. The conundrum is why the right-wing dislikes it so much when the BBC pushes right-wing orthodoxy a lot of the time.

Scotland got the worst attention of any UK country. One could be excused for thinking the weather in Rockall and Dogger got more attention that Scottish affairs. The BBC did the dirty years earlier when just before the first vote on devolution it transmitted a third-rate drama serial entitled *Scotch on the Rocks*. Adapted from his novel by Tory Minister, Douglas Hurd, one ultimately close to Thatcher, it portrayed Scotland full of erstwhile tartan terrorists. The central group was a paramilitary organisation "operating on the fringes of" – but really affiliated to, the SNP, ready to blow up anybody in their quest to rid Scotland of the English. It put the fear of the loose lunatic with an axe among us and helped blight the reputation of a legitimate political party. A stushie blew up over the blatant racism and political bias in *Scotch on the Rocks* – if 'blew up' is the best phrase. The corporation got very nervous indeed and declined to commission more episodes, announcing it had wiped the tapes. (They exist to this day. What the BBC says publicly is not what it does privately.) But the damage was done. The myth of a Tartan Army laying in wait among the heather or behind a privet hedge with a gun and a bomb was given substance.

The second rout of SNP influence happened internally. One of its most respected departments, its education wing, was led by a nationalist sympathiser, Sinclair Aitken. He employed producers of a like-mind, mainly because they had excellent knowledge of Scottish culture and history, and knew how to weave their erudition into entertaining and informative programmes for Scottish schools. They were not preaching independence, they were teaching Scottish history.

Sinclair was a character and a half; outspoken, fearless, protective of his staff, a man able to get the best out of them creatively, and a confirmed lover of the malt. Whether that or a natural confidence fired his boldness is uncertain, but he was often heard telling senior management where to go when they dared tell him to tone down the Celtic, or make do with less money. Eventually, Sinclair Aitken succumbed to the war of attrition between BBC London and BBC Scotland. He left to enjoy more malt.

Sinclair was always asking for greater financial support from BBC London. Two BBC Scotland controllers who tried to do just that were brutally banished into the wilderness, Alistair Hetherington, sacked in 1978 – a respected former editor of the *Guardian* newspaper, and Alasdair Milne, sacked in 1986 – by Joel Barnett of 'Barnett Formula' notoriety, *Barnett* the loaded calculation by which Scotland gets a third of what the UK Treasury takes from it in way of an annual allowance. Both were Scots who asked BBC London for greater programme autonomy, and by smear and wars of attrition found themselves outlawed for their attention to their brief.

In one of the many vengeful attacks on the BBC, the Tory party appointed a right-wing walking calculus as director general, John Birt, elevated to the House of Lords as Baron Birt, a businessman and an ice cold accountant. He cut costs as one would cut a lawn. He did that while wearing £2,000 Armani suits. He implemented a draconian system of internal commercialisation. By a combination of budget cuts and inter-departmental competition for funds (including hiring facilities rather loaning them as was the normal practice), morale among staff plummeted while vast inflated salaries for executives and producers, the bonus culture, increased. From that moment on things went from bad to worse.

Under Birtian cost cutting BBC Scotland lost any relevancy to Scottish culture, and its education department lost its presence in the Diaspora of Scottish life. What little respect was left for educational programmes was lost under Sinclair Aitken's successor, the deep fried dullness of James Boyle, BBC Scotland Radio Controller, the man who went on to give birth to the bureaucratic sleeping policeman of Scottish arts that is *Creative Scotland*.

Other happenings conspired to fix in the public's mind that BBC Scotland was a provincial simpleton outpost. There was a call for a *Scotland at Six*, an international angle to Scottish news, extinguished in double-quick time by BBC London, though a pilot programme was adjudged excellent. BBC London brooks no international outlook from a 'region'. BBC's then director general, Greg Dyke, encouraged by a BBC Trust report, concluded a *Scottish Six* filled with international news was a good thing. In his autobiography

John Birt – that clothes horse again – thought the idea 'totemic', motivation for the potential break-up of the Union. Once more, the colonial usurper decides a colony must remain a colony. The idea had the backing of the Broadcasting Council of Scotland, a group consisting almost exclusively of Tory and Labour sympathisers, and *only one* SNP supporter, but they too were over-ruled. To a limited extent, Gaelic Television's news flagship *Eorpa* fulfills the indigenous cultural role although more of a documentary series rather than hard daily news. It enjoys a niche group of viewers. In any event, London's power elite probably think it has too little influence to be a threat to their colonial hegemony. Besides, who wants to read subtitles?

What did BBC do prior to the Referendum vote on the 18th of September 2014 that places it squat in the latrine of infamy? It showed in Times bold font it was a state broadcaster not a public broadcaster. It did all it could to promote and protect the status quo, upholding conventional wisdom and authority. "If the BBC is for the people, and the government is for the people, it follows that the BBC is for the government" said Lord Reith, its stern first director general – 'Reith' a name derived from the Pictish meaning a prosperous man.

Alarmed by a poll that showed the Yes vote in the lead for the first time, 50% for, against 49%, with only days to go to the vote, BBC exploded into action. 'Exploded' is the only adjective to use because the BBC had little time left to alter the course of events. Faced with a challenge to its very existence by the SNP government BBC had to move swiftly, knowing an alternative broadcasting service would be the outcome of independence. Protest groups began to form almost as a monthly occurrence outside its new headquarters in Glasgow's Pacific Quay headquarters. Something had to be done to alter the course of events. After running a series of specious programmes on how Scots felt about their democracy presented by shallow celebrities and stand-up comedians that amounted to an expenses paid jaunt to the tourist spots of Scotland, the BBC gave an hour's prime time television to Gordon Brown, a man without a role in the Referendum. A Scot detested by the British Establishment, considered a grossly inept prime minister, he had barely attended the House of Commons since his humiliating exodus from Number 10 Downing Street, and never visited Scotland's parliament once.

For television and press, Brown gave an oration to a hand-picked group of the elderly and the meek, held behind closed doors, no press to ask awkward questions, an oration packed to the gunnels with untruths, disinformation, and terrifying tales of lost jobs, careers, freedoms, and pensions. His core announcement was pure fantasy. He personally would guarantee more powers for Scotland if it voted No, and he would agree a timetable with Cameron and his cohorts to implement those powers. No similar uninterrupted, non-analysed hour was given to Alex Salmond, Scotland's First Minister.

One oddity in this morass of propaganda stood out for its brazen fabrication. The journalist and erstwhile presenter of BBC 2's *Newsnight*, Gavin Esler, presented a glaring piece of puffery about an obvious to all except Esler, fake "grass-roots" organisation curiously without membership or even grass tufts, an alleged anti-independence movement called 'No Borders.' The organisation amounted to one man, Malcolm Offord, a smug, well-heeled financier and businessman unable to explain who his backers were. The enterprise smacked of a phony British intelligence unit without a shred of credible evidence to support its claims. Probably backed by Tory largess, dark money, Offord was a member of the Tory party. Esler's narrative was without scepticism. To increase puzzlement further, Esler presented his location interview to viewers *before* 'No Borders' had announced its arrival to the public. Gavin Esler's news feature *was* the announcement. In 2022 Boris Johnson elevated Malcolm Offord to the House of Lords, thus giving him power over Scotland's affairs. He is now Baron Offord of Garvel. His role is to stymie the rights of Scotland. Esler went on to do more unreliable investigation elsewhere.

The BBC's next move allowed Jackie Bird, a newsreader not known for trenchant interrogation of flaky politicians, to interview the 'leader' of the No campaign, the ill-at-ease Alistair Darling. She began the chair-to-chair, toe-to-toe interview asking a loaded question. "What do you feel about more powers for Scotland?" adding "Let's call them Devo-Max." Using the ambiguous term 'Devo-Max' placed in the viewer's mind more powers meant greater control of our affairs. Devo-Max was not on the ballot paper, nixed by Prime Minister David Cameron as his condition for signing the Edinburgh Agreement. Nor should it have been discussed because the terms of the Referendum barred politicians from offering additional incentives in the last days of the debate. Waiting in the wings ready to exploit the interview, arch enemy of more democracy for Scotland, his ermine calling, Alistair Darling seized on the topic and waffled. The Union was a benign relationship. He was not challenged about his claims and assertions. He offered no evidence how Scotland benefits from being colonised economically and culturally. Darling said he was 'all for' more powers but with Scotland remaining in the Union. This was misleading. He was on record stating the opposite contention, we should expect a 'flood of tears' if new powers were granted. In another biased interview, a concerned Jackie Bird, faced with the 'shocking' rise of the Yes vote, asked her Tory politician guest in genuine alarm, 'What are *we* to do?' On leaving the BBC, Bird announced she'd like to become a Tory MP.

The next day the *Daily Record* tabloid paper published its infamous 'Vow' on the front cover, a promise made by the three Unionist party leaders of more unspecified powers if Scotland voted 'No' to autonomy. BBC gave the empty Vow full coverage in all news bulletins, radio and television, plus political discussion 'shows,' in contravention of Referenda rules. Almost immediately Gordon Brown announced he had a swift timetable agreed for a commission to pull together a list of new powers. He gave no evidence of how he had secured a timetable. He would see to it Westminster kept its promise. To make the claim he hijacked an already existing Internet-based petition, a promise he would guarantee. This was self-deception on a grand scale. He had no influence. He could barely stop a taxi in the street let alone swing the British State to an understanding with Scotland. Nevertheless, the BBC made the most of his self-aggrandisement

The BBC's intervention was topped by one of their London-based political reporters – Nick Robinson, a confirmed Tory – who asked Scotland's first minster, Alex Salmond, why the public should trust his judgement rather than the barons of big business who deal in millions of pounds every day, as if they were honest businessmen and he looked after the canteen sweets and chocolate dispenser. The question arrived when Salmond was in a temper at the false news the Royal Bank of Scotland was moving staff south, in truth only moving its brass plaque. The BBC omitted to make the truth known.

Every week, in news items and political debates, BBC journalists dutifully repeated how Scotland's North Sea oil was running out no matter where that falsehood emanated. This was topped by false alarms of the SNP cutting emergency wards in hospitals. One piece of black propaganda followed another. The Mad Hatter's tea party was now in full swing, and the result was obvious on the bleak morning of September 19th when it became clear a large number of 'Yes' voters had switched to 'No' in the final days before the vote.

In a page 5 column, alert readers discovered John Boothman BBC Scotland's Head of News and Current affairs had been transferred back to BBC London. He lost a grievance complaint against him taken out by Zoe MacDonald, a BBC camerawoman, daughter of the late admired nationalist politician Margo MacDonald, after she recorded him being abusive about her and her mother. Claim of impartial news gathering took another blow.

The backlash to the BBC's aggressive anti-independence stance did not abate. Still in auto-pilot anti-SNP mode, BBC Scotland reported Unionist thugs attacking peaceful, disappointed 'Yes' voters in Glasgow's George Square as a battle *both* had started. For once, the BBC was forced to retract the lie. A politicised nation energised for empowerment was not going to take the crap and go home to watch BBC television, hoodwinked. The BBC had acted as a mouth-piece for the British government, a third force against liberty, successful in altering the course of Scotland's history, delaying the modernisation of its democratic structures and economy. The BBC's reputation was in tatters. It would never recover.

In Alex Salmond's autobiographical account of the 2014 independence referendum *The Dream Will Never Die* he remarks upon the general behaviour of the BBC. He has a few pleasant things to say of BBC Scotland's handling of a couple of panel-audience participation debates, but of BBC News reports he thinks otherwise – 'malicious' is his judgement. And that is how many people saw the BBC's output and from it adduced BBC's attitude to a country the corporation assumes is North Britain but retains an ancient name.

One final colonial insult: the ultra-naive guardians of the City of Edinburgh, preparing for the build of Scotland's parliament at the foot of the High Street, gifted a large area of land a mile away, at the top of Leith Walk, given to the BBC to sit its new Scottish headquarters. Where else should the United Kingdom's premier news gathering service be but next to Scotland's resurrected seat of democracy? Parliament construction underway, the BBC reneged on the deal and sold the land off to a developer for a reputed £10 million, and skulked off to Glasgow, money it its London coffers. The city's councillors did not include legislation in the contract of sale for the land to be handed back to the city in event of BBC bosses changing their mind. The city fathers and mothers had not decolonised their minds. They were duped by the duplicity of the British State's mouthpiece.

For all its feverish propaganda and disinformation to defame and divert, BBC London and BBC Scotland succeeded in informing Scots they desperately needed their own broadcasting company.

31

THE GOSPEL ACCORDING TO THE ALBIONITES

AND it came to pass that there existed a fertile land called Caledonia, a wild and verdant place abundant in all the fish of the water and the sea around, and all the fowl of the air and the cliffs, and the fruits that grow upon bush and tree in the earth below, and the beasts of the field, an infinite cornucopia of nature's bounty, enough that any man or woman or child doth want and need never ask for more.

AND it was that Caledonia lived in troubled peace with its Neighbour, Albion. Caledonia did not prosper, for the people of Caledonia were a purblind people who did accept their place under Heaven's vast firmament was to serve the superiority and the power of Albion. And they giveth Albion all that Caledonia owned and created in return for Albion's protection and their survival so that they may ward the people's fearfulness of untold, and unknown enemies as Albion did warn. It was so written in the Scriptures according to Albion.

AND there arose a Man of the People in Caledonia named Dissent who did spake his thoughts to them. "Why is it we maketh one thing, and we groweth another, yet all things thereby and therein remaineth the Albionites possession?"

AND hearing this, the Albionites did answer thus: "It is written, all that you maketh, and all that you groweth, must be pooled and shared, for it doth unite us as one. And we are stronger for the mutual nourishment."

AND the Man Named Dissent was not content for he did ask again, "If we are as one why is it that as you groweth stronger we groweth weaker? You taketh our tithe, and dill and cumin, our kindling, our cattle and our amphora of oil, and have neglected the weightier matters of justice and mercy and faithfulness that you promised in return for all we giveth thee. These you ought to have done, without accepting the others."

AND the Albionites did answer thus, "It is written we are stronger because we are stronger together. A righteous mind will not question these things, but accept what must be, must be. Be thee not full of envy or deceit for we Albionites have removed the burden of life's weightier matters from thy shoulders. Rejoice, rejoice for thy freedoms."

AND the Man named Dissent did consider the Word of the Albionites, and seeing it the image of a circle, revolving infinite and forever to the beginning from where it began, was disconsolate and not comforted, and did ask again, "We giveth thee all that we maketh, and all that we growth and yet we are servants, vassals and nomads whereas thee are kings and queens, lords and gods. Pooling and sharing becometh fooling and scaring."

AND the Albionites answered thus, "Be content, for it is written in the Commandments that so long as we are your Neighbour no other tribe dare smite thee, so long shall thee be safe in all that you do, and in all that thee think, and so it shall be for thy children, and thy children's children. Our laws sayeth we inherited thy Kingdom. Furthermore, if you love us, so you will keep our Commandments. And we know that for those who love Albion, all things work together for good, and for those who are called according to Our purpose."

AND the Man named Dissent did ponder upon the Albionite's Word but was greatly vexed, and did ask again, "If it is written We are stronger together, why is it that *Thou* do not give unto us all that *Thou* maketh, and all that *Thou* groweth?"

AND at this the Albionites grew impatient and did answer thus, "We are The Chosen One. Hast thou a problem with that, Mate?"

And their anger did abate and they soften and added, "Do nothing from rivalry or conceit, but in humility count others more significant than yourselves. It is your humility that makes you a good Neighbour."

AND the Man named Dissent did consider the rebuke, and told of Their message unto His People. And He answered truthfully saying, the Word of the Albionites passeth all understanding.

AND the People did speak of the Man named Dissent as a leader, and yet others as a false Pharisee, a proselytiser, and a vagabond, and others asked, "Please, what is a proselytiser?"

AND it was that the Man named Dissent promised there was a better land than the one they tilled and seeded and harvested, not out with their land but actually their land, and that it should belong to them one and all. And He did scorn the naysayers, Jeremiahs and Jonas as Ministers of Fear who were forsaken and lost. And unmoved by the wails and woes of unbelievers, stood up again and did ask the Albionites, "By whose hand were thee anointed The Chosen One, for nowhere is it written in any Commandment there is a Chosen One?"

AND it was that the Albionites became agitated and angry, and spake unto the People of Caledonia a parable thus, "Imagine that all we give thee is like an oval of Divine Bread we have baketh. The Bread is divided into two. One half is ours to use for fashioning weapons to keep our lands safe from our enemies. The other half is ours to use for our money lenders so that they may thrive and bring wealth to our households. But the third part of the Divine Bread, that shall be yours that you may rejoice and prosper, for so it is written."

AND the Man named Dissent was deeply troubled by this Scripture, and did repeat the parable of the Albionites to the people of Caledonia saying, "One and one doth not, *in all bloody eternity*, maketh three, but it doth maketh us poor and poorer."

AND the people of Caledonia did recognise the Man named Dissent as a prophet except every thirteen who, favouring the Albionites, countenanced him a troublesome meddler. And there began a great contemplation in the land of Caledonia, and a great gnashing of teeth, and drinking of fermented grape waters, followed by a gushing of Truth, and hearing of this the Albionites did blow a great release of esteem, and warn the Caledonians their heads would not be anointed or their cup overfloweth if they denied the Albionites their place in the firmament. In anger they did say, "Thy prophet is only flesh and blood. Forsake him or we shall divert the river of life from thy fertile banks and thy banks from thy cities until thee bridle and fall down before us."

AND it was then that the People of Caledonia knew the Albionites were a haughty People, and an abomination. And they stood up *as one*, and did say with *one voice*:

"We shall write our own Word and live by our own Law; and we shall keep all we grow and all we earn, and all we maketh with our hands and the sweat of our brow, yet shall we not covet our Neighbour's land, nor the goods therein, for *no one* is The Chosen One."

AND so it came to pass that the land of Albion did cease to be neither senior nor superior to the people of Caledonia, or live off the sweat and toil of Caledonia. And the Caledonians ceased being grieved by various trials, so that the tested genuineness of their faith in them self grew and they became wise and confident, and learned how to be themselves and speak in their own tongue, that overthrowing servitude was more precious than gold that perishes though it is tested by fire. And the People did finally inherit the Kingdom of Caledonia as theirs not only in name, and they did begin to create a heaven in their land and prosper under the sun's beneficent balm, and the people did eat of the fruit of the trees, and the wheat in the fields, and the fish in the sea, giving respect to the land and beasts thereon that shared the green earth and the blue ocean. And the People begat sons and daughters of virtue and merit who carried the Word to Their Children.

AND Albion did understand that neither man nor woman could be a slave to their commandments, that all people were free to think for themselves and enjoy liberty to the fullest extent of their laws for the common good. And the Albionites did say "Let no man seek his own good, but the good of his neighbour."

And thereby did both tribes live in mutual respect and harmony, for so it was written.

Amen.

32

GEORGE FORREST, PLANT HUNTER

Next time you wander through a garden centre hunting for a particular plant and leaving with ten you never meant to buy, or visit a botanical garden, you are sure to have bought or admired a plant discovered in a far off land by a daring, fearless Scottish plant hunter. Too many lost their lives in the pursuit of beautiful flora and the arboreal. I would think the name of botanist David Douglas is a good example of the breed, remembered because of one tree named after him, now growing all over Scotland, the Douglas-Fir.

Pseudotsuga menziesii or *P. douglasii* is a conifer species from the Pacific north-west of North America. It was brought here in 1857 and liked Scotland so much it stayed and proliferated. I have five growing on the hillside near my home, stout and wide spreading winter protection from the fierce chilling winds that blow through the glen. Owls love its cover from the elements. A barn owl has taken to one as its hooting and hunting post. Douglas had an eye for an unknown spruce or fir: Sitka Spruce, Sugar Pine, Western White Pine, Ponderosa Pine, Lodgepole Pine, Monterey Pine, Grand Fir, Noble Fir and several other conifers that transformed our landscape and timber industry, as well as collecting numerous garden shrubs and herbs such as the Flowering Currant and the primrose genus *Douglasii*.

In 1832 Douglas, born in Scone in Perthshire, wrote a letter home saying "You will begin to think shortly I manufacture pines at my pleasure." Douglas was ferocious tree collector in the great Victorian mould, only he stole nothing, no great works of art, tribal totemic images or gold. He did not tear sculpture off buildings and sit it in a museum in Glasgow or London. He gathered seeds and cuttings. It was just as well he was a man of singular obsession. Our gardens and parks would be the barer without him. He died an early death when he visited the Sandwich Islands by falling into a wild bull pit when an angry bull was still in it. He was thirty-five years of age. The lingering rumour that he might have been killed for his purse of money and thrown in the bull pit by a disgruntled local is not an ameliorating substitute to being gored by a mad bull. (Nor does it help to find a biography of Douglas praised as an *English* botanist.)

There is another plant hunter almost unknown to the general public, a botanist who collected thousands of plants and shrubs like a kid might raid a sweetie shop, superior to the better known Sir Joseph Hooker, the twenty-year director of Kew Gardens, and Frank Kingdon-Ward, the latter a man who had no sense of direction, forever getting lost for days in search of a plant, forced to eat them to survive until rescued. If Beethoven or Mozart is considered top of the 'A' List classical composers, George Forrest is at that level, his life cut short like Mozart's by the physical challenges of his profession.

He was a great plant hunter, a true renaissance man of the early nineteenth century, with the near perfect name for a person whose whole career was hunting for new shrubs and plants. He brought to Scotland thousands of botanical specimens and seeds, often at high risk to himself, among them the beautiful blue Himalayan poppy, *Meconopsis betonicifolia*, and lent his name to hundreds of specimens that grace our municipal parks, private gardens and window boxes. There are thousands of his dried seed and root specimens stacked to the ceiling in the shelves of Edinburgh's Royal Botanic Garden where he worked. His is story is one of flower power. But he had a self-imposed quest, an obsession, which he never realised, to find the hidden valley, the Shangri-La of unique rhododendrons and flowers.

Forrest sought plants in remote, unexplored regions of China, particularly in the remote south-western province of Yunnan generally regarded as the most bio-diverse province of that vast land, a dangerous country for a 'long nose' to wander with a dog and two pack mules. Forrest was an Indiana Jones character, right down, or up, to his battered fedora hat. He carried a whip, a rifle, a leather satchel, wore a leather jacket, and often rode a horse or mule. I tried BBC television on the idea of a dramatised series of Forrest's exploits, a cross between Indiana Jones and Monty Don, or between *Gardener's World* and *David Attenborough Gone Wild*. But the BBC did not take the bait. Commercially, it has to be a winner, grabbing two already established audiences, the horticulturalist and the action man fan.

There's a claim film producer and director George Lucas modelled his adventurer on Forrest, but it's highly unlikely Lucas ever heard of him. He's more likely to have based his Indiana Jones on Professor Challenger, a fictitious character the creation of another Scot, Sir Arthur Conan Doyle in his novel *The Lost World*. Lucas was reared on old movies, and he's on record as saying he half-based the character on Ian Fleming's anti-hero James Bond, but placed him decades earlier.

If one has never heard of George Forrest that's probably because of Kew Gardens and the BBC. Had he worked at Kew Gardens and not Edinburgh's Botanic Gardens we would know all about him and his black Labrador dog. They would feature in gardening books, BBC travel documentaries, and an exotic Scottish-Chinese drama series *The Plant Huntsman* would be raking in thousands worldwide. Yet Forrest is revered by botanists on both sides of the border, but for London researchers, Kew Gardens is BBC's first stop, and that institution has its own plant hunters to promote.

Forrest was a son of Larbert, north of Falkirk, born in 1873. Later his parents moved to Kilmarnock and opened a drapery store. The area proved a good training ground for Forrest's natural inclination to explore. His father's side had tough craftsmen and businessmen in his family, his grandfather a blacksmith. On his mother's side he had seafarers and adventurers. Exploring was in his blood.

Education was compulsory in Scotland until aged thirteen. Forrest was so smart he stayed on until he was eighteen. He showed early interest in plants by collecting seeds from the Isle of Arran, but a probable need of cash stopped him attending university. In his twenties he took work in a pharmaceutical chemist which turned out to be great serendipity. Plant-derived drugs were the order of the day and new products always in demand. He soon got down to collecting plants and testing them for any efficacy against ailments.

What happened next was sheer luck. A prosperous uncle left him a small inheritance and George used it to visit Australia. There he contacted relatives, tried his hand at sheep farming and then gold digging. Digging for gold was a rough, tough existence, but George gained the respect of older men for his resilience, and his cleverness in finding water to sustain him while camping under trees in the bush, weeks on end. He found nuggets of gold but not his fortune.

When he returned to Scotland he had blossomed – if that's the right description – into an explorer of 'true grit', according to relatives. Australia had whetted his appetite for more travel only it was the diversity of plants that interested him.

George settled in a cottage in Loanhead, outside Edinburgh, back then a small mining village. It was a typical wee Scottish parish, with a smiddy, a store, a greengrocer, a kirk, and a horse trough in the main street. For a young man keen on faraway place overseas Loanhead must have seemed like a boring tool hut at the end of the garden.

Forrest was a man who arrived at the right time in history. China was opening up to foreign traders and tourists. Missionaries were the first out there. It was a place ready to be explored by plant hunters. He met his botanical destiny by a series of welcome coincidences, and some luck. His brother introduced him to a Glasgow natural history society for whom George was asked to collect plants. No sooner started, Forrest found a stone coffin and inside some human bones on a weekend's walk at a reservoir near Loanhead. He took the bones to the National Museum of Scotland. The secretary of the Antiquaries of Scotland, John Abercromby, was impressed by Forrest's "appealing, open, friendly, uncomplicated, and enthusiastic manner" but above all "his eager curiosity for plant hunting." In short measure he introduced him to Professor Isaac Bayley Balfour, Regius Keeper of Edinburgh's Royal Botanic Gardens (RBG).

"Dear Professor Balfour, Do you know of any society looking for a collector of botanical specimens abroad? I have recently come acquainted with a young fellow by the name of Forrest who lives out at Loanhead. He is collected specimens of plants in the three Lothians for a society in Glasgow. He would rather travel than stay at home. If you care to see him he looks the right sort of man. Yours sincerely, John Abercromby."

Balfour made Forrest a tentative offer, "It occurred to me you could take care of the dried plants in the Herbarium here. The lad who has left got ten shilling as week …" Forrest leapt at the chance. The job offered security and training. The year was 1895. Balfour was a dynamic leader, dedicated to the advancement of Edinburgh's burgeoning botanic gardens. In that goal he was ably assisted by well qualified staff, all of whom came to be close loyal friends of Forrest. The Herbarium was in the RBG's Caledonian Hall. Dried, pressed plants were sent there from all over the world. Forrest had arrived at plant heaven, even if they were all dead specimens wrapped in blotting paper.

He began work carefully mounting, labelling, and classifying them – learning Latin part of the experience! It was there he assimilated the vast diversity of the plant kingdom, tropical plants, Himalayan specimens, American plants, many known only to grow where they were discovered. New specimens fascinated him.

It was at the RBG that Forrest met his future wife, Clementina Traill – a fine name for a female botanist. She was intelligent, tall, slim, elegant, and like Forrest shared a sense of humour and a passion for flowers. Until that stage in his life it was debateable George realised so few plants had ever come out of China for the rest of the world to marvel and admire. One day some seeds arrived from missionaries working in Yunnan province. Forrest studied them and got hooked. Clementina encouraged him to seek more in China's Yunnan district.

As luck would have it another instance of serendipity arrived at his feet. Arthur Bulley was a Liverpool cotton broker keen on large gardens and, as was the fashion of the times, large collections of plants no one else had in their gardens. He had just bought a large area of land near the Welsh border, now known as Ness Gardens. He wrote to Balfour at the RBG asking if any of his staff would be keen to explore the Yunnan province of China where he had heard "Gentians, Peonies, Anemones, and Iris grew in profusion." Bulley wanted his collection of rare flora to rival the best. He didn't want to waste money on slow postage to and from missionaries. "Send a man to collect plants!" Balfour wrote to him, "There is a man here, George Forrest, who is on the lookout for a billet such as you describe. He will write to you." And the rest, as they say, is history.

A lot of Forrest's time in China collecting plants was not only arduous, but dangerous. There is something ironic about surviving journeys full of hardship and then setting up camp among amazing plants and shrubs in mountain valleys surrounding by beautiful exotic flowers, while French missionaries you stayed with only days before are slain. The Yangtze and Mekong rivers harboured groups of brigands and robbers making travel in those regions highly risky.

Filled with confidence and a sense of adventure, Forrest managed to reach Dali, Yunnan in 1904. He used the winter's months to learn Chinese and helped with a vaccinating campaign to immunise the local villagers against smallpox. There, in 1905, he recruited a small team to assist him on his first expedition. As is the colonial Englishman's habit, English mercenaries had entered Tibet and upset Tibetan lamas by their crassness and exploitation sufficient to turn them militant. The lamas began exciting the locals into revolt. British nationals were hunted out and killed, as were French incomers. Foreign dwellings were burned to the ground, possessions looted. Forrest knew nothing of these bloody events on his arrival and only by timing avoided them in his search for the 'land of exotic rhododendron'. But a group of lamas got wind of Forrest's expedition and followed it. Forrest thought he was safe by staying at the mission was Père Jean Armand Soulé, discoverer of the rhododendron species *R. Souliei*. (A predominately white with pink edged shrub with round trusses.) Forrest had gone to meet Soulé to discuss where the hidden valley of his dream shrubs might lay. Soulé asked Forrest to leave for his life was in danger. The Tibetans might not distinguish a Scot's accent from an English one, or care.

Forrest was loath to cut and run, and would not to leave people behind who might be killed. Hearing raiding parties were not known for their acts of mercy, Forrest's natural leadership skills took over, and he appealed to all 100 men, women and children staying and working at the mission to follow him into the valley's jungle vegetation to hide. A desperate flight took place, the straggling line moving past a lamasery in Batang where a single loud sound would alert their potential killers. They got about a couple of miles distance or so and looked back only to witness their beloved mission burning. In defeatist mood, the people he had led sat down to await their fate. Forrest had gone to a vantage point to see where the armed Tibetans were that were following the party, saw them in the near distance and shouted a warning which the group ignored. Forrest's expedition team fled. The main group were slaughtered.

Alone, Forrest writes that he "crashed through the dense undergrowth, found a large rock, hid behind it into the dark night hours, and readied his rifle for his last moments on earth". Happily, a Tibetan scout party passed him by. In the morning's light he hid his boots for fear the prints would betray his direction. He hid in the valley for nine days. Several times he was almost caught and killed. On one occasion it is said he was warned by a French missionary miming on a slope above him that some Tibetans were not far away and he should move downstream. Throughout all this time Forrest survived on peas and wheat grains he found on the ground. Finally, he staggered into a village expecting to be chopped into pieces when he asked for food but the people gave him sanctuary and nursed him back to health from a bout of malaria. He was saved by Lisu villager, an indigenous people who also lived in the mountains of northwest Yunnan. They facilitated his concealed journey back to the safety of Talifu where they arranged to have him smuggled to safety over arduous mountain paths dressed as a Chinese peasant, a disguise he was to employ many times. Unfortunately his collection of thousands of plant specimens was destroyed. He never had time to study the beauty of the rhododendron valley through which he had moved and hidden for over a week, an irony that was not lost on him.

A lesser plant hunter would have fled China and not returned but Forrest organised the local Lisu people from his sick bed to find plants. The entire experience moulded Forrest into one of the toughest plant hunters in world and he attracted loyal trackers to his future monthly expeditions. Many of the collections he amassed were made by that hard working team led by Zhao Chengzhang whom Forrest called "Old Chao".

Back home in Scotland, he was written off as dead. Bulley his sponsor wrote to Balfour, "I feel very sick. The vile feeling that this fine young fellow was working for pay for me, and did it because he was poor, and that he lost his life in the endeavour to earn some beastly money."

Forrest returned many months later to wild celebration, joy evinced by Clementina. Together with his mentor and his sponsor, Forrest handed the RBG director bags of seeds.

Established as a superb plantsman, he married his fiancé Clementina. He refused an immediate return to China on another expedition to be at the birth of his first child. By 1920 he had made four trips to China, usually with his close friend George Litton, Forrest still searching for that heavenly valley, his reputation rising with each trip.

Forrest guarded his plant finds by staking out the ground; trip wiring the area, and camping near it toting a rifle, guarding against thieves and loss of rare specimens. Unlike Indiana Jones, Forrest didn't have a convenient seaplane waiting on a river to rescue him, but escape he did, time after time, often dressed in Chinese attire as paddy field farmer. Though it played havoc with his health, managing to escape death saved by local villagers, "my ower guid luck", he always continued his quest to bring back plants and seeds new to the western world. He never turned back or gave up. He knew discovery of rare plants would make his name if not his fortune, together with his friend Old Chao, the most prolific plant hunter known to the world of botany. His experiences formed his character, his Scots tenacity a strong motivation to plough on through good days and bad. He wrote:

> "Wild looking fellows, they were, dressed as Tibetans, and armed with swords, guns and crossbows, and the hated poisoned arrows – death from the slightest scratch. All that after a terrible, trying journey ... I lost a mule, it fell over a precipice breaking its back, the two cases it carried smashed to pieces. I carried some of the baggage myself."

Yet only days later he was writing:

> "I witnessed several species of meconopsis, all surprisingly lovely, miles of rhododendrons, and acres of primulas, of which I counted over a dozen species in flower, many of which I have never seen before. Those mountains have, quite rightly in my opinion, been called the flower garden of the world."

Though Forrest is best known for discovering many rhododendrons and azaleas (one he named after his wife), plants Forrest introduced included buddleias, anemones, asters, berberis, alliums, cotoneasters and primulas.

Among admiring colleagues Forrest was known for walking to his work at the Botanic gardens from Loanhead and standing at his desk. But in time, the privations of foot-slogging travel, climbing mountainous slopes, sleeping out under thunder storms, and bringing pack mules carrying sacks of plant seeds back to camp, before transferred to sailing ships from India, took its toll on his health. He died suddenly while on a field trip in Yunnan province in 1932. He was only 49 years of age when he died of a massive heart attack.

Forrest, nor the Scots family nursery grower James Veitch who came to prominence at that time, would have foreseen that the wild rhododendron, *R. ponticum* – the pale pink variety seen everywhere – would become such a scourge in Scotland. Poisonous to animals, sheep and cattle learn to avoid eating the wild variety, but in winter and snow may be forced to chew a leaf or two if starving. If caught early enough, the poison can be cured by nothing more than administering a brew of black tea by bottle and teat. Farmers and shepherds have known about the antidote for years, tea combined with a little bicarbonate of soda. In the Isle of Arran infestation was reputed to be so bad a report recommended shrubs bulldozed out the ground at a few million pounds cost, but if left too long, would cost many millions more. A campaign of eradication was attempted by Arran council but not sustained. The problem is the seeds of the shrub thrive in disturbed ground.

Forrest could well have watched Nepal fisherman use the leaves of *R. arboreum* to incapacitate fish caught for food, and the juice used to repel bed bugs. In China the flowers of *Rhododendron molle* are pulverised and used as an insecticide sold in drug stores. It is effective in wiping out vegetable chewing insect pests including the rapacious Colorado beetle. As insects develop resistance to synthetic pesticides the toxin in *molle* could acquire commercial use. Rhododendron are used by the Chinese, Nepalese and Turks for all sorts of medicinal purposes, the flowers turned into chutney to cure diabetes, diarrhoea, rheumatism, headaches and stomach aches, but great care must be taken in how the toxicity of the plant is used. I have a specimen of black rhododendron. In full bloom the flowers are dramatic and visually stunning. Legend has it that Chinese warriors soaked their swords in the juice of the crushed flowers of the black variety before going into battle.

Forrest's legacy is phenomenal. You won't find a statue erected to George Forrest's memory – too many erected to generals on horsebacks – but you are likely to have plants he discovered in your garden, or flowers in a bowl in your house. When you delve into his plant collecting career you realise he put Indiana Jones to shame.

George Forrest thought his success at finding over one hundred rhododendron species "only scratched the surface." And without realising it, his quest to find the rarest of rarest rhododendrons was achieved although he was never to live long enough to understand how or why. He reckoned the rhododendrons must have a place of origin undreamed off by plant hunters, the place he had thought of a Shangri La. He never found his fabled home for the simple reason we know now rhododendrons are 20 million years older than the Himalayan Mountains. Yunnan did not exist when rhododendrons proliferated in the lush valleys of China. Botanists believe the species began 90 million years ago when the common ancestor of the family *Ericaceae* evolved a way to interact with fungi and create a wide range of flowers and colours, including the black rhododendron

I end as I began; there is a wonderful drama series awaiting an ambitious producer and a talented scriptwriter – the adventurers of the world's greatest plant collector, George Forrest. Please cast a Scot in the role.

33

THE TWILIGHT OF THE IMPERIUM

Empires expand voraciously in a never-ending search for sustenance: the greater the number of nations controlled by the imperium, the greater the cost to keep the natives docile and subservient. The invading soldiers billeted among the people to keep control have to be fed and housed. The flaw in pursuing universal domination is the one the imperium overlook – in time, the centre of the empire implodes. Just ask the Romans.

There comes a time in history when empires cease to exist and become symbolic. It begins with a disintegration of social systems, the poor getting poorer, the rich richer, food shortages, spiralling costs of everything. The circulation of money becomes scarce while ever increasing taxes are spent on acquiring more and more armaments to keep up a pretence at impenetrable strength, the wealthy protecting their privileges by pulling back to safe ground. Corruption is endemic. People of ability and conscience withdraw from the fray. With the strain of conducting wars around the empire's borders, and putting down internal skirmishes in the territories, the best talent is sent to quell the uprisings leaving the mediocre to take over positions of power at the empire's centre.

When dire warnings of the coming of Goths or Reds stop frightening the populace you invent internal demons out to destroy our harmonious lifestyle and steal our pensions. Muslims we brought to Britain are our current evil. It used to be the Irish. Battered by so many existential spectres, governed by people of high ambition and low ability, who'd never be employed anywhere in positions of authority, respect for leadership collapses, and in turn leaders turn against the people for being so ungrateful.

Reds, why do those pesky critters get elected to parliament? Some politicians are unable to tell the difference between communism and socialism. It doesn't matter, as far as they are concerned, they are one and the same, nasty ideas to create a minimum living wage, protect the national health service and labour unions, each calculated to undermine the capitalist system.

We are witnessing the demise of England's empire, the last derelict sunset, with Scotland yet to be set free. I can't see Wales wanting free of England anytime soon, but there are some among them trying hard to turn a principality into a free state. Wales being close to the centre of an empire, London, sees them easily controlled. There was a mid-nineteenth century report on Welsh education, the outcome of which was easily predicted – it was conducted by three English education inspectors for the House of Commons in 1846. The inspectors saw the Wales as a backward nation. The colonial adjudicators grabbed the opportunity to tell the indigenous people how to better themselves. A glance at the section on the Welsh language illuminates their mentality:

> *"The Welsh language is a vast drawback to Wales and a manifold barrier to the moral progress and commercial prosperity of the people. It bars the access of improving knowledge to their minds. Because of their language, the mass of the Welsh people are inferior to the English in every branch of practical knowledge and skill. The Welsh language distorts the truth, favours fraud, and abets perjury."*

That is some indictment; the people's language keeps them poor and dim. The inspectors sum up stating "The Welsh language is a disastrous barrier to all moral improvement and popular improvement in Wales." They were able to speak in those authoritarian terms because they had outlawed the Gaelic language in Scotland

and shut down Old Scots spoken in schools and universities. The first task of the usurper is to ban or demolish the local language, depict it as inferior to that of the invader. The inspectors did not like the Welsh non-conformist religion. They thought there was something lacking in the character of the Welsh. They could have been writing about the plantation African whose entire thoughts and life were out of step with the white man. The Scots are quite familiar with those tactics.

The Irish will be plain daft to subsume Northern Ireland in the Republic in a day, taking on its poverty and religious bigotry and screwing their recovery from the 2008 bank crash. They need time to allow the Northern Irish to understand they are one of the same people and the British happy to see the back of them. A United Ireland is a fine ideal, but drive across the border south to north and to my eyes even the quality of light degrades. The European Union will need to fork out a lot of cash to assist the north unite with south without too much pain. People will accept the inevitable if they see their rights increase.

Almost every civilisation except the Chinese, more concerned with keeping 'big nose' Europeans out, 'you all look the same to us' – has tried to build and retain an empire and lost it, but not before impoverishing the land it left behind, scorched and burned, removed of its treasures. The treasures amassed by Venice's Doges Palace are an example of how imperialists steal everything. Scotland stands in jeopardy of the same fate if not clever and swift to block England's wealth grab.

The Spanish in South America is a case in point. Spanish conquistadors all but wiped out one civilisation after another, by sword and syphilis. Chased out of Mozambique by the forces of independence, the Portuguese wasted everything they left behind them. We know what Hitler and his Nazi troops did to make Europe a German state. Everybody has had a go at colonialism one time or another. The French, pretty well linked to the emperium, was once the dominant power in Europe under the gifted general of generals, Napoleon. It had a second empire overseas, the eastern seaboard of Canada and chunks of north and east Africa, easy pickings.

The only reason Britain got to own a few thousands scattered Aborigine tribes and a lot of kangaroos, collectively called Australia, was because Captain James Cook notified the Admiralty of French ships sniffing around the Great Australian Bight. That was warning enough for the English government to send thousands of cheap and not so cheerful convicts from England's over-crowded prisons to colonise that great continent, laying claim to it for the British Crown, two aims achieved in one simple colonial move.

To have an empire you first must convince the populace they are under attack from outside sources; their taxes best spent in making weapons and sending legions of soldiers and sailors to faraway lands. Here we are with England rekindling its hatred of the French, and anything remotely European it cannot patronise. This is a massive contradiction in the English political psyche. The scouting wing of western expansionism, NATO, warns of Russian evil while it itself expands as far as its useless aircraft carriers can take it. (Useless, meaning we have few war planes to put on its deck.) England withdraws from Europe while paying for NATO to protect Europe of which the French are a large part.

NATO was created so that the United States could dominate Western Europe, militarily, politically, and economically. When the Soviet Union's economy collapsed, and President Gorbachev announced he would create a democratic Russian Federation, NATO had no role, so it found another while continuing to do the same job. At its July 11, 2018, meeting, NATO approved new steps to contain Russia. Those included two new military commands and expanded efforts against cyber warfare and counter-terrorism. No wonder Russia under President Putin is ruthlessly proactive. NATO is under American control.

As I said, the centre collapses into itself because the edges of the once impenetrable empire stretch and stretch and get thinner and thinner. Paying for NATO's upkeep is ruinous but it helps deluded politicians feel they still have an empire, and the coffers of America's expensive weapon makers like Lockheed Martin filled to the brim.

Observing England's petty politicians battling among themselves for absolute power and control, and lying to secure it, is an ignominious sight. They talk of freeing us from government while eliminating freedoms. They extol equality while sowing the seeds of poverty. They talk of transparency while closing doors as fast as they can bolt them. They sell us open democracy while supporting tyrants, despots and dictators. They offer the poor and the vulnerable security while acting like cuckoos in the nest.

Our neo-liberal government tells us we should pay taxes. The society Margaret Thatcher said did not exist, but does – the wealthy society – do not want to pay taxes. They are given tax havens to hide their wealth from the taxman. Society sees infrastructure degrade, roads, buildings, schools and hospitals, thus procuring the downfall of English power. The rich show little concern because they are rich and have no use for our public roads, schools or hospitals. If you work hard you too can be like us, they try to convince. By appealing to our worst instincts, greed and envy, we participate voluntarily in our own downfall.

By 1956 almost 80% of British citizens paid tax. Coincidentally, it was the greatest decade of liberal and material advances. Britain has the greatest expansion of tax haven colonies in the world. None of the unionist parties have suggested closing them down, merely 'disciplining' them. (We were pulled out of the EU weeks before legislation was introduced to outlaw tax havens.) The powerful and the privileged will always protect their assets.

On the disintegration of empires you are sure to have wars. Our warlords are always ready to squander what little savings we have on killing people to keep our nation great. The Covid pandemic helped to put away thousands of us, and suck taxes from the Treasury to cope with the near cessation of working life. The UK Government, on the other hand, blew millions in gifts given to Tory-friendly companies to provide medical equipment during the pandemic, a lot of which went straight into accounts in tax havens.

Scotland attaining its independence for the umpteenth time in its ancient existence accelerates the death of England's empire. When

Scotland finally achieves political liberty England will become a very small country indeed. This can only be a good thing for Scotland, Wales, and the Irish, and for the rest of the world, pretty miserable for the English. We can give a sigh of relief in our quest for civilised self-reliance, which is the best wisdom I can muster to avoid finishing on a sententious note.

34

DEFINE WOMEN

I begin with the obvious, a woman is an adult female human, her reproductive organs fully matured ready to conceive. A man who likes to dress in women's clothes is *not* a woman. A man who wants to be a woman and act like one is a man who is *not* a woman but enjoys pretending he is one.

When I first heard the odd term *trans* spoken I took little notice, another diminutive that would drift out of sight to make way for the latest fashionable word. It was not a new intercontinental language spoken in progressive circles, like the early twentieth century attempt to have Esperanto taught in schools as an international auxiliary tongue. The British Empire saw that English was the accepted single homogeneous tongue the world's nations must use for trade, commerce, science and technology. Since withdrawing from the European Union people living in the EU are abandoning English for their own language as primary means of communication. On the other hand, ***trans*** is an umbrella term to describe people whose gender is not the same as, or ***does not*** sit comfortably with, the sex they were assigned at birth. Who could have guessed it would be used to impose laws on entire countries, firebomb women's rights and see the career of individuals destroyed.

A lot of men and some women are scared to challenge the 'transgender' nonsense that fills pages of newspapers, has members of institutional committees at each other's throats, and dominates

Internet social site discussions. I readily admit I was bewildered by the arguments and apprehensive about writing on the subject.

The disparate terminology and opinions bandied about cause the curious to withdraw, others repelled by the aggression used to push transgender claims on inequality, especially when some transgender people are quick to settle a score with society. The reality of regressive laws mean we should speak out and reverse what is nothing less than claiming apples fall up the way when they leave the tree. By devious routes and stealth this warped doctrine has managed to become legislation in various countries, advocated by politicians for reasons that are obscure. Scotland's national administration has embraced it with a vigour one wishes they had applied to securing Scotland's independence.

In effect, the SNP has declared war on women, the First Minister stating that objections to proposed laws are "not valid". Seeing a cash-strapped City of Edinburgh Council put £5 million of the rates into creating single sex public toilets should tell women fighting to retain their rights they have a battle on their hands. When our institutions are against women's very existence they should regroup into a mass movement if they are to repeal laws, bills, and heal the damage done so far. And men should not stand idly by.

As a male of the species, one who penned a much praised screenplay exploring the sources of male aggression on women, physical and psychological, I cannot believe the fiasco has gotten to the point where outbursts of candour are denounced by the transgender lobby, or that entire swathes of female society feel lost for political representation. The surprise is t knowing the transgender lobby is very small but very loud.

Do parents know what is being taught in our schools on this subject? Some of the subject is confused with the trans-sexual, also cross-dressing men and drag queens. Somewhere, lurking among the confusion, are men who prey on children, keen to have the age of consent lowered to suit their sexual obsessions and inadequacies. I wish children to be knowledgeable *not* kept innocent, but trans gender theory is a dangerous muddle. Scots are supposed to be famous for our down-to-earth common sense. And yet women working for the Stonewall organisation are leading the transgender contortions as if biological fact.

Experts tell us the '*trans*' gender does not exist. The existence of the creed alarms. How did it get so far, so fast and so easily accepted? I see it as a patriarchal invention to make the categories of women *and* men invisible, to substitute feminism with something more generic. It undermines the feminist struggle for equality. As one feminist put it, "The word '*gender*' has replaced those of '*women*' and '*men*'; '*gender violence law*' has replaced patriarchy, feminism, feminist struggle." To my certain knowledge, trans people share the same civil and human rights as the rest of us, which makes the screams and squeals from certain frantic quarters very odd.

A man can become a woman just on saying that's what he wants to be. And he can retain his beard and join all-women sports. The radical feminist Germaine Greer who knows her subject inside out and is not someone to annoy by spouting waffle (I am six feet, she's taller) does not mince her words. "If I put on a long brown coat with big black buttons and a pair of ear muffs, that doesn't make me a fucking bloodhound!"

As the gender debate has escalated so has the tiny trans lobby increased its demands. The debate is bitter. Suddenly 'queer theory' is defused, sexuality a fluid thing. I do not recall any societal threat to their existence, but here we are liable to be faced by a long-running perverse conflict. Having worked in theatre with trans actors, and having known a few in ordinary professions, one an accountant, another an antique dealer, their existence is part of life's rich pattern. What I see now is a profound detraction from far greater pressures on society, namely Scotland's destiny and climate change. I cannot recall voting for this grotesque trans policy, or the SNP explaining their intentions in detail to the public before an election. Like a meat hors d'oeuvres brought to vegetarian diners it arrived at our table without ordering it.

Anybody trying to study the arguments is confronted by incomprehensible discussions about the meaning of the term '*gender*'. It has gone so far that women are now the people marginalised and oppressed. A massive amount of the national party's time has been devoted to, and invested in, pushing forward legislation that will see a small group dominate the mass of the population and effectively have women disappear.

The Scottish Government has shut down honest criticism and dissent about ways and means. They have also weaponised the trans 'gender' debate and used that too to declare war on women. The first minister – still female as I write this – dismisses protest as 'not valid'. Politicians are not elected to wave aside protest, but to listen and understand its source. Helping the SNP to build this Trojan horse is their political partners, the Scottish Green party, and yet that party is also riven by the debate it has helped create and nurture.

The biological disaster that is gender identification belongs at the door of Stonewall and compliant institutions and governing bodies, using arrant nonsense to further its financial ends. Writer Sarah Ditton put the issue succinctly: "You might consider those consequences good, bad or irrelevant. But as a society we *never* got the chance to discuss them, because rather than wait for parliament to pass a bill, Stonewall simply wrote its own version of the law as it would like it to be, and then disseminated it through the training it provides to various public bodies, which have promptly fallen into line."

Ask an acquiescing politician to define what a woman is and they choke on their words, scared, as I mentioned earlier, to give a straight-forward answer. The Scottish Government has allied itself with a fraudulent cause invented by the controllers of capitalist propaganda. We are liable to be faced by the absurdity of passing laws to eliminate any reference to women and men. As it is, women are to be seen no longer the exploited class. This puts the women's equality cause back a hundred years and more.

I hear tell I will be categorised as 'transphobic' by Stonewall's supporters for expressing an opinion contrary to Stonewall's twisted orthodoxy. Galileo was offered a lighter jail sentence by the Pope Urban VIII's interrogators if he recanted, that he agreed the Earth did *not* go around the sun. He agreed. He demolished the integrity of every scientist that followed him. One has to hold tight to the truth. When archaeologists dig up the bones of a human, they can tell whether the person was male or female. They cannot tell what the person was thinking or what they believed in, but the DNA of their gender remains intact in their bones.

Whether by plan or stupidity, Stonewall has given female-hating men the opportunity to make women and motherhood vanish. A woman is merely someone who wears a dress. Astonishingly, we read that some hospital staff members face disciplinary action for not falling in line with this anti-biological, anti-human, anti-female gobbledygook. The Inquisition lives on.

35

DEATH OF A MONARCHY

Royal watchers are privileged to observe the faults of the Royal family before the rest of us, the rest of us too busy trying to get through our day always a few pound notes short of what we need to survive. When a member of the British aristocracy is caught doing something naughty they are depicted as human like you and me, so forgive them their wee peccadilloes. The current monarch, Queen Elizabeth, or Lizzie as she's affectionately called in some quarters of Scotland, has named her successor, Prince Charles. He has waited a very long time to be passed the royal chamber pot. So the time has come for us to regard the umpteenth bum on the British throne in the light, if not in eternity, of the twenty-first century, and ask if the English monarchy in Scotland's eyes is drawing to a close.

The royal family have never featured in my thoughts to the extent I felt the need to go out, buy a Union Jack and stand at the roadside waving it furiously and cheering while one of them passed by half-hidden in a bullet-proof black limousine. The earliest memory I have of anybody remotely aristocratic was Lizzie, a woman born with a face pre-modelled to be on every coin, note and stamp ever produced, ageless.

I watched the coronation of Elizabeth II in Westminster Abbey in June 1953 on a bulbous black and white goggle box in the corner of the room supplied by Radio Rentals. I was too young to question why she went around the back of the chair and off camera to be sworn in before God and His Church of England Archbishop as Elizabeth I of Scotland. She is Queen of the United Kingdom only in the mind of the colonially inclined but holds only a few powers over Scotland.

The next time I was aware of royalty's hold over our lives was the forced removal of the democratically elected prime minister of Australia, Gough Whitlam, in 1975. Like Macavity's cat that is never there, a good example of how the Queen's fingerprints are never found at the scene of the crime, the household stratagem, was the way no one was able to link her to the outrage. Whitlam, a radical liberal, wanted an end to colonial rule. He had the backing of the mass of the Australian electorate. Only recently did we discover the Queen's then personal secretary was involved. He would not put himself in such a position unless officially blessed to do the dirty deed. The Queen is never seen to be directly involved in politics but is in reality up to her diamond earrings in controlling events.

It is almost impossible to put the Queen into any perspective other than, hard working, gracious, and well rehearsed, so well protected and projected is she by the media. No one knows if she is impatient, cranky, or has a temper other than her closest intimates. An approved documentary aimed at having us believe she is mother to her siblings like any other, showed her holding a picnic with her direct family, and how she loves horses and breeding a dog with stumpy legs called a Corgi. Our media establishment figures are not about to help us get to know her better. Other than reading out loud the headlines from her latest government's manifesto at the state opening of parliament in that terribly, terribly standard nasal southern accent, we do not see what she says or does behind the mask. Yet she will remain for many in the top of the royal cavalcade of mediocrity.

She dropped her guard once when it seemed she was going to lose Scotland to a free thinking society. Her secretary coined the phrase "Think carefully about the future" spoken as she made her way past an admiring crowd of the faithful outside Crathie Kirk, her Scottish Presbyterian haunt at Barmoral Castle, a few days prior to Scotland's independence referendum. (How odd that the royal family can switch religions so easily.)

On that occasion she could not deny she had nothing to do with swaying public opinion. Not only did she utter the fateful words, but her personal secretary boasted about composing the sentence that she should speak, a journalist just happening to be nearby to emblazon the royal utterance across the front pages of newspapers and television news bulletins and divert the debate from one of Scotland's lack of democracy, to a useless debate asking what the Queen meant by the cryptic remark. We knew what she meant. It was a clever, calculated move, but a gross interference in the sovereignty of Scotland. Nowadays we know Prince Charles writes letters in support of lots of personal causes, and others letters belittling public projects he dislikes. He will not drop the habit once king.

A visit to a friendly aristocrat, Lord Carew-Pole pricked my natural subversive character. Carew Pole lives at Antony House in Cornwall, used many times as a backdrop for drama films. John is a very tall, pleasant, daffodil growing horticulturist, a man who bustles through the day with a thousand small domestic things on his estate to see to, and chairmanships to attend. When I knew him he was President of the Chelsea Flower Show. Aware of my keenness on garden design, he kindly offered two free tickets for my wife and I to beat the Chelsea crowds. They were for 6am. Misreading, I arrived at 6pm. But that's another story.

Sir John Richard Walter Reginald Carew Pole, 13th Baronet, OBE, DL was holder of the Pole baronetcy and his palatial home gifted to the English National Trust for them to pay the bills – his son has the responsibility these days to make the home zing and ring with paying visitors and remain water-tight. The baronetcy was granted to Carew Pole's ancestor by King Charles I in 1628. (All aristocracy are hyper-proud of their lengthy heritage, although not always quick to explain how the first in line got the title or what they did to be given it.) Invited to his pile, my wife got talking to his wife, Mary, Lady Carew Pole, his second wife, a lady-in-waiting to Princess Anne. His wife asked if I had signed the Visitor's Book when

I first entered the Palladian pile. "You'll find it on the Serpentine table at the main door." I knew instantly this was a command.

Off I went through a series of double-door rooms across the top floor, apprehensive of getting lost, down to the next level traversing right to left this time through more wide, high ceiling, flock wallpapered rooms festooned with oil painted portraits, and finally, breathless, down a staircase to the entrance table. There I opened a large black book and looked for a clean page to sign. On my return upstairs, Carew Pole's wife asked if I had found the book.

"Yes, and I duly signed it, 'Gareth'. I smiled as if I had accomplished a great test for the state.

"Gareth?" she asked quizzically.

"Yes, just 'Gareth'. The page was blank."

"What was written on the opposite page?" she asked.

"Charles," I said.

She took a deep breath and scowled. "I think *everyone* knows who *Charles* is!"

I cannot imagine why anyone would want to spend their adult life as a 'royal expert', but there is enough of the English variety making a living at it to fill Buckingham Palace and leave no room for its actual inhabitants. They appear out of the wainscoting like woodworm, ready to be interviewed for every programme about each and every member of Britain's royalty, garrulous about everything they do and everything they own. But they must be wondering if their comfortable days are almost at an end. They had a field day in the 1930s discussing the Yankee mountebank who was chasing one of their own. After ruling for less than one year, the feckless wastrel and confirmed partygoer Edward VIII decided he did not want the responsibility of waving to crowds from a horse-drawn carriage or limousine. He became the first English monarch to abdicate the throne voluntarily in order to marry a raunchy American divorcee, Wallis Warfield Simpson. The outraged British Government, public, and the Church of England condemned his decision. Hey presto, within a couple of years and some massaging from the press, all was well. Proud English thanked God they were ruled by a new king in line and demeaned by a suffocating class system again even though the new king, George VI, suffered from a bad stutter that curtailed his public speeches. That was a good thing.

I was well aware of the royal family as a bunch of interfering ne'er-do-wells having affairs and flings long before Princess Diana found she had married beneath her status. Princess Margaret was known to be on the lookout for a suitable fuck buddy whenever away from Buckingham Palace and usually found one. In fact, though the British press did their best to screen the adulterous adventures of the royals from our attention and us guessing what they were up to, there were so many affairs and marriage breakups and rampant sexual encounters I thought the lives of the British aristocracy resembled bouncy castles.

Lots of royal disruptions, *faux pas* and bloomers have happened since. One divorce after another caused Her Majesty to comment that she had had a year that was an *annus horribilis*. Considering the disasters that had befallen her and shaken her normal demeanour of stately stability and tranquillity, a death, the destruction of an ancient building by fire, a divorce, this comical understatement elicited rapturous applause from her dinner guests, the phrase repeated in opinionist columns for years after. With one bound she was free of gossip. The monarchy is an institution so well oiled and relentlessly self-preserving it would carry on if T-boned by a runaway express train.

In the year of the Queen's silver jubilee, or 'Royal Jubbly' as a gloriously inept misprint would have it, the offending clanger printed on thousands of commemorative teacups and saucers, we have reached an unexpected impediment in the history of the royal family. This anniversary is different from all the others. When the Queen is entombed in Westminster Abbey the question uppermost in minds is, will the Monarchy survive?

The answer is, of course it will. The English monarchy has managed to reinvent itself ever since the first Queen Elizabeth, played by Glenda Jackson or Kate Blanchet, put Scotland's Queen in a castle jail for almost two decades and then had her beheaded to exterminate any chance of competition for the English throne.

Termination by assassination has been the English way of doing business for hundreds of years: extirpate rivalry in any form, in any quarter, in any way possible. This is how it treated Scotland on learning the discovery of North Sea Oil in Scottish waters would make Caledonia one of the richest nations in the world. The British Government hid the report and downplayed any thought of oil anywhere near Aberdeen except on a house driveway from a leaky car sump. The Queen did not speak out to protect the sovereign seas of Scotland, but she did turn up to open our newly re-established parliament.

The ability to regenerate a image of rectitude and stability and regain love and affection from the masses was most evident when Princess Diana, a not very bright woman but a fine clothes horse, married into the royal family only to find her husband, Prince Charles, agreed to the marriage because his father told him to do it. Britain's top aristocrats needed an heir. Prince Philip knew Charles had another suitor waiting for him down the corridor behind the arras, Camilla, Duchess of Cornwall, who by 2022, was rehabilitated not as His Royal Squeeze, but as the future queen to Charles's king. Henry VIII would have enjoyed the shananigans.

> "When, in the fullness of time, my son Charles becomes King," the queen stated, "I know you will give him and his wife Camilla the same support that you have given me. It is my sincere wish that, when that time comes, Camilla will be known as' queen consort' as she continues her own loyal service." Elizabeth II

When Diana was dispatched to that royal heaven, which I think is called Mystique, in a car accident at high speed by a clumsy driver – whether her chauffeur or an assassin – the Queen, tiring of Diana's confessions to the paparazzi of her husband's faithlessness and scummy domesticity in the halls of his great houses, took days to lower the flag over Buckingham Palace, an oversight that smacked of relief displacing etiquette. The Queen was spared more toe-curling

'Diana Spills All' interviews to camera. The grieving masses who had wailed and wept and pulled out their hair at Diana's tragic death, who had shouted abuse through the iron gates of the royal family, forgave the absentmindedness. She bloomed for another generation, handbag over her permanently dog-legged arm, privileges intact.

And then along came Prince Andrew and his lucky addiction to pizzas and an inability not to sweat when under stress, his alibis for not being anywhere near an underage American girl loaned to him a few times for a quick royal bonk, a gift from a scumbag American blackmailer he had befriended. Caught red-handed by a photograph of Handy Andy with his arm around the unfortunate victim's waist, he paid up a few million pounds of his own money to avoid a messy court case in New York that would embarrass a queen in her coffin, never mind a live one on a throne. Stripped of every dignity except his clothes – a fate not given to his trafficked bed mate, he managed to separate himself and his sleazy antics from his mother. The Queen knew of his Dick Diggler antics and saw sent him to Scotland and Balmoral to avoid receiving a summons from a New York litigation lawyer. She protected a known paedophile. Escapade laid to rest; the jubbly celebrations were free to go ahead without fear of press diversion. As I said earlier, the royal family regenerates and reinvents itself after every crisis faster than Superman can change his clothes in a telephone booth. They arise stronger than before. This time, however, things might be different. There is trouble brewing in the remnants of the Commonwealth. The territories once slavishly loyal to the monarchy are not happy. They have been educated about their colonial history, and knowledge as we have been taught to understand, can be a dangerous thing. The natives are restless.

Sitting across from the prime minister of Antigua and Bermuda – a former British colony where the Queen is still the head of state – partway through a royal tour to celebrate the Queen's platinum jubbly, Prince Edward was filmed laughing awkwardly. Next to him sat the Caribbean nation's political leader Gaston Browne. He had asked the prince whether he and his wife Sophie, also at the ceremony, would use their "diplomatic influence" to push for the payment of slavery reparations to Britain's former colonies. "We believe that all human civilisations should understand the atrocities that took place," he is recorded as saying without genuflecting or apology. "One day," the prime minister told the couple, Antigua and Barbuda will cut ties with the monarchy and become a republic. Squirming, Prince Edward responded, "I wasn't keeping notes, but thank you for your welcome today." Fair to guess the Earl of Wessex replied through clenched teeth.

Antigua and Berbuda's wish to cut ties with the monarchy followed from two other Commonwealth realms that indicated they wished to become a republic, St Kitts and Nevis. "The advancement of the decades has taught us that the time has come for St Kitts and Nevis to review its monarchical system of government and to begin the dialogue to advance to a new status," said Shawn Richards, the deputy prime minister. All this happened after a disastrous tour earlier by the Duke and Duchess of Cambridge to the Caribbean, the Duke decked out with medals, riding high in the back of a very British Landover and glad-handing the poor through a wire fence to keep them from who knows what, the very epitome of colonial days of old?

The way the British State deals with these matters is to manufacture a crime that accuses the prime minister of stealing taxes – unlike the British Government – or having salacious affairs with many women – unlike the royal family – and he should be replaced, preferably by direct rule. Having territories of the realm ask for reparation for decades of slavery is just not on. In the first collection of essays I wrote about how the example made by Barbados, led by the Prime Minister Mia Mottley, would cause other Commonwealth countries to see republicanism both as a route to freedoms and compensation for being plundered with impunity, their people enslaved, impoverished and murdered. It took only a few months to become the reality. Calls for slavery reparations – and the fury of the *Windrush* scandal that encompassed Belize, Jamaica and the Bahamas where passports were refused and people living in England for decades were sent back to their country of origin – undermined a royal trip aimed at strengthening the Commonwealth and discouraging other countries from following Barbados's example in becoming a republic.

When he becomes king, what will Charles make of the inevitable march to democracy and liberty? Will he write more letters to the UK prime minister of the day demanding he intervene and teach those upstarts to behave? What has he written about halting the same mass movement in Scotland? Will we have to wait thirty years before his documents are released? These are questions members of the Commonwealth will not be asking. They will be busy *taking* their independence.

Some people in Scotland have no negative opinion of the royal family because like causality they think they do no harm. This is no reason not to question their existence in a modern world, and in a new Scotland. We should recognise that members of the royal family from Charles II to William IV were involved with and supported slavery and the slave trade, and that this is part of their past. If the monarchy ever says sorry, we must ask the question, 'How sorry?' Ordinary indigenous Scots were trafficked as slaves, but we whisper that, not declare it because we are told some Scots were slave traders.

In Scotland we are at the stage of wondering if we should remove Victorian street names and statues to men who benefitted from slave traders yet we still line the streets to cheer at royalty when they visit us, or we add the prefix 'royal' to anything we can to give it a spurious 'class'.

Velma McClymont, a writer and former Caribbean studies academic who was born in Jamaica and was five when the country gained independence, has this to say, "My grandparents could trace generations back to slavery, but they died believing Jamaica was fully independent. Imagine, sixty years later and it's still an extension of the British Empire".

Aye, and that goes for Scotland too, but not, I hope, for much longer. The existence of a monarchy is not only an anachronism, it is abhorrence. They are a relic of a bygone age. Our relationship with it is pointless.

36

DREAMS

Last night I had a dream. I dream a lot and always in colour. The colour is vivid, the landscapes I find myself show up in green if there is grass and ochre if there is stone. The light is warm and bright, occasionally dark and foreboding if inside a building. The dreams can turn from one to the other in an instant. I have met people who dream little and always in black and white. How odd. Unless living in a coal shed with no electric light, life is in colour.

    I discovered in youth how to master irrational fears that appear in my dreams. Awake, I repeated to myself three times, "It's only a dream, it's only a dream, it's only a dream." In the next rapid eye movement sleep (REM dreaming) where I experienced a feeling of dread I invoked the chant. The young people around me shared the fearfulness I experienced, but as soon as I spoke the magic words all fear disappeared. This became increasingly handy when finding myself standing on a high cliff, a dark valley way below. I knew to throw myself off the edge meant I was waking up. I threw myself off like a bird.

    Dreams are an array of images, emotions and feelings that the brain is telling us we have not resolved in reality. They sit in our subconscious coming out at night to invade our mind.

    I had two recurring nightmares as a child, both surreal images. The movement of the abstract objects or people in them was minimal, each action taking place in slow motion. The first was a large white ball sitting on top of a high, wide chute. I knew it would rush towards me at speed and I would be fixed to the ground unable to move. This it did, zigzagging from side to side as it sped up rushing in my direction. But instead of hitting me hard as was my dread, when it reached me I awoke. In youth the dream never revisited me.

The second nightmare was far more disturbing. Against a misty grey background of infinity, I saw my mother sitting sideways in a white hospital nightgown on a plain pine chair, only her long dark brown hair showed its colour. She was impassive. What looked like a medical man of some sort, also in white apparel, strode into the image and stood behind her, hammer in one hand, a large six-inch nail in the other. He held the nail to the back of her head and began hammering it into her skull in measured beats. There was no blood, no squeals of pain. When the steel nail was embedded deep, he stopped and rested his arms by his side. My mother turned slowly to look at me, expressionless. In my childhood, and most of her life, my mother was mentally ill, frequently given electric shock therapy to reduce her paranoia a terrible treatment adopted by torturers around the world. A child is ill-equipped intellectually or emotionally to help a mother in those circumstances.

What was my brain saying? There are bad men in the world? Of that we can be sure. My mother had something inside her head that caused her to scream and shout, symbolised by the nail, an alien object? Or was the dream saying she would never be capable of showing love or affection to her first-born? In truth, she did. It was fleeting, never to be forgotten.

The dream I have as an adult is a recurring one. I am the producer-director of a film that I have written. The assistant director is showing me around the production set up, people busy making ready for the first take. I have the screenplay in my hand only I cannot remember what is in it or what the film is about. I try to tell the assistant of my dilemma only no one is listening. The crew and actors get ready to start. I make a quick exit.

There is an amusing story in the movie industry similar to my dream of perpetual torment. A producer dies and goes straight to

Hell. Do not ask why; I do not know why, he must have led a dissipated life to fall into the pit of everlasting fire. The Devil welcomes him and shows him around. To the producer's surprise in every room and in every corner of every room a film is being prepared to go into production. Scene painters are at work, camera crew ready a crane, costume designers help actors try on their garb. "This is great!" says the producer. "If this is Hell what must Heaven be like?" Old Beelzebub continues to show him around the facilities and says, "Oh, in Heaven – up there, they get to *make* the pictures."

Whichever damn priest or monk envisaged Hell as a giant Nazi incinerator had to be troubled by the most terrible torments when he slept. The visions of Hell depicted in so many medieval paintings, fashioned in stain glass in cathedral windows, and drummed into us as a child, are impossible to shake off. "You'll go tae Hell!" shout the hurt and the cheated, a warning that loses most of its power in a secular society where following one God is not a solemn obligation any more if one expects to be accepted by society. Applied to daily life, rather than a particular religion, knowledge of a human-devised heaven and a hell ensure we have a conscience of sorts, but they do not hold us back from committing every folly of which we are capable. In any event, wittily, Irish writer George Bernard Shaw thought Hell a good place to go if one has led a venal life. Hell was made for the bad.

There is one more dream to talk of, the dream of Scotland recovering nationhood. It need not be a dream. It can be recreated overnight if the Scottish Government had the courage to withdraw from the one-way, abused Union. One day, a politician will arise and do just that, they will make an appeal to the United Nations to place Scotland under the category of a colonised country, for we fall easily within the UN's criteria.

As a semi-invalid handling the accumulating effects of incurable cancer I will never see that day though I thought it near to hand. I watch with deepening sadness people I know and those I have only read of, die before the great day arrives, old age, heart disease, the Covid virus and cancer the stalkers that caught them, one by one. The

British State is a ruthless opponent. There ought to be a wall erected in a public place where the names of confederates can be etched, those who dreamt of a better Scotland, the fallen, people we should remember. They gave so much of their lives to a democratic ideal.

The Right Honourable Alex Salmond MP entitled his memoire of the run-up to the 2014 referendum, *The Dream Will Never Die*. The line originates in a speech given by Senator Edward Kennedy, one of the Kennedy dynasty of American politicians. It was part of a speech he gave in 1980, in Madison Square Garden, New York City, for the Democratic National Convention election. Kennedy was supporting a bill for Equal Rights for all Americans. The full quotation is: "The work goes on, the cause endures, the hope still lives, and *the dream shall never die*."

I wish Salmond had found a line from our national poet, Robert Burns (he wrote an anti-monarchy poem entitled *A Dream*), or a good Gaelic equivalent from the work of Sorley MacLean. Salmond did actual quote one of Scotland's poets. The quotation appears at the end of his memoire – a book published in a hurry without an index; the nobleman James Graham, 1st Marquis of Montrose, poet, soldier and lord lieutenant and later viceroy and captain general of Scotland.

> *He either fears his fate too much,*
> *Or his deserts are small,*
> *That puts it not unto the touch*
> *To win or lose it all.*

Salmond has given most of his adult life to the cause of greater democracy for his country. He did not know a majority of indigenous Scots voted in favour, but the accumulated total, incomers and short-stays and all, was seen by our colonial masters as proof positive Scots reject full democracy, and this was the end of the matter. But Salmond was astute. The blurb on the back of the book's cover reads "The people who emerged from the hundred days' campaign are different from those who embarked upon that journey". Of that there is no doubt. Mass movements for liberty rarely cease and die away.

Once the flame of expectation is lit, there is no stopping determination. They may be suppressed by the ruling class, or retreat for a while, but the belief people hold that their civil rights are curtailed drive them forward. Scotland's journey has no less continuity.

One can find countless history books in every library and bookshop relating how indigenous people of colonised countries are forced into armed uprising, bloody battles, or prolonged civil disobedience. In the end the usurper vacates the premises, as it were, the cost of sustaining a governing presence too much to shoulder. In that equation the colonial's own citizens take a decisive role, public pressure commanding politicians to withdraw from repression that shames their own people. I hope Scots never resort to violence to see our full rights reinstated, not in the way the English nation has suppressed rebellion in Scotland in the past, and by malicious campaigns in the modern age to incinerate dreams of equality.

Man is essentially a dreamer. We surround ourselves with comforting beliefs, whether respect for a friend's politics or their religion, either of which we might dislike if asked. We wish so-and-so would materialise and we soon believe that wish to be truth. We like to suppose that the bulk of our beliefs are derived from hard facts, from rational ground, and that crude desire is only an occasional intruder. The exact opposite of this would be nearer the truth: the great mass of beliefs by which we are supported in our daily life is merely the force of desire, corrected here and there at isolated points by the rude shock of fact. Sigmund Freud has a thing or two to say about dreams, and he had things to say of day-dreams which we might wish to call beliefs.

An independent Scotland is not a day-dream. What we do with independence is a dream that will have to face the harshness of reality and competing beliefs when the time comes. The colonial tells us the systems they have put in place are harmless and comforting, they should be left undisturbed. This is a lie. They cause people misery. We can see it every day in the lives people lead. We have to find better systems. Clearing a country of its imposed systems gives us that opportunity to create better ways of living and of justice.

There is one more aspect of dreams and dreaming I wish to place in perspective. I received a letter responding to an essay. It was a delight to read, the unexpected that stops one in one's tracks. It mentioned the Scottish Youth Theatre I knew well, and it expressed how learning about ourselves can turn a feeling of overwhelming inevitability into powerful resolve. The writer mentions he has a dream. Here is the letter, slightly abridged.

> *"I was going to say this to Gareth privately, but circumstances being what they are, I feel I should do it publically. If you know me, you know I think the world of my mammy. She was, after all, the first Scottish Nationalist I ever met, and I met her before I was born. She supported Scottish independence even before she met my father.*
>
> *Mammy did a spell in the Scottish Youth Theatre (SYT), founded and run as the first artistic director by Gareth. Most of her pals at the time were Labour or Liberals depending on their income bracket, but my father's sister was SNP. She was instrumental in my mammy joining, Gareth was another. Back then, Scottish independence was a minority movement, a curiosity at best. My mammy often told me about how much support she received from my aunt, and from Gareth himself, while she was at SYT.*
>
> *My aunt passed away many years ago. Mr McGillivray, who was mum's link to Inverclyde's SNP collective, also passed away. Gareth is one of a small group of folk who brought my mammy into the Scottish independence movement and, by extension, me. I want everyone to know that, through a few degrees of separation, Gareth is one of the reasons I've dedicated so much of my time, life, and dreaming for Scottish Independence.*
>
> *I will be forever grateful. We will get there. Not in time to see it for Auntie Susan, nor Mr McGillivray, nor it seems for Grouse Beater – but they laid the bricks we will use to build the nation we dream of. Thank you, Gareth. I hope we do you proud."*

Al Harton

I do not want to see fleeting, distorted shadows of a better Scotland, as if in a prison cell staring at the sky through a small, barred window, catching glimpses of passing birds or planes. Like the creation of a garden, we shall have to put our backs into fashioning a new Scotland. We will get as much wrong the first time as we get right, we are human, we are not infallible, but what an exciting prospect. The thing to remember is, we have the knowledge, and we will gather more as we move along the pathway.

There is no need to 'dream on'. We are at the threshold now. September 2014 saw facts intrude into our nation's aspirations but did not dispel the dream. Onward!

37

POSTCARDS OF WISDOM

Emulating the chapter in the first collection of essays, crafted carefully into a couple of hundred characters, here are more bon mot, epigrams, sayings from a fertile mind too lazy to take all of them on a journey to a dissertation or conclusion.

In my travels I found the Irish most adept at coining memorable phrases; they slipped off their tongues like honey off a knife. I became aware of their natural linguistic talent when reading the plays of Oscar Wilde, and later the booze bedevilled adventures of Brendan Behan, a man of great wit who refused to wrestle with his compulsive gene that caused him to drink to excess. "I'm a drinker with writing problems," he said. He also said "There's no such thing as bad publicity except your obituary," which has a great deal of truth to it.

I never accepted George Bernard Shaw's dictum that 'those who can do, and those who cannot teach', because good teaching takes considerable skill, knowledge and expertise, but he did write, "I have no more right to consume happiness without producing it, than to consume wealth without producing it". Completely lost in Dublin airport, I asked a security officer how to get to the Domestic gate. "If I was you," he said, "I'd not bother looking. I'd go out the building again and come back in." He was right. I found the lounge in an instant. And while dipping into the Irish gift for poetic loquacity, on a sketching and painting expedition in the west coast of Ireland, my wife stopped her car to ask directions from a farmer. She was driving a car with a powerful engine. The farmer thought for barely a minute, "You're twenty miles from your destination, seven in your car."

One of the best aphorisms I ever was lucky enough to hear came out of the mouth of a retired Texas Ranger. He was hired to guard a film company's equipment and location in a corner of dusty Texas. He carried the full panoply of intimidating prison guard authority straight out of Paul Newman's movie, *Cool Hand Luke*; well over six feet tall, holstered gun hanging from a bejewelled tooled leather belt, white wide-brimmed cowboy hat and the one-way sunshades. Both of us leaning against his V8 pick-up bonnet watching proceedings, he spoke to me without turning his head, in the manner of a stranger at a bar unburdening himself to someone he felt would listen. "What number you on?" I had no idea what he was talking about.

"Pardon?"

"What number?"

"Number of what?"

"How many wives have you had?"

"Just the one," I answered, apologetically.

"I'm on my fifth."

Five wives? I commiserated. Lost for something positive to say, I hoped his latest proved the best. "Nope", he said. "She ran off with a drug-headed, goddamn loser. Can you believe that?" he asked rhetorically, without spitting a gob of chewed black baccy at his feet. He then proceeded to give me the perfect aphorism encapsulating his view of women.

"A woman's love is like the mornin' dew. It can settle on a horse turd as easily as on a rose."

When my sojourn among the location shoot was over I never met him again, but learned stories of his idea of justice, taking his horse across the Mexican border to hunt down fleeing felons and rapists and drag them back to a jail in El Paso.

There are plenty of Scots sayings to regurgitate, too many lost in our eagerness to assume the language of the English invader, such as

"Better the heid o' the commons than the tail o' the gentry," which means, better to be top of your social class than the bottom of the privileged class. Another, "Aw's welcome that come wi' a crookit oxter," meaning, everyone is a welcome guest who brings a gift tucked under their arm. Giving some thought to that saying makes me wonder if it means a chicken or a lamb carried as a gift. And finally, "A nod's as guid as a wink tae a blind horse," translated: be sure to make your meaning clear!

Here are few of my own or refined from what somebody said, *en passant*, that I hope are clear, their profundity or usefulness a matter for the reader to judge:

There are good teachers and there are bad teachers. Good teachers teach you how to walk tall, be confident, make your own decisions and stand by them. Bad teachers teach you that you will never survive without their advice and guidance.

There is a recurring motif. The first minister and Scottish Government make decisions but rarely suffer the consequences of bad decisions. To whom are they accountable? It is us the electorate, yet bad MSPs hang on, and the first minister is excused her lapses of judgement.

Of all the things Scots have done, the one history will record as the principal contribution of our generation – is sustaining the struggle to restore our autonomy after setbacks; we know winning is essential to create the mentality to build a new society.

The man so proud to be British he is happy to hold back the rights of millions of Scots will be the same shouting for the independence of Ukraine to be respected. "Let the people choose," he will say, without a hint of irony.

In an independent Scotland the state must be the first to be organised and committed to serving the interests of the people. The SNP will never accomplish this while employing Whitehall civil servants and former opponents of freedom as key advisers.

Every country that has left England's rule embarked on decolonisation, Barbados the most recent example. They understood imperialism, colonialism, is more than political and economic exploitation. It is about culture, language and the survival of communities.

Referenda are not a requirement to attain autonomy. A majority government and a nation's sovereignty are enough. Scotland has attained both, but SNP ignore that. We are free to dissolve the union to negotiate a new accord based on our reinstated independence.

The referendum of 2014 was based on a local government franchise. This was a fatal error. Local government voting is based on residency, meaning, no matter how long one is here, a week a year, you got a vote. No other country would allow that franchise.

After the defeat of Culloden, the attempt at genocide, the Gaelic culture was all but wiped out and followed by the Clearances, imposing master and servant roles, each part of British State policy. Scotland lost more of its people than any other western nation.

The motivation for independence is uncomplicated: to install people power able to construct a new society devoid of exploitation, for the happiness and benefit of those who feel themselves to be Scottish. To *know* you are a Scot, you need to *think* like a Scot.

English love to venerate failure. If the Darien Adventure had been engineered by an English expeditionary force there would be statues erected to key leaders praised as courageous, books, coffee mugs, a whole sales industry, the pioneers held up as heroes.

After independence what people do with their freedom is up to them. Self-determination is not about upholding a free market economy, nor creating a socialist utopia or a green revolution. We are liberating the people. That is the sole and sacrosanct goal.

In a colonised country inconvenient facts are suppressed with surprising effectiveness, those things it will not do to speak, or think. One taboo subject is expressing concern at living in a colonised country. You are liable to be mocked and probably silenced.

England, the usurper of Scotland's rights, has first dibs on Scotland's resources. Only England gets to recycle wealth. Scotland's parliament is the colonial's facade. This causes eternal conflict. Scots don't understand why they are not the beneficiaries of their wealth.

The British press will always headline news of voting or opinion polls with 'Scotland still divided on constitutional lines' until the day autonomy is reinstated, and they will continue doing the same after.

There are always reasons for optimism. Things may look grim but there are ways out. We know the ways. Engage a basic morality, show courage not compromise, and we can convince others to follow our example.

After independence what people do with their freedom is for them to decide. Self-determination is not about upholding a free market economy, nor creating a socialist utopia or a green revolution. We are liberating the people. That is the sole and sacrosanct goal.

The British State's normal appeal to jingoism is to the altruistic side of the argument, not to the imperialistic. Scots are told we share a common humanity, never that "England needs Scotland's wealth and resources, your youth for wars".

When an SNP politician or party member condemns your right to challenge government policy, as any concerned citizen should, they ask for your obedience, and worse, imply you're a separatist. Does the SNP realise they sound exactly like our colonial masters?

The act of analysing, the need to discern possibilities, to give warnings and seek out solutions is the very lifeblood of hope, shame on those who prefer silence, who demand obedience. The society they want is censorious and authoritarian.

Politicians in the West are terminally addicted to cold war politics. They are prey to the powerful armaments industry, ignoring that we demand peace, not perpetual enmity. To be conciliatory in a dispute we argue with lethal logic; we first threaten to go to war and then pull back.

A defining characteristic of colonialism is denigration of local culture. Displays of superiority undermine the native's will to resist imposed rule. Failure to secure equality or promotion tend to be internalised, blamed on personal inadequacy, the régime is not to blame.

I see a shining vision, a confident Scotland, industrious, innovative and self-sufficient. We have all we need to begin the task and all we need to sustain the ideal. I do not say it can happen tomorrow, or the day after independence, but I do say it's attainable if we put our minds to it.

In the debating chamber there is the baying of dispute, in the finance house there is the buzz of money, in the market place there is the chatter of voices, but under the cherry blossom tree there is contentment.

The serious error made by SNP's politicians is to assume the enemies of England must, *ipso facto*, be the enemies of Scotland. In doing this, in meekly following England's xenophobia, they remove Scotland's right to make its own decisions and tar us with the same brush.

The outcome of the British State moving to consolidate its power absolutely over Scotland, and by imposed law constrain Scotland's progress, the mass movement determined to restore self-governance will have to be less tolerant, more militant and revolutionary.

Gradualists and meliorists like me discuss peaceful commingling and educating our English opponents to accept Scotland's right to self-determination. They didn't accept it in 1707 and have reject it ever since, so why will they welcome it when the indigenous population is the minority subsumed into an English colony?

Humankind is an infinitesimally tiny spec in a vast firmament of stars and planets and gaseous elements. We have no idea why we are here, but some of us are smart enough to make the best of it.

Insects have two irresistible driving forces, food and procreation; they forage for food, and they share food and shelter. The continuation of the colony is paramount. Nothing else matters. There are no slackers among ants or bees like lazy folk in human society.

One has to stay on guard against the assimilation of black propaganda into everyday speech, things meant to sell a lie as truth, but it becomes blatant fascism not asked but instead instructed, that 'a person who gives birth' must be substituted for 'mother'.

Every time a boss threatens to remove his company south to England if Scotland regains full democracy, each time a CEO blackmails his staff into voting against Scotland's interests, which are their own, he is reminding us we are a colonised country.

England's rich conservative class likes to think itself liberal, and devolution as genuine separation of powers to Scotland. But Scots know the difference between revolution and a bag of soor plooms from a colonial power too far away to govern well or fairly.

I had a guardian. She taught me respect for the female of the species. My wife taught me not to ignore those who love you. My daughters taught me how to provide verbal affection. Fashioned by women? You bet I was.

The novelist J.B. Priestley wrote a meditation on the Monarch's coat-of-arms. He opined loss of the empire freed England to lose the lion. He suggested a unicorn was better; it was "an elegant beast, representing magic and art". The Scots beat them to it.

Of English civilised behaviour while exercising colonial rule, given the history of the British Empire and recent interventions in the affairs of Scotland, there is room for improvement. Aime Cesaire wrote: "between colonization and civilization there is an infinite distance."

A political party denounced me publically in my absence; they then excommunicated me in my absence, in which case they can damn well expect vigorous retaliation in my absence.

A totalitarian state is, in effect, a theocracy; its ruling caste wants to be seen as infallible. As no one is infallible, it is necessary to revise past events to fit the image and show no errors were made. In that situation objective truth is the casualty.

Critics are only good for pointing out a relationship that does not work in your novel, stage play or screenplay, a lack of humour in the right places, or a tone you misjudged, but they cannot tell you how to fix it.

In decolonisation there are only two protagonists: the colonized and the colonizer. Colonialism is primarily about economic and political exploitation as well as cultural and linguistic imperialism, all of which Scotland has been subjected for over 300 years.

The SNP's promises to secure Scotland's liberty are a great way to calm political frustration. The thin paper they are printed on, with some sweet baccy rolled in between, is as decent a smoke as you will ever enjoy.

The USA has been at war continuously from its inception, first with its indigenous societies, disastrously so to the point of genocide, and then with various nations around the world. America began as a group of nations but once unified decided the rest of us should cooperate with its foreign policies or be severely penalised or punished.

In a long eventful life I have yet to meet a member of the Tory party who did not join it either for personal social advancement or to protect their business privileges. None joined the Tory Party to enhance civil rights. They think 'civil rights' freedom from prosecution.

When people say to me the science of economics is beyond their expertise, my response is simple: forget trying to understand economic theories. Know what is right, and know what is just for the common good. After that most things fall into place.

"A better world is possible if only we all work harder to achieve it," said every millionaire hiding their loot in a tax haven facilitated by sleazy lawyers and accountants, wealth we worked hard to create and never saw a penny invested back in the community.

Forget the past, says the colonial usurper. To remember will have the populace know of attempts at genocide, land theft, political oppression, cultural suppression, economic control, and multi-breaches of the Act of Union and that will be, in their words, 'divisive'.

If the Declaration of Arbroath was consummated this day, its many earls and clan chiefs signed and sealed, you can expect some cock womble of a colonial to be the first to jump up claiming the signatories "do not speak for Scotland" as if the invader is the only person qualified.

That England's elite may live in comparative comfort, almost four million Scots must forego full civil and constitutional rights, our taxes taken and not used for our betterment, leaving tens of thousands of Scots poverty-stricken and hungry. We acquiesce in the crime when we venerate English royalty.

Writing essays is akin to composing music. You begin with an expression of ideas, your first movement. The second movement is the development of those ideas, the third movement variations of gathered evidence, light-hearted even, and the last movement a profound conclusion of your thoughts. One hopes it all makes cohesive sense, flowing one to another.

When I am dead I won't be bothered by my death. I won't know I am dead. This is the same state as when I was not born. I did not know anything about that either. It pleases me to have discovered one good thing about not being alive.

I do not care why I am here. I care only about what I do while I am here. There is no meaning to our lives. None. We must create meaning in our lives. For me, it was helping others make a life for themselves. I found a kind of happiness creating happiness in others.

Living a full life and being generous in love is everything. All the rest pales into insignificance. The society that creates the best opportunities for happiness is an ideal society. That so many of us bottle up those instinctive qualities is the pity. Free your mind, free your spirit. Be a citizen of the universe.

38

MY COUNTRY TO GOVERN

If a Scot says, I want my back country to govern again, he is judged a fool, and everything is done to demean him and mock him. When an Englishman says he wants his country back to govern again, and shouts freedom into the face of Europeans, his countrymen praise him and call him patriotic.

Our neighbour allows us the small things, the junior sports event, the touring production, the regional organisation, the provincial television station, and a parliament with next to no economic powers and absolutely no formal participation in international affairs. They gift us a life as ersatz English folks. The charade tells us England has scant respect for us as a people. Question, complain, rebel, and we are warned Westminster will punish us when independent if we dare use the very pound sterling we helped create. They will place border controls to corral us if we resist their rule, or they will fine us, reduce the annual allowance they give us taken from our taxes if we do anything they dislike. And then they have the effrontery to demand to know why we feel artificially constrained or oppressed.

We have an England that saw fit to recruit Scottish men and women in two world wars to fight and die for liberty and freedom, but will not allow us freedom to govern ourselves. What kind of freedom is that? We have an England that saw fit to use Scotland as a guinea pig for unpopular policies, for a place to bury nuclear waste and an island to test anthrax bacterium. What kind of ally is that? We have an England that destroyed a nation's heavy industry rather than support it. What kind of equality is that? It is a tyranny.

The English have a set of assumptions, a reality, different from Scots. Their reality is based on two centuries of rampant colonialism, of English nationalism wrapped up in glorious empire, of wars and battles and heroes made and heroes sacrificed, territory captured, ruling the wide waves, a domination of indigenous cultures. To English, the Scottish man or woman, you, me, standing before them, protesting, holding a placard, asking for political change, we are deemed to be stupid, presumptuous to resist their system to which they think we owe our identity. They defend an English system, an English reality.

There was a time last century when the Labour party, always a Unionist party, fought for Scotland's corner. But here's the rub, they *had* to *fight* for our rights, for a share of the wealth we generated, it was not Scotland's by right. And while their elected representatives were banging their desk for Scotland, behind the scenes they were doing their best to discourage their membership supporting Home Rule for Scotland. The Labour Party held the legendary John MacLean and Keir Hardie in high regard, hoisting them up onto a plinth for us to idealise like martyrs on a crucifix, whilst behind the clamour they kept Scotland's independence a bottom drawer issue within the party.

Back in the 1960s, before they infected themselves with the disgusting ideology of neo-liberalism, a cobbled together phony philosophy where we feed the best oats to a horse and we are expected live of what comes out of the other end, the English Conservative Party recognised they had ignored Scotland's material and social plight for too long. Too long was two hundred years. The British Treasury was draining Scotland of its earnings, squandering it on imperial wars and weapons of mass destruction to enhance the power of *Great* Britain. The Celtic fringe, as we were known, let it be known Scots were not happy. To encourage votes for the Tory party the British Treasury gave Scotland £600 million to help clear our city slums, to create outer city communities, to encourage the entrepreneur. Colleges flowered like spring bulbs. Our new found hyper-activity was mirrored in our culture. The Edinburgh International Festival of the Arts grew in all directions in activity and fame. Our artists were feted in London. BBC Scotland adapted and produced some of our greatest novels. New, bright Scottish filmmakers made their name. James Bond was a Scotsman.

The working class were still called the working class but saw a ladder to middle-class if they were willing to take it. We called it social progress. Meanwhile emigration continued unabated. In 1967 over 47,000 people left Scotland.

Running an empire is a costly business. Within a decade England's parliamentarians checked their pockets. They couldn't sustain the expenditure. The British government discovered they couldn't balance their books by giving Scotland back more of what it earned; there was civil war in Northern Ireland to fund. So they took to stealing Scotland's oil. They hid an official government report for thirty years that said the oil would see Scotland one of the richest nations in the world. England was not only a tyranny, it was a thief.

As I write the Tory party is considered a pariah and shunned, a minority cabal detested because it is unelected and yet governs Scotland. The national party, out of weak leadership, is considered no more than a reproduction of the Labour party of yesteryear. Now we have food banks for the destitute, described counter-logically by our colonial masters a 'good thing', a sign of a caring nation. England took back everything we had built with our own hands for our own needs, everything except our bridges over the river Forth, and they might have removed them had they not been bolted together and pile driven into Scotland's bedrock. Scotland is an internal colony.

On the days you wonder what the future is for your children, remember this: when you say you are British, that is the day you have given up the fight for Scotland's political and social justice. To be Scottish and British means you will never govern your own country.

England will never let Scotland leave the rotten un-United Kingdom voluntarily. Holding tight to resource rich territory over 330 years tells us the brutal reality. Scotland is England's cash cow. We can reinstate self-governance by our own choice of mechanism. We do not have to restrict ourselves to only one path to freedom, one route easily dismissed by the British State.

If you are happy to kneel before the grotesque indifference of the colonial, ready to die for another nation's wars, you chose that destiny. The rest of us have had enough. No nation demands it is governed by another nation. No nation rose up to demand its abolition.

39

THE COLONIAL

They swarm over my homeland like maggots
Searching for what they can consume
They leave the earth rancid and the bones dry.
They make nothing but keep us apart.
They leave only tears and pain in the heart.

They look for those who believe in themselves
They look for the confused, one person with two cultures.
Confusing us is their cause, lying until we embrace their will.
They do not like us respecting one another
Or caring for our land, as we do a sister and a brother.

They called me Jock but I did not like that name
They called me Separatist, but I did not like that either.
In time my name grew longer: I became 'Person of Interest'.
But I remember their lies, each and every fear monger,
The dead weight of their tongues saw me grow stronger.

They tell us we fail at everything even at failure.
They tell us they know better and are our betters.
See the clouds swirling around us, we are the power.
They are the dregs, the faeces, the sludge,
With resilience and truth, we will see them budge.

We are spiritual people; never forget the ways of our ancestors.
We are spiritual people; do not feed the ways of the invader.
Be friendly with silence to hear what is happening.
Scotland is our talisman against drowning, a wordless spell.
Our cry is liberty, fraternity, a dream too vivid to dispel.

ACKNOWLEDGEMENTS

As with the first book of essays, typesetter Laura Kincaid has been as ultra-skilled and efficient as a master Swiss horologist and a wise adviser. Gratitude goes to immediate family suffering my insularity for months. "Granddad does a lot of thinking," remarked a puzzled grandson. "Granddad is someone who lives in his head," answered my daughter, with affectionate insight. Thanks also are due to Scotland's National Library in old Edinburgh for many hours sifting through musty old books as a student, and in past years studying documents and records for articles and essays, lately by Internet. I am proud my National Library has a copy of both books of essays. Poland, long associated with Scotland's culture, has my thanks, the books published in Wroclaw. And I have to bow to my talented wife, Barbara, for the book's beautiful jacket and that on the front of the first collection, part of her studies of Edinburgh Castle. The art that flows from the hand and imagination of an artist is as sweet as that from a fine composer.

ABOUT THE AUTHOR

Born in Edinburgh into a family of pioneering professional musicians, Gareth is half-Sicilian by his father, and half-Irish by his mother, "a combination that works wonders for writing polemic and poetic prose". A classic runaway from a broken home, he sought out knowledge and fun, training at the Royal Scottish Academy of Music and Drama, Jordanhill College of Education (graduating with distinction) and Glasgow University, beginning a drama career in writing and directing for the theatre, and teaching and lecturing. For a time he studied philosophy. It provided him with "a framework to attach a conscience but beyond that, is not very useful for a practical-minded Scotsman."

He founded and became the first Artistic Director of the Scottish Youth Theatre which nurtures gifted actors, writers and performance musicians. After a spell as an executive producer for the BBC in London, Northern Ireland and then Scotland, he established his own film production company *Jam Jar Films* produced a number of highly praised original dramas, the youth series *It's Our World*, the political thriller *Brond*, and the film *Conquest*. Finding little work in his homeland, he moved to Los Angeles for several months a year as a screenwriter and script doctor. He wrote and produced the first music video for folk-rock duo The Proclaimers. He returned to Scotland permanently in 2014 to take part in the independence referendum, and began publishing essays in support of Scotland's civil rights.

His literary work includes screenplays, television scripts, and a radio work. He founded and edited the magazine *Information for Drama*, wrote the *Louis Vuitton Guide to Los Angeles* at a month's deadline whilst still in Edinburgh, publishes movie reviews, countless columns for magazines and newspapers, and written and edited books for the Royal Academy of Arts. He broadcast regular radio programmes on classical music. Described as a polymath, and given the generous accolade of "Scotland's foremost intellectual on independence" by Professor Alfred Baird and "Scotland's Mark Twain" by ribbing students, his first collection of 'ESSAYS' was published in 2021 to high acclaim.

Married to the Royal Academician painter and master printmaker, Dr Barbara Rae, he has two daughters, Emma and Nora, and no pets. He names coffee and happiness as his two drugs. As a 'relaxing hobby' he designs and plants large gardens, his current project a Roman garden on Roman archaeological ground. He rates his best work for the community the regeneration and landscaping of a hitherto dilapidated, ignored backwater, Circus Lane, an 18th century mews in the centre of Edinburgh, now a tourist destination, voted "The Most Beautiful Street in Edinburgh", and the "most photographed street in Scotland".

*

ESSAYS and ESSAYS 2
The first collection of Grouse Beater *ESSAYS* is available from Amazon Books, or signed copies from the author at: garwarscot@hotmail.com. *ESSAYS 2* can be purchased from the same outlets.

"Truly insightful, possessing a strong sense of right and wrong, his sound ethics and finely-tuned moral compass get to the heart of the matter. As a Scot in America it's a joy to read."

INDEX OF NAMES

A. Douglas Willcox 11
A. S. Neill 67
Abbott Bernard 227
Adam Smith 11
Adolf Hitler 138, 142
Adrienne Corri 16–26
Agatha Christie 109
Al Harton 313
Alan Sharp 130
Alan Taylor 33
Alasdair Milne 266
Albert Finney 23, 110
Albrecht Dürerr 143
Aldous Huxley 165, 166
Alec Douglas-Home MP 33, 34
Alec Guinness 23
Alex Salmond 47, 209, 210, 241, 268, 270, 271, 311
Alexander de Lamberton 231
Alexander III 228
Alison Rowat 30
Alistair Darling 241, 269
Alistair Hetherington 266
Allan Massie 30, 31, 33
Allan Pinkerton 80, 160
Andre Deutsch 27, 40
Andrea Jenkyns 59
Andrew Carnagie 160
Andrzej Szarko 252, 254, 255
Angela Soper 224

Angus MacMillan 160
Annie Hirst 224
Anthony Burgess 19
Anthony Hopkins 25, 26
Antonia Fraser 23
Antonio Gramsci 13
Arnold Schwarzenegger 174
Arthur Bulley 282
Arthur Campbell 230
Arthur Donaldson 140, 143
Arthur Griffiths 121, 125
Avril Blair 168
Ben Shephard 58
Benito Mussolini 138, 139
Bertrand Russell 51, 99, 155
Betty Stark 224
Bigfoot 196–200
Billy Connolly 132
Blair McDougall 91
Bob Boothby 22
Bonne Maman 150
Bonnie Prince Charlie 78, 161
Boris Johnson 268
Brendan Behan 130
Brian Barr 263
Brian Redhead 258
Brian Spanner 91
Bridget Reilly 2
Brigadier General Earl Haig 10
Bryce Wilson 184

ESSAYS 2

C. B. Benson 223
Camilla Parker 304
Captain James Cook 187, 291
Carl Eduard von Sachsen-Coburg 142
Carlo Bernini 5
Catherine Destivelle 219
Catherine Middleton 306
Cecil Rhodes 86
Charles Dickens 183, 193–95
Charles Gray 23
Charles II 307
Charles Rennie Mackintosh 81, 213
Chris Sawyer 73
Christine Robertson 25
Christopher Devine 3
Christopher Isherwood 142
Clara Ford 239
Claude Debussy 8
Clementina Traill 281, 282
Craig Murray 43, 47
Crown Prince Wilhelm 141
Cubby Broccoli 24
Cynthia Grindley 224
Daniel Defoe 82
Daniel Massey 17, 26
David Brynmor Jones 119
David C. Hutton 11
David Cameron 210, 269
David Douglas 58, 277, 278
David Garrick 22, 23
David Graham 231
David I 243
David Lean 21
David Lloyd George 118, 121–24
David McWilliams 244
David Mundell 92
David Starkey 139
David Suchet 110
David Walker 24
Davy Byrne 200
Delia Smith 61
Detective John Trench 39
Diana Quick 23
Dick Diggler 305
Don Watson 160
Donald Francis Tovey 10, 11
Donald Mackay 160
Donald Trump 58
Douglas Hurd MP 40, 265
Dr John Rae 183–95
Dr Richard Beeching 31
Dr Ronan Toolis 216, 217
Duncan Campbell 263, 264
Èamon de Valera 121, 124–26
Ed Davey 58
Ed Miliband 61
Edgar Allan-Poe 20
Edward Degas 143
Edward Elgar 55
Edward I 230
Edward VIII 302
Edwin R. Pope 11
Eileen Blair 168
Elon Musk 240
Elton John 164
Emily Buchanan 11
Emperor Antoninus Pius 76, 215
Emperor Publius Hadrianus 76, 214, 217
Ennio Morricone 114
Eric Shlosser 99
Esther Brookes 168
Esther L. Cruickshank 11
Evelyn McNicol 224
F.W. de Klerk 86
Ferdinand Karl Piëch 237–39
Fintan O'Toole 33
François Boucher 143
Frank Kingdon-Ward 278
Franz Kafka 36
Fraser Nelson 60
Frédéric Chopin 6
Frederic Lindsay 27–36, 38–44
Frederick Graff Snr 174
Friedrich Engels 13
Friedrich Hegel 144
Gabriel Fauré 3
Galileo Galilei 297
Gareth Ward 4

INDEX

Gareth Wardell 134, 136, 147, 151, 313
Gaston Browne 305
Gavin Esler 268
Gavin McCrone 90
General Franco 139
George Bernard Shaw 310, 315
George Cunningham 84
George Forrest 277–87
George Litton 284
George Lucas 279
George Monbiot 62
George Orwell 61, 163–72, 256
George Osborne 241
George VI 303
Georges Simenon 31, 39
Germaine Greer 296
Gilbert Harding 262
Glen H. Snyder 99
Glenda Jackson 303
Gordon Brown 29, 91, 268, 269
Gore Vidal 40, 43
Gough Whitlam 300
Greg Dyke 267
Grzegorz Jaworski 252, 254
Gustavo Dudamel 68
Guy Woolfenden 108
Hamish MacInnes 220
Hector Berlioz 109
Heinrich Himmler 141, 142
Helen Steven 225
Henry David Thoreau 50, 51
Henry Ford 239
Henry V 110, 111
Henry VIII 139
Hercule Poirot 110
Hermann Göring 141
Hermann Khan 99
Honora Reilly 5, 6, 7, 12, 13, 15
Horatio Walpole 79
Hugh Grant 60
Hugh MacDiarmid 203
Hymie Bierman 7
Iain Christie 88
Ian Botham 58

Ian Fleming 279
Indiana Jones 279, 284
Irvine Welsh 131
Isabella Reilly 5, 6, 12, 13, 15
Isambard Kingdom Brunel 224
J. H. Smith 11
J. M. Barrie 161
J.K. Rowling 90, 152
Jacek Ogórek 252, 254
Jack the Ripper 21
Jackie Bird 268, 269
Jacques Offenbach 3
James Bond 61, 234, 279
James Drummond 78
James Graham 311
James Joyce 200
James Maxwell of Kirkconnell 78
James Rae 80
James Reilly 2
James Veitch 286
Jane Inglis Clark 220, 222, 223
Janet Street Porter 59
Jascha Heifetz 13
Jean Anouilh 21
Jean Renoir 18
Jean Sibelius 108
Jean Sibelius 13
Jean-Édouard Vuillard 25
Jeffrey A. Larsen 99
Jeremy Corbyn 60
Jeremy Paxman 61
Jill Stephenson 91
Jim Sillars 89
Jimmy Savile 262
Joe Cairns 7
Joel Barnett 266
Johannes Brahms 13
John Abercromby 280
John Aitkenhead 67
John Barrow 187
John Birt 266
John Boothby 270
John Byrne 112
John de Inchmartin 231

John Dickie 160
John Duraunt 231
John Farrell 2
John MacLean 13, 203
John Osborne 21
John Reilly 5
John Updike 40
John Williams 115
Julie Christie 21
Julius Agricola 75
Justice Lord Neuberger 50
Karl Marx 11
Kate Blachet 303
Kate McNiven 82
Kate Watson 91
Kathleen 5
Keith Haring 65
Kenneth Branagh 109, 110–16
Kenneth Leighton 12
Kevin Bridges 242
King Charles I 301, 304, 307
King James II 74
Klaus Knorr 99
Kray Twins 22
Lady Jane Franklin 183, 187–89, 192–95
Lady Macbeth 192
Lady Mary Carew-Pole 301
Lewis Grassic Gibbon 257
Liz MacKean 262
Lord Beaverbrook 140
Lord Horatio Nelson 56
Lord John Carew-Pole 301
Lord John Reith 141
Lord Jonathan Sumption 209
Lord Palmerston 188
Lord Reith 267
Louisa Reilly 5
Lucy Smith 220
Ludwig van Beethoven 13, 278
M. P. Lunn 11
Mabel Inglis Clark 220, 225
Magdalene Seton 11
Mahatma Ghandi 181
Main Coon 196

Malcolm Lennox 231
Malcolm McDowall 19
Malcolm Offord 268
Malise Strathearn 232
Marcel Proust 150
Marchioness of Breadalbain 221
Margaret Ann Reilly 2
Margaret Maid of Norway 228
Margaret Thatcher 207, 246, 263, 292
Margo MacDonald 270
Mariusz Szarko 252, 254, 255
Mark Carney 246
Mark Rothko 68
Martin Scorsese 147
Mary Lou MacDonald 117
Mary O'Donnell 1
Mary Reilly 3
Mary, Queen of Scots 48
Maureen Constance Reilly 6
Maurice Binder 24
Maurice Ravel 8
Maurice Utrillo 143
Max Schmeling 7
Meikle 249
Melanie Philips 60
Merion Jones 262
Mia Mottley 306
Michael Collins 121, 124, 125
Michael Foucault 143
Michael Gove 61
Michael Ochiltree 74
Mikhail Gorbachev 98, 178–80, 205, 291
Milton Freidman 180, 244
Monty Don 279
Morag Aitkenhead 67
Mr E Dearnley 11
Muriel Gray 91
Muriel Mackie 11
Murray Foote 90
Nelson Mandela 86–88, 92
Nicola Benedetti 204
Nicola Sturgeon 63, 92, 210
Nicolas Hayek 236, 237, 240
Nicole Farhi 62

INDEX

Noam Chomsky 52
Norman Tebbit 258
Old Chao 285
Oscar Slater 39
Oscar Wilde 315
Oscar-Claude Monet 143
Otto Preminger 21
P. R. Meny 11
P.W. Botha 86, 87
Pablo Picasso 65, 139, 151, 153
Pádraig Joseph Reilly 1, 2, 5, 11, 15
Patricia Gibson 228
Patrick Corri 20
Patrick Doyle 109–116
Patrick Dunbar 231
Patrick Filmer-Sankey 20
Patrick Reilly 1, 3
Paul Dacre 60, 62
Paul Mason 264
Paul Newman 316
Père Jean Armand Soulé 283
Peregrine Worsthorne 61
Peter Jackson 105
Peter Paul Rubens 25
Peter Purves 61
Peter Stefanovic 58
Peter Ustinov 261
Pierre Bonnard 143
Pierre-Auguste Renoir 18
Piers Morgan 60
Piotr Szarko 252, 254, 255
Pope John XXII 227, 229
President Barack Obama 181
President Boris Yeltsin 179
President George W. Bush 180
President H. W. Bush 179
President Ronald Reagan 178, 179
President Samora Machel 87, 88
President Vladimir Putin 180, 181, 291
Primo Levi 137
Prince Andrew 305
Prince Charles 299, 301, 307
Prince Edward 305
Prince Hamlet 114

Prince Phillip 304
Prince William 306
Princes Margaret 303
Princess Diana 164, 303–05
Professor Arthur Herman 220
Professor Challenger 279
Professor George Bryce 185
Professor Ian Ritchie 213
Professor Isaac Bayley Balfour 280
Pyotr Ilyich Tchaikovsky 109
Queen Elizabeth II 141, 182, 204, 299, 300, 303
Queen Victoria 55, 79, 142
Ralph Waldo Emerson 51
Raymond Briggs 99
Reginald le Cheyne 230
Rembrandt H. van Rijn 25
Rev. Ian Paisley 260
Richard Blair 168
Richard Murphy 244
Richard Rodney Bennett 110, 111, 114
Robert Barnet 99
Robert Burns 192, 311
Robert Davidson 239
Robert Falk 99
Robert Louis Stevenson 4, 160
Robert the Bruce 214, 228
Rolf Harris 262
Ronald Mason 263
Rumer Godden 18
Rupert Brooke 57
Rupert Murdoch 259
Ruth Davidson 58
Ruth Raeburn 221
Sarah Corri 20
Sarah Ditton 297
Scott Joplin 6
Sean Connery 16
Senator Edward Kennedy 311
Sergeant Pepper 62
Sergei Prokofiev 109
Shawn Richards 306
Sherlock Holmes 21

Shirley Lindsay 38
Sigmund Freud 312
Simón Bolívar 67, 68
Simon Heffer 60
Simon Jenkins 62
Sinclair Aitken 265
Sir Alexander Fraser 231
Sir Alexander Seton 232
Sir Arthur Conan Doyle 279
Sir David Brechin 230
Sir Edward Keith 231
Sir George Simpson 186
Sir Gilbert Hay of Erroll 231
Sir Henry Wood 59
Sir Ian Lang 91
Sir Ian Wood 90
Sir Ingram de Umfraville 232
Sir James Clark Ross 188
Sir James MacMillan 206
Sir John Back 191
Sir John Franklin 187, 192, 194
Sir John Ross 187
Sir Joseph Banks 187
Sir Joseph Hooker 278
Sir Nicholas McPherson 91
Sir Oswald Mosley 137
Sir Roger de Moubray 231
Sir William Oliphant 231
Sir William Stirling 75
Sir William Wallace 48
Sonia Orwell 172
Sophie Rhys-Jones 305
Stanley Kubrick 19, 20
Suddam Hussein 96
Sydney Lumet 110
Tagak Curley 195
Ted Galen Carpenter 181
Tennessee Williams 262
Thea Musgrave 108
Theresa May 60
Thomas de Menzies 231
Thomas de Morham 231
Thomas Gainsborough 22, 23, 24
Thomas Harris 43

Tommy Beltrane 42
Tommy Sheridan 47
Tommy Weddell 4
Tony Blair 96, 210
V. S. Naipal 40
Velma McClymont 307
W. Barry Furniss 11
W.G.H. Kingston 62
Wallis Warfield Simpson 302
Walter Reilly 3, 5, 9
William Clark 221
William Edward Parry 187
William Hill 200
William IV 307
William MacIlvanney 130
William McGregor 73
William Wordsworth 163
Willie McRae 87
Winnie Ewing 207
Winnifred Reilly 5, 6
Winston Churchill 4, 118–26
Winston Graham 166
Winston Smith 99
Wolfgang Amadeus Mozart 278
Wong Gee Chic 7
Yanis Varoufakis 244, 246
Zbigniew Brzezinski 143
Zoe MacDonald 270

Printed in Poland
by Amazon Fulfillment
Poland Sp. z o.o., Wrocław
17 July 2022

8b2656f3-3758-4ec6-8053-4cfe79246c5eR01